30°E   60°   90°   120°   150°

ARCTIC OCEAN
166 –167

Europe-Asia Boundary

A S I A
100 –123

E U R O P E
82 –99

A F R I C A
124 –139

PACIFIC OCEAN
160 –161

INDIAN OCEAN
164 –165

AUSTRALIA
NEW ZEALAND
OCEANIA
140 –151

PHYSICAL WORLD *18 –19*
POLITICAL WORLD *32 –33*
WORLD OCEANS *156 –167*

A N T A R C T I C A
152 –155

YOU ARE HERE.

NATIONAL
GEOGRAPHIC
KiDS

World Atlas

Fourth Edition

NATIONAL GEOGRAPHIC

WASHINGTON, DC

Table of Contents

South America:
Llama, page 73

North America: Grand Canyon, page 56

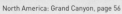

Europe: Colosseum, pages 88–89

Antarctica: Penguins, page 154

Australia, New Zealand, &
Oceania: Maori man, page 144

Africa: Mother and child, page 129

GETTING STARTED

How To Use This Atlas

This atlas is a window on your planet. Through it you can explore the world. To learn about maps, use the first section, Understanding Maps. Next, basic facts about Earth as a planet are presented in the section called Planet Earth. The section Physical World includes world maps that focus on different aspects of nature and the environment. The Political World contains world maps about how humans live on the planet. In the pages that follow, the maps, photographs, and essays are arranged by continent and region. You can look up specific places or just browse. Remember, it's your planet— learn it, love it, explore it!

"YOU ARE HERE"
Locator globes help you see where one area is in relation to others. On regional pages (shown here), the area covered by the main map is yellow on the globe, and its continent is green. On pages with continent maps, the locator globe shows the whole continent in yellow. The surrounding land is brown.

STATS & FACTS
At the left-hand edge of each continent opener and regional page is a bar that includes basic information about the subject. This feature is a great first stop if you're writing a report.

CHARTS & GRAPHS
Each region includes a chart or graph that shows information visually.

SOUTHWEST ASIA

THE CONTINENT:
ASIA

THE BASICS

STATS

Largest country
Saudi Arabia 756,985 sq mi (1,960,582 sq km)
Smallest country
Bahrain 277 sq mi (717 sq km)
Most populous country
Iran 78,868,000
Least populous country
Bahrain 1,326,000
Predominant languages
Arabic, Farsi (modern-day Persian), Kurdish
Predominant religion
Islam
Highest GDP per capita
Qatar $98,900
Lowest GDP per capita
Yemen $2,300
Highest life expectancy
Bahrain, Qatar 78 years
Highest literacy rate
Qatar 96%

GEO WHIZ

Rub' al Khali (Empty Quarter), the world's largest sand desert, covers 225,000 square miles (583,000 sq km), an area larger than France.

More than 4,000 years ago, the Sumerians built the first cities in the world on the plain between the Tigris and Euphrates Rivers in what is now Iraq.

The ancient Romans called Yemen "Arabia Felix," meaning "Happy Arabia."

Five times a day, every day, Muslims all over the world face the city of Mecca, in Saudi Arabia, to pray. Mecca is the birthplace of the prophet Muhammad, the founder of Islam.

Iran drilled the first oil wells in the region in 1908.

Causeways connect Bahrain Island—the largest of the 33 islands that make up the country of Bahrain—to two others and to the mainland of Saudi Arabia.

Southwest Asia

This region, made up largely of deserts and mountains, includes the countries of the Arabian Peninsula and those that border the Persian Gulf. Islam is the dominant religion in each, and the two holiest places for Muslims—Mecca and Medina—are here. Arabic is the principal language everywhere but Iran, where most people speak Farsi. While water has been the most important natural resource here for millennia, global attention has focused in recent decades on the region's oil wealth. With the majority of the world's reserves found here, oil has brought outside influences and military conflict. Long a cradle of civilization, Southwest Asia continues to hold the world's attention.

○ **GIRL TALK.** Young Iranian girls get together at a film festival in Tehran. The scarves they are wearing are part of the Islamic dress code hijab, which says that women and girls must cover their heads and dress modestly.

○ **HE'S GOT THE BEAT.** This Omani drummer plays at a dance in the Arabian Sea port of Qurayyat. Though modernizing in many ways, Oman works hard to preserve its traditional culture.

○ **DIFFERENT WORLDS.** A contrast between horse and horsepower, this roadside meeting in Qatar also displays both traditional Arab and Western clothing styles. This Persian Gulf country preserves a rich history of Arabian horse breeding and continues to produce champions.

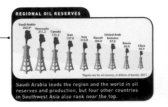

REGIONAL OIL RESERVES

Saudi Arabia 262.6 | Venezuela 211.2 | Canada 175.2 | Iran 137.0 | Iraq 115.0 | Kuwait 104.0 | United Arab Emirates 97.8 | Russia 60.0 | Libya 46.4

Figures are for oil reserves, in billions of barrels, 2011

Saudi Arabia leads the region and the world in oil reserves and production, but four other countries in Southwest Asia also rank near the top.

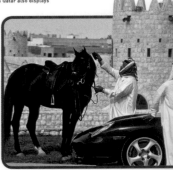

ABOUT THE CONTINENT

SOUTH AMERICA

more about
South America

ABOUT THE CONTINENT

SOUTH AMERICA

WHERE THE PICTURES ARE

WHERE ARE THE PICTURES?
If you want to know where a picture in the regional sections of this atlas was taken, look for the map in the photo essay. Find the label that describes the picture you're curious about, and follow the line to its location.

Maps use symbols to stand for political and physical features. At right is the key to the symbols used in this atlas. If you are wondering what you're looking at on a map, check here.

INDEX AND GRID

Look through the index for the place-name you want. Next to it is a page number, a letter, and another number. Go to the page. Draw imaginary lines from the letter along the side of the map and the number along the top. Your place will be close to where the lines meet.

Río Muni (region), Equatorial Guinea **135** F7
Rivera, Uruguay **81** D4
Riverside, California (U.S.) **62** E2
Riviera (region), Europe **84** F3
Rivne, Ukraine **95** D6
Riyadh, Saudi Arabia **117** E4

COLOR BARS

Every section of this atlas has its own color. Look for the color on the Contents pages and across the top of every page in the atlas. Within that color bar, you'll see the name of the section and the title for each topic or map. These color bars are a handy way to find the section you want.

North America

South America

Europe

Asia

Africa

Australia, New Zealand, & Oceania

Antarctica

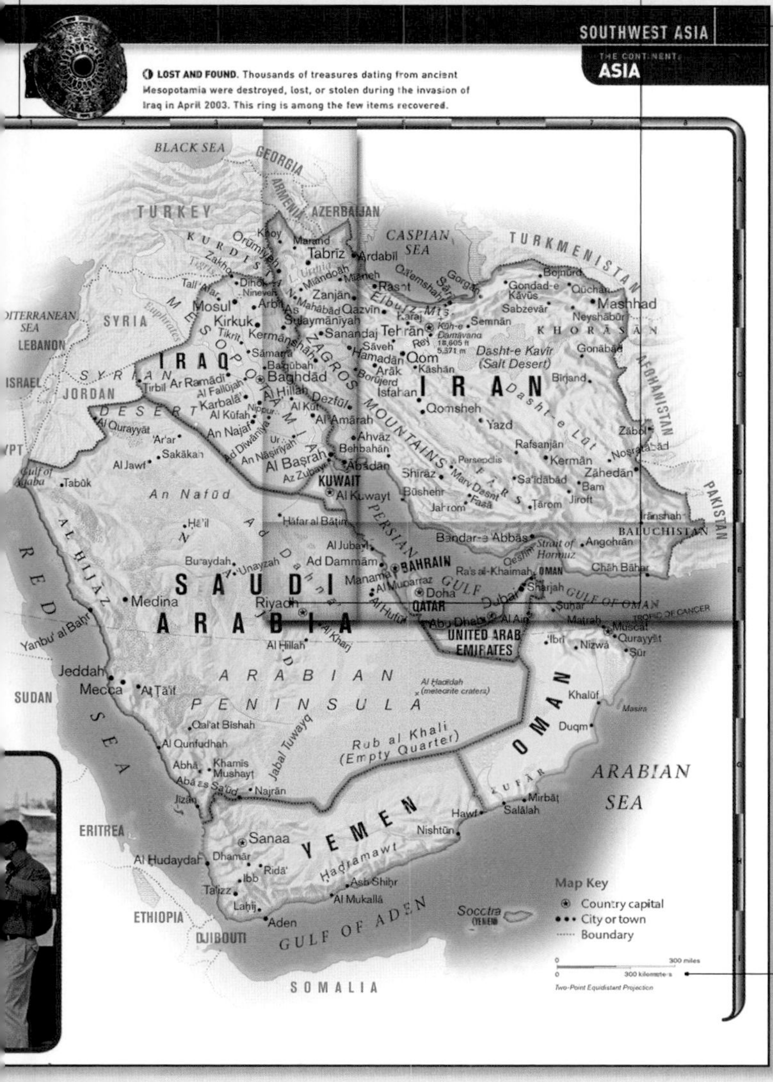

SOUTHWEST ASIA
THE CONTINENT: **ASIA**

● **LOST AND FOUND.** Thousands of treasures dating from ancient Mesopotamia were destroyed, lost, or stolen during the invasion of Iraq in April 2003. This ring is among the few items recovered.

Map Key
⊛ Country capital
●●● City or town
······ Boundary

0   300 miles
0   300 kilometers
Two-Point Equidistant Projection

BAR SCALE

If you want to find out how far it is from one place on a map to another, use the scale. A bar scale appears on every map. It shows how distance on paper relates to distance in the real world.

MAP KEY

●●● City / Town	791 ft / 241 m + Mountain peak with elevation above sea level	⊶ Waterfall	Dry / Salt Lake
⊛ Country capital	-282 ft / -86 m Low point with elevation below sea level	Dam	Glacier
⊙ State / Provincial capital		⊔⊔ Canal	Swamp
◆ Small country	········ Defined boundary	Ice Shelf	Sand
∴ Ruin	··· ··· Undefined boundary	Reef	Tundra
▪ Point of Interest	······· Claimed boundary	Lake	Lava
	～ River	Intermittent Lake	Below sea level

Exploring Your World

Earth is a big place. Even from space you can't see it all at one time. But with a map, you can see the whole world or just a part of it. Thanks to the Internet, you can download programs that allow you to experience Earth from space, pick a place you want to explore, and zoom closer and closer until you are "standing" right there! These screenshots (right) take you from space to Chicago at the click of a mouse. You can even find a satellite view of your house (see below).

Compare the computer-enhanced satellite images with the maps on the opposite page, and you will see how the same places can be shown in very different ways. You will want to explore all these ways to really get to know your world.

COMPUTER ENHANCED VIEWS OF...

THE WORLD

CONTINENT & COUNTRY

Chicago•

REGION & STATE

Chicago•

METROPOLITAN AREA

Chicago

CITY & SKYLINE

FIND YOUR HOUSE

This image from SkylineGlobe shows the National Geographic offices in Washington, D.C. To see your house, go to www.skylineglobe.com, one of several websites that allow you to view satellite imagery of the world.

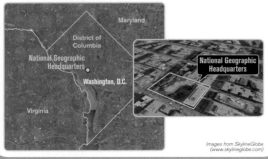

Maryland

District of Columbia

National Geographic Headquarters•

Washington, D.C.

Virginia

National Geographic Headquarters

Images from SkylineGlobe (www.skylineglobe.com)

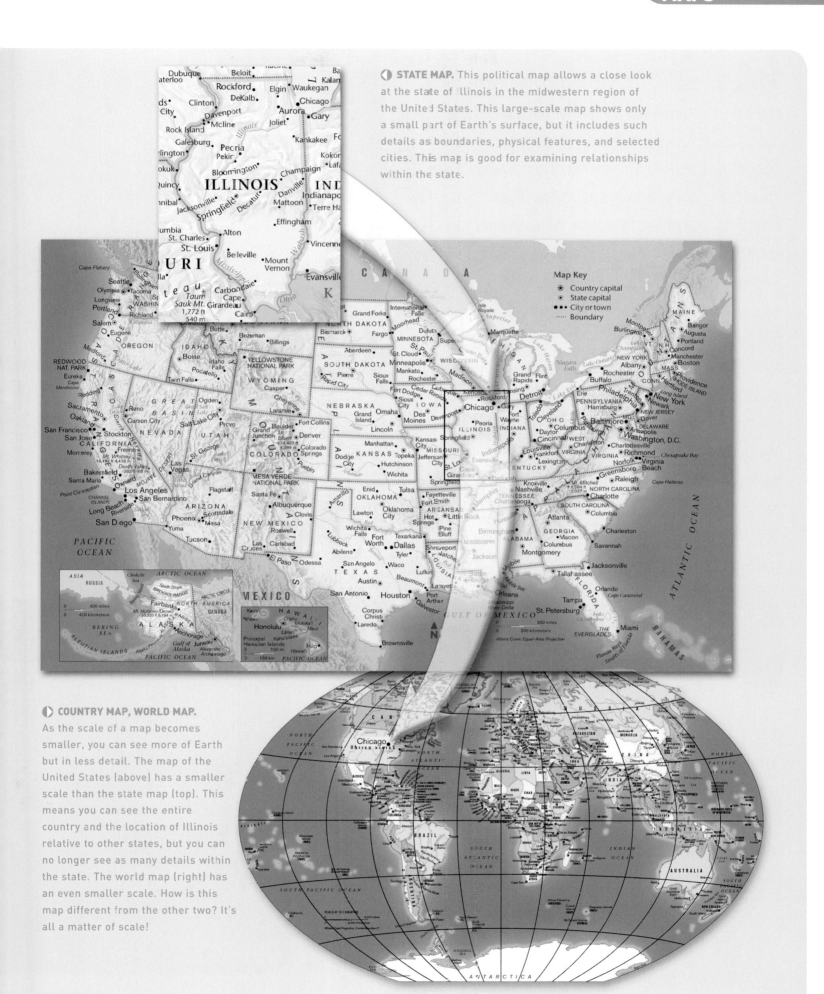

STATE MAP. This political map allows a close look at the state of Illinois in the midwestern region of the United States. This large-scale map shows only a small part of Earth's surface, but it includes such details as boundaries, physical features, and selected cities. This map is good for examining relationships within the state.

Map Key
- Country capital
- State capital
- • • City or town
- ⋯⋯ Boundary

COUNTRY MAP, WORLD MAP.

As the scale of a map becomes smaller, you can see more of Earth but in less detail. The map of the United States (above) has a smaller scale than the state map (top). This means you can see the entire country and the location of Illinois relative to other states, but you can no longer see as many details within the state. The world map (right) has an even smaller scale. How is this map different from the other two? It's all a matter of scale!

Kinds of Maps

Maps are special tools that geographers use to tell a story about Earth. Some maps show physical features, such as mountains or vegetation. Maps also show climates or natural hazards and other things we cannot easily see. Other maps illustrate different human features on Earth—political boundaries, urban centers, and economic systems.

Maps are not perfect. A globe is a scale model of Earth with accurate relative sizes and locations. Because maps are flat, they involve distortions of size, shape, and direction. Also, cartographers—people who create maps—make choices about what information to include. Because of this, it is important to study many different types of maps to learn the complete story of Earth.

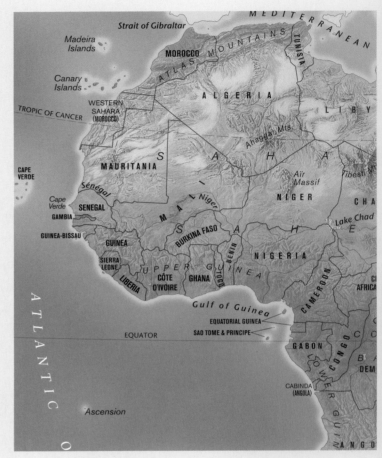

PHYSICAL MAPS. Earth's natural features—landforms, water bodies, and vegetation—are shown on physical maps. The map above uses color and shading to illustrate mountains, lakes, rivers, and deserts in western Africa. Country names and borders are added for reference, but they are not natural features.

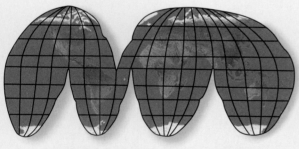

MAP PROJECTIONS. To create a map, cartographers transfer an image of the round Earth to a flat surface, a process called projection. All projections involve distortion. For example, an interrupted projection (top map) shows accurate shapes and relative sizes of land areas, but oceans have gaps. Other types of projections are cylindrical, conic, or azimuthal—each with certain advantages, but all with some distortion.

MAKING MAPS

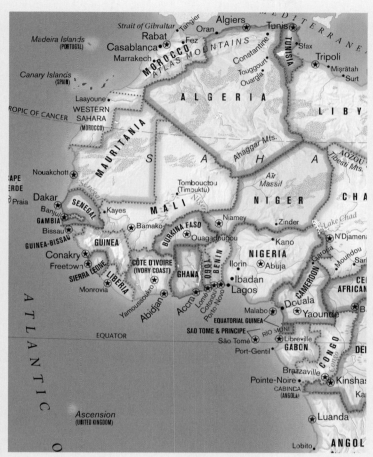

POLITICAL MAPS. These maps represent human characteristics of the landscape, such as boundaries, cities, and place-names. Natural features are added only for reference. On the map above, capital cities are represented with a star inside a circle, while other cities are located with black dots.

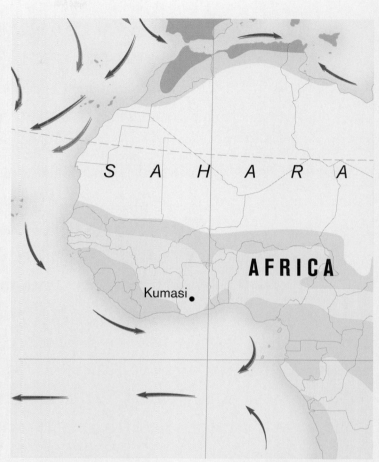

THEMATIC MAPS. Patterns related to a particular topic, or theme, such as population distribution, appear on these maps. The map above displays the region's climate zones, which range from tropical wet (bright green) to tropical wet and dry (light green) to semiarid (dark yellow) to arid or desert (light yellow).

Long ago, cartographers worked with pen and ink, carefully hand-crafting maps based on explorers' observations and diaries. Today, mapmaking is a high-tech business. Cartographers use Earth data stored in "layers" in a Geographic Information System (GIS) and special computer programs to create maps that can be easily updated as new information becomes available. The cartographers at left are changing country labels on a map of the Balkans.

Satellites in orbit around Earth act as eyes in the sky, recording data about the planet's land and ocean areas. The data is converted to numbers that are transmitted back to computers that are specially programmed to interpret the data. They record it in a form that cartographers can use to create maps.

How to Read a Map

Every map has a story to tell, but first you have to know how to read the map.

Maps are useful for finding places because every place on Earth has a special address called its absolute location. Imaginary lines, called latitude and longitude, create a grid that makes finding places easy because every spot on Earth has a unique longitude and latitude. In addition, special tools, called Global Positioning Systems (GPS), communicate with orbiting satellites to determine absolute location.

Maps are also useful for determining distance and direction. Maps have a scale, often a bar scale or a verbal scale, that shows the relationship between distance on the map and distance on Earth. Maps often have a compass rose to show direction. Many people think north is at the top of a map, but this is not always true. The compass rose indicates north for each map.

Maps represent other information by using a language of symbols. Knowing how to read these symbols provides access to a wide range of information. To find out what each symbol means, you must use the map key. Think of the map key as your secret decoder, identifying information represented by each symbol on the map.

◖ **LATITUDE AND LONGITUDE.** Latitude and longitude lines help us determine locations on Earth. Lines of latitude run west to east, parallel to the Equator (below, left). These lines measure distance in degrees north or south, from the Equator (0° latitude) to the North Pole (90°N) or to the South Pole (90°S). One degree of latitude is approximately 70 statute miles (113 km).

Lines of longitude run north to south, meeting at the Poles (below, right). These lines measure distance in degrees east or west from 0° longitude (prime meridian) to 180° longitude. The prime meridian runs through Greenwich, England.

Latitude

Longitude

◖ **ABSOLUTE LOCATION.** The imaginary grid composed of lines of latitude and longitude helps us locate places on a map. Suppose you are playing a game of global scavenger hunt. The clue says the prize is hidden at absolute location 30°S, 60°W. You know that the first number is south of the Equator, and the second is west of the prime meridian. On the map at right, find the line of latitude labeled 30°S. Now find the line of longitude labeled 60°W. Trace these lines with your fingers until they meet. Identify this spot. The prize must be located in central Argentina (see arrow, right).

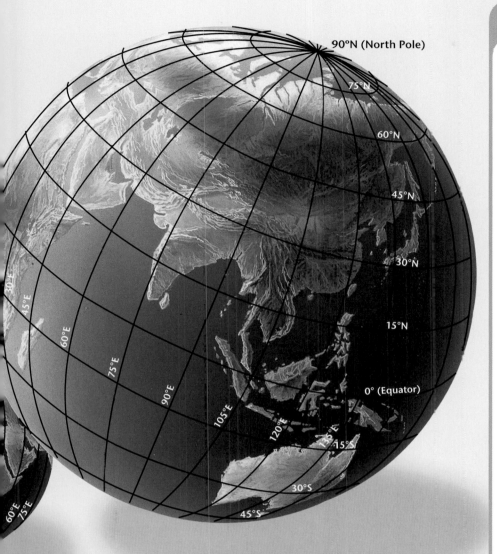

SYMBOLS

There are three main types of map symbols: points, lines, and areas. Points, which can be either dots or small icons, represent the location or the number of things, such as schools, cities, or landmarks. Lines are used to show boundaries, roads, or rivers and can vary in color or thickness. Area symbols use patterns or color to show regions, such as a sandy area or a neighborhood.

POINT
A point symbol, a black dot, indicates a city, such as Omdurman.

LINE
Sudan's country boundary appears as a line symbol: a dotted line with a colored edge.

AREA
Sandy places, such as parts of the Saharan desert, are shown by a tan, speckled area.

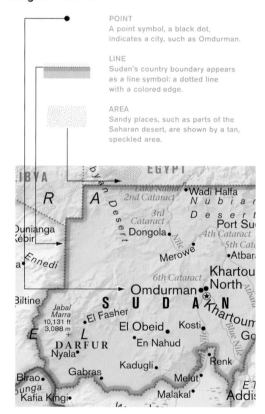

SCALE & DIRECTION

The scale on a map can be shown as a fraction, as words, or as a line or bar. It relates distance on the map to distance in the real world. Sometimes the scale identifies the type of map projection. Maps may include an arrow or compass rose to indicate north on the map. Maps in this atlas are oriented north, so they do not use a north indicator.

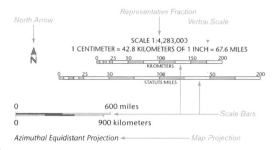

North Arrow
Representative Fraction
Verbal Scale

SCALE 1:4,283,000
1 CENTIMETER = 42.8 KILOMETERS OF 1 INCH = 67.6 MILES

0   25   50   100   150   200
KILOMETERS

0   25   50   100   50   200
STATUTE MILES

0   600 miles

0   900 kilometers

Azimuthal Equidistant Projection   *Map Projection*
Scale Bars

▶ **APPLYING WHAT YOU'VE LEARNED.**
Now that you know how to read a map, can you find places on the maps in this atlas? What about Sapporo in the eastern Asian country of Japan? The index at the back of this atlas tells you that Sapporo is on "page 113 B10." Along the edges of the map are letters and numbers. Place one finger on the B at the side and another finger on the 10 at the top. Now trace straight across from the B and down from the 10. Sapporo is where your fingers meet!

Earth in Space

Earth, the planet we call home, is part of a cosmic family called the solar system. It is one of the planets that revolve around a giant solar nuclear reactor that we call the sun.

The extreme heat and pressure on the sun cause atoms of hydrogen to combine in a process called fusion, producing new atoms of helium and releasing tremendous amounts of energy. The sun is the essential source of energy that makes life on Earth possible. It provides us with light and warmth.

Time on Earth is defined by our relationship to the sun. It takes Earth, following a path called an orbit, approximately 365 days—one year—to make one full revolution around the sun. As Earth makes its way around the sun, it also turns on its axis, an imaginary line that passes between the Poles. This motion, called rotation, occurs once every 24 hours and results in day and night.

Io

Ceres

Mars

Earth & Moon

Venus

Mercury

10 A.M. 9 A.M. 8 A.M.
11 A.M. 7 A.M.
12 NOON 6 A.M.
PRIME MERIDIAN 5 A.M.
4 A.M.
3 A.M.
DATE LINE 2 A.M.
1 A.M.
12 MIDNIGHT
11 P.M.
7 P.M. 8 P.M. 9 P.M. 10 P.M.
5 P.M.
6 P.M.
4 P.M.
3 P.M.
2 P.M.
1 P.M.

ASIA

PACIFIC OCEAN

INDIAN OCEAN

TIME ZONES. Long ago, when people lived in relative isolation, they measured time by the position of the sun overhead. That meant that noon in one place was not the same as noon in a place 100 miles (160 km) to the west. Later, with the development of long-distance railroads, people needed to coordinate time. In 1884, a system of 24 standard time zones was adopted. Each time zone reflects the fact that Earth rotates west to east 15 degrees each hour. Time is counted from the prime meridian, which runs through Greenwich, England.

Callisto

Titan

Triton

Charon

Haumea

Jupiter

Saturn

Uranus

Neptune

Pluto

Makemake

Eris

Note: Art shows relative sizes of the sun and planets, but distances are not to scale.

◓ **SOLAR SYSTEM.** The sun and its family of planets are located near the outer edge of the Milky Way, a giant spiral galaxy. Earth is the third planet from the sun and one of the four "terrestrial" planets. These planets—Mercury, Venus, Earth, and Mars—are made up of solid rocky material. Beyond these inner planets are the four gas giants—Jupiter, Saturn, Uranus, and Neptune. Recently, astronomers—scientists who study space—have named a new category called "dwarf" planets that includes Pluto, Ceres, Eris, Haumea, and Makemake. More of these dwarf planets may soon be identified. Many planets, including Earth, have one or more moons orbiting them. The art above names a few: Io, Callisto, Titan, Triton, and Charon.

◑ **ENVELOPE OF AIR.** Earth is enclosed within a thick layer of air called the atmosphere. Made up of a mix of nitrogen, oxygen, and other gases, the atmosphere provides us with the life-giving air that we breathe. It also protects us from dangerous radiation from the sun. Weather systems move through the atmosphere, redistributing heat and moisture and creating Earth's climates.

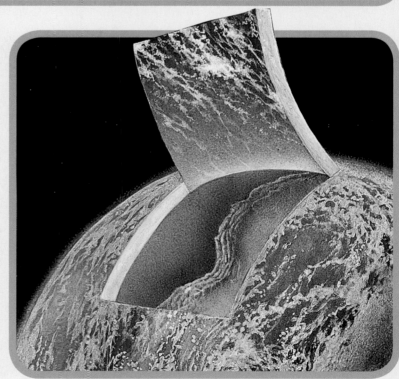

Earth in Motion

If we could step into a time machine and travel 500 million years into the past, we probably would not recognize Earth. Back then, most of the landmasses we call continents were joined together in a single giant landmass called Pangaea. So how did the continents break away from Pangaea and move to their current positions? Where will they be in another 500 million years?

Deep within Earth, pressure and heat cause rocks of the mantle to become partially molten, but near Earth's surface a thin shell of solid rock forms the crust. Currents of heat rise and fall within the mantle, causing the crust to break into large pieces, called plates, which very slowly move about on Earth's surface. These powerful forces are at work today, creating and destroying land features and reshaping Earth's surface.

CRUST IN MOTION. Earth's major plates are outlined in red on the map at right. Plate edges are the most active parts, with volcanoes and earthquakes (yellow dots on the map) resulting from plates moving together or grinding past each other.

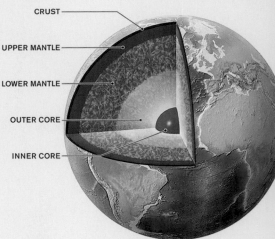

CRUST ——
UPPER MANTLE ——
LOWER MANTLE ——
OUTER CORE ——
INNER CORE ——

A LOOK WITHIN. The distance from Earth's surface to its center is 3,963 miles (6,377 km). There are four layers: a thin, rigid crust; the rocky mantle (upper and lower); the outer core, which is a layer of molten iron; and finally the inner core, which is solid iron.

CONTINENTS ON THE MOVE

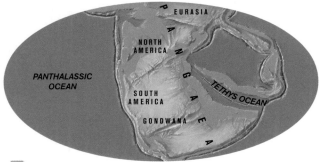

1 PANGAEA. About 240 million years ago, Earth's landmasses were joined together in one supercontinent that extended from Pole to Pole.

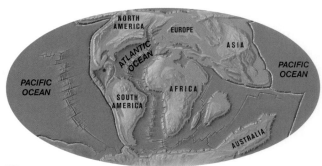

3 EXTINCTION. About 65 million years ago an asteroid smashed into Earth, creating the Gulf of Mexico (red * on map). This impact may have resulted in the extinction of half the world's species, including the dinosaurs—one of several major extinctions.

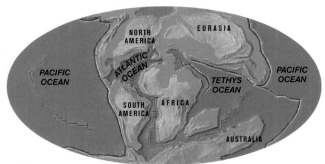

2 BREAKUP. By 94 million years ago, Pangaea had broken apart into landmasses that would become today's continents. Dinosaurs roamed Earth during this period of warmer climates.

4 ICE AGE. By 18,000 years ago, the continents had drifted close to their present positions, but most far northern and far southern lands were buried beneath huge glaciers.

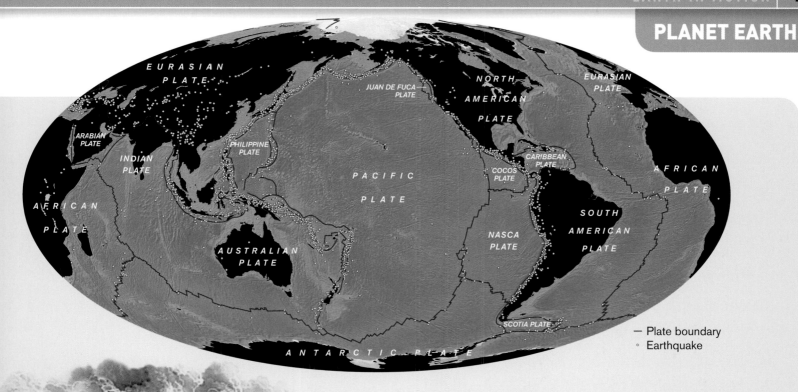

— Plate boundary
∘ Earthquake

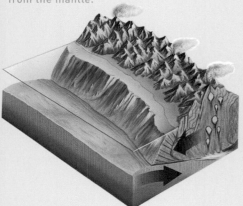

⬙ **VOLCANOES** form when molten rock, called magma, rises to Earth's surface. Some volcanoes occur as one plate pushes beneath another plate. Other volcanoes result when a plate passes over a column of magma, called a hot spot, rising from the mantle.

Earth Shapers

Earth's features are constantly undergoing change—being built up, destroyed, or just rearranged. Plates are in constant, very slow motion. Some plates collide, others pull apart, and still others slowly grind past each other. As the plates move, mountains are uplifted, volcanoes erupt, and new land is created.

⬙ **FAULTING** happens when two plates grind past each other, creating large cracks along the edges of the plates. A famous fault is the San Andreas, in California, where the Pacific and North American plates meet, causing damaging earthquakes.

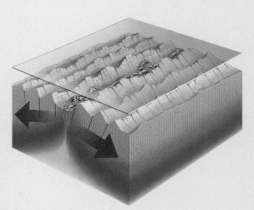

⬙ **SPREADING** results when oceanic plates move apart. The ocean floor cracks, magma rises, and new crust is created. The Mid-Atlantic Ridge spreads a few centimeters—about an inch—a year, pushing Europe and North America farther apart.

⬙ **COLLISION** of two continental plates causes plate edges to break and fold, creating mountains, Earth's highest landforms. The Himalaya are the result of the Indian plate colliding with the Eurasian plate, an ongoing process that began 50 million years ago.

⬙ **SUBDUCTION** occurs when an oceanic plate dives under a continental plate. This often results in volcanoes and earthquakes, as well as mountain building.

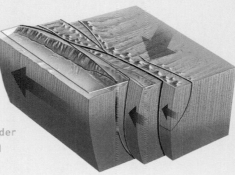

PHYSICAL WORLD

The Physical World

Earth is dominated by large landmasses called continents—seven in all—and by an interconnected global ocean that is divided into four parts by the continents. More than 70 percent of Earth's surface is covered by oceans; the remaining 30 percent is made up of land areas.

Different landforms give variety to the surface of the continents. The Rockies and Andes mark the western edge of North and South America, and the Himalaya tower above southern Asia. The Plateau of Tibet forms the rugged core of Asia, while the Northern European Plain extends from the North Sea to the Ural Mountains. Much of Africa is a plateau, and dry plains cover large areas of Australia. Beneath massive ice sheets, mountains rise more than 16,000 feet (4,877 m) in Antarctica.

Mountains and trenches make the ocean floors as varied as any continent (see pages 156–167). A mountain chain called the Mid-Atlantic Ridge runs the length of the Atlantic Ocean. In the western Pacific Ocean, trenches drop to depths greater than 35,000 feet (10,668 m).

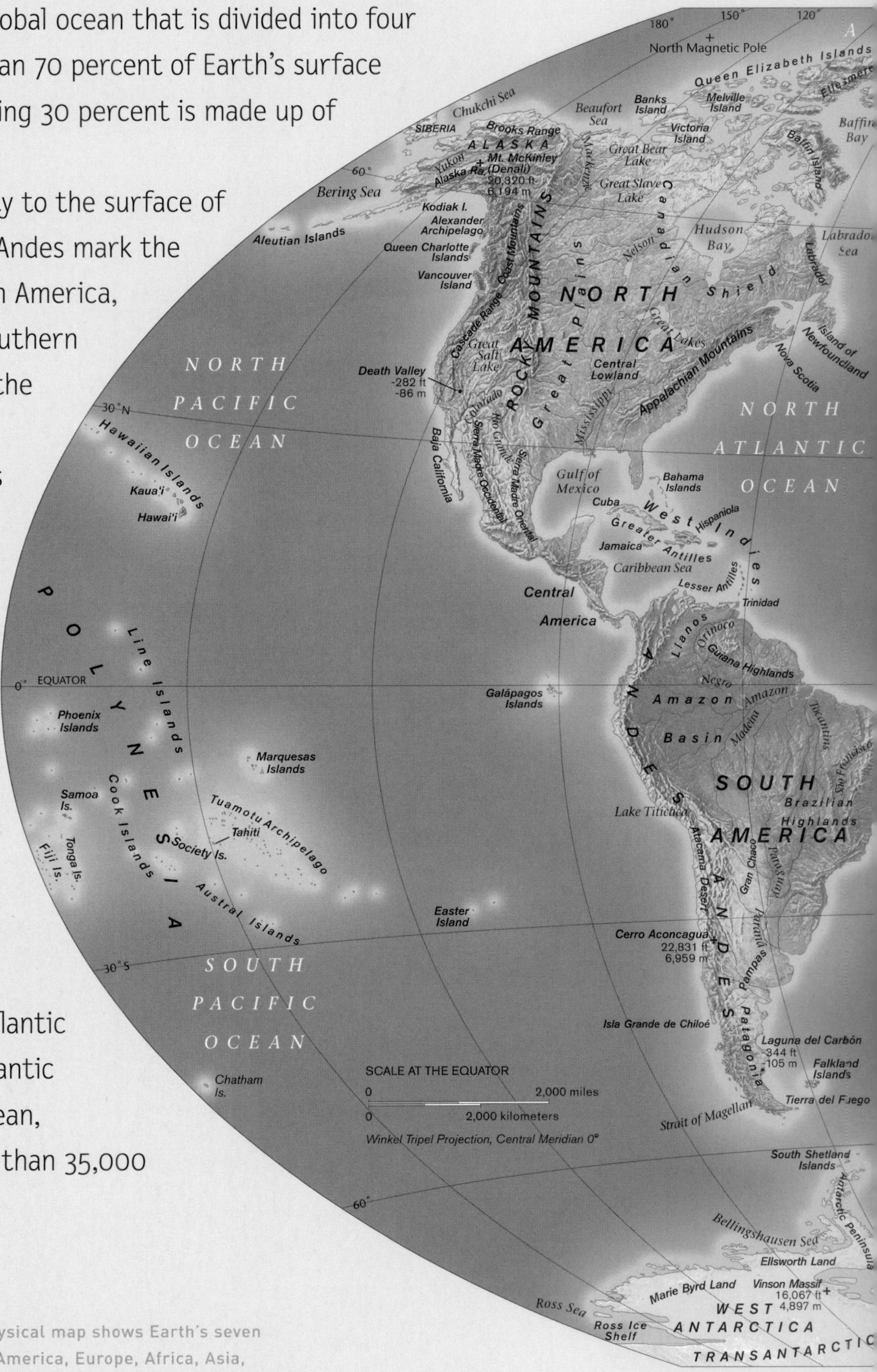

○ **LAND AND WATER.** This world physical map shows Earth's seven continents—North America, South America, Europe, Africa, Asia, Australia, and Antarctica—as well as the four oceans: Pacific, Atlantic, Indian, and Arctic. Some people regard the area from Antarctica to 60°S, where the oceans merge, as a fifth ocean called the Southern Ocean.

SCALE AT THE EQUATOR

0   2,000 miles

0   2,000 kilometers

Winkel Tripel Projection, Central Meridian 0°

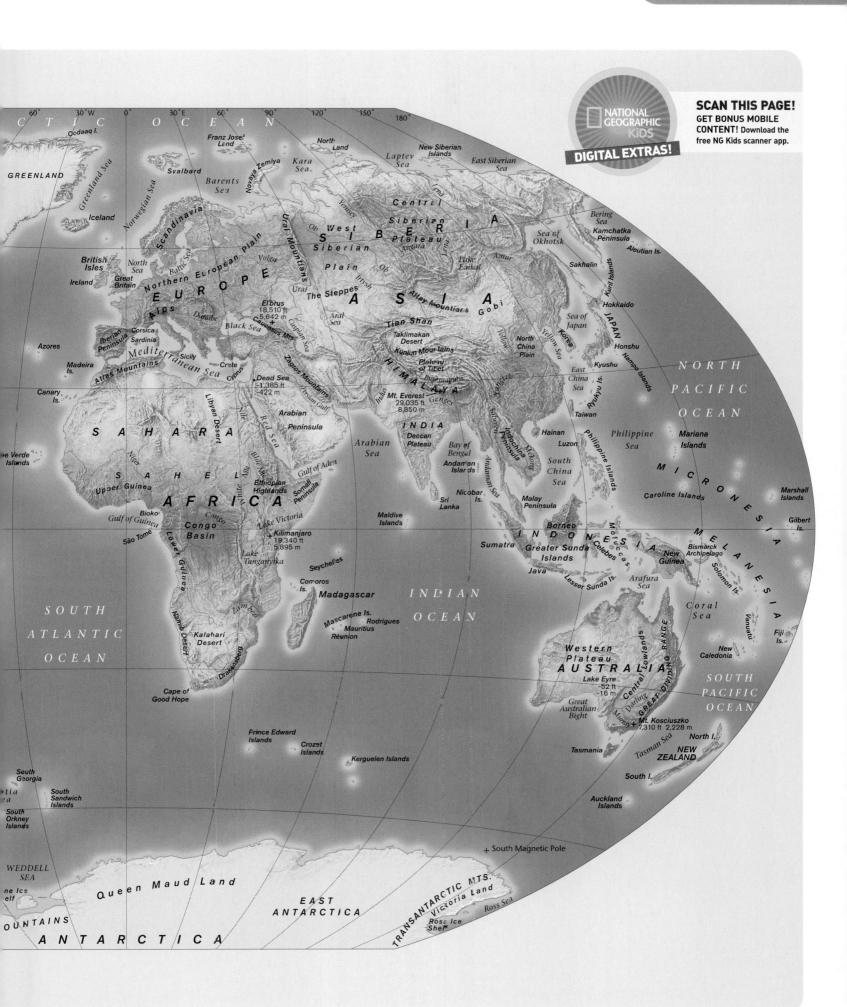

60°   30° W   0°   30° E   60°   90°   120°   150°   180°

ARCTIC OCEAN

GREENLAND

Oodaaq I.

Franz Josef
Land

North
Land

New Siberian
Islands

Laptev
Sea

East Siberian
Sea

Greenland Sea

Iceland

Svalbard

Novaya Zemlya

Kara
Sea

Central

Siberian

Bering
Sea

Kamchatka
Peninsula

Norwegian Sea

Barents
Sea

Lena

Plateau

Aleutian Is.

British
Isles

North
Sea

Baltic Sea

Northern European Plain

Scandinavia

Volga

Ob

West
Siberian

Plain

Yenisey

Angara

Lena

Lake
Baikal

Amur

Sea of
Okhotsk

Sakhalin

Kuril Islands

Ireland

Great
Britain

EUROPE

SIBERIA

Ob

Hokkaido

Alps

Danube

Ural Mountains

Ural

The Steppes

Irtysh

ASIA

Altay Mountains

Gobi

Sea of
Japan

JAPAN

Iberian
Peninsula

Corsica
Sardinia

El'brus
18,510 ft
5,642 m

Caspian Sea

Aral
Sea

Tian Shan

Korea

Honshu

Nampo Islands

Azores

Caucasus Mts.

Black Sea

Taklimakan
Desert

North
China
Plain

Yellow Sea

Kyushu

NORTH

Madeira
Is.

Mediterranean Sea

Sicily

Crete

Zagros Mountains

Kunlun Mountains

Plateau
of Tibet

Yellow

East
China
Sea

Ryukyu Is.

PACIFIC

Atlas Mountains

Cyprus

Dead Sea
-1,385 ft
-422 m

Persian Gulf

HIMALAYA

Brahmaputra

Yangtze

Taiwan

OCEAN

Canary
Is.

Libyan Desert

Nile

Red Sea

Arabian
Peninsula

Indus

Mt. Everest
29,035 ft
8,850 m

Ganges

Salween

Indochina Peninsula

Hainan

Luzon

Philippine
Sea

Mariana
Islands

SAHARA

SAHEL

Upper Guinea

AFRICA

Blue Nile

Niger

Ethiopian
Highlands

Gulf of Aden

Somali
Peninsula

Arabian
Sea

INDIA

Deccan
Plateau

Bay of
Bengal

Andaman
Islands

Mekong

South
China
Sea

Philippine Islands

MICRONESIA

Cape Verde
Islands

Bioko

Gulf of Guinea

São Tomé

Congo

Congo
Basin

Lake Victoria

Kilimanjaro
19,340 ft
5,895 m

Maldive
Islands

Sri
Lanka

Nicobar
Is.

Andaman Sea

Malay
Peninsula

Caroline Islands

Marshall
Islands

Gilbert
Is.

Lower Guinea

Lake
Tanganyika

Seychelles

Sumatra

Borneo

Greater Sunda
Islands

Java

Celebes

Moluccas

INDONESIA

Lesser Sunda Is.

New
Guinea

Bismarck
Archipelago

Solomon Is.

MELANESIA

SOUTH

ATLANTIC

OCEAN

Namib Desert

Zambezi

Comoros
Is.

Madagascar

Mascarene Is.

Rodrigues

Mauritius

Réunion

INDIAN

OCEAN

Arafura
Sea

New
Caledonia

Coral
Sea

Vanuatu

Fiji
Is.

Kalahari
Desert

Drakensberg

Western
Plateau

AUSTRALIA

Lake Eyre
-52 ft
-16 m

Central Lowlands

Darling

GREAT DIVIDING RANGE

SOUTH

PACIFIC

OCEAN

Cape of
Good Hope

Prince Edward
Islands

Crozet
Islands

Kerguelen Islands

Great
Australian
Bight

Murray

Mt. Kosciuszko
7,310 ft 2,228 m

Tasmania

Tasman Sea

North I.

NEW
ZEALAND

South
Georgia

...tia
...a

South
Sandwich
Islands

South
Orkney
Islands

South I.

Auckland
Islands

+ South Magnetic Pole

WEDDELL
SEA

...ne Ice
...elf

Queen Maud Land

EAST

ANTARCTICA

TRANSANTARCTIC MTS.

Victoria Land

Ross Sea

...OUNTAINS

ANTARCTICA

Ross Ice
Shelf

The Land

A closer look at Earth's surface reveals many varied forms and features that make each place unique. The drawing (right) captures 41 natural and human-made features in an imaginary landscape that shows how these different land and water features relate to each other. For example, a large moving "river" of ice, called a glacier, descends from a high mountain range. A river passes through a valley and empties into a gulf. And a harbor, built by people, creates safe anchorage for ships.

Features such as these can be found all over the world because the same forces are at work wherever you might go. Internal forces such as volcanoes and the movement of the plates of Earth's crust are constantly creating and building up new landforms, while external forces such as wind, water, and ice continuously wear down surface features.

Earth is dynamic—constantly changing, never the same.

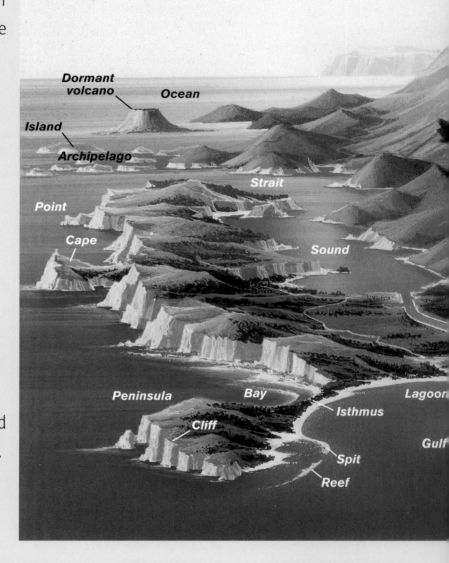

RIVER

As a river moves through flatlands, it twists and turns. Above, the Rio Los Amigos winds through a rain forest in Peru.

CANYON

Steep-sided valleys called canyons are created mainly by running water. Buckskin Gulch (above) is the deepest slot canyon in the American Southwest.

DESERT

Deserts are a land feature created by climate, specifically by a lack of water. Above, a camel caravan crosses the Sahara, in North Africa.

OASIS

Occasionally, water rises from deep below a desert, creating a refuge that supports trees and sometimes crops, as in this oasis in Africa.

PHYSICAL WORLD

Mountain peak

Mountain range

Glacier

Iceberg

Basin

Desert

Mesa

Oasis

Divide

Plateau

Valley

Waterfall

Escarpment

Lake

Canyon

Canal

Plain

River

Fork

Beach

Hills

Delta

Harbor

Tributary

Breakwater

A NAME FOR EVERY FEATURE

Land has a vocabulary all its own, each name identifying a specific feature of the landscape. A cape, for example, is a broadish chunk of land extending out into the sea. It is not pointed, however, for then it would be a point. Nor does it have a narrow neck. A sizable cape or point with a narrow neck is a peninsula. The narrow neck is an isthmus. Such specific identifiers have proven useful over the centuries. In the early days of exploration, even the simplest maps showed peninsulas, bays, and straits. Sailors used these landmarks to reach safe harbor or avoid disastrous encounters.

◀ **EXPLORING THE LANDSCAPE.** How many land and water features can you identify in the imaginary landscape at left? Definitions for these terms can be found in the glossary on pages 186–188.

MOUNTAIN
Mountains are Earth's tallest landforms, and Mount Everest (above) rises highest of all at 29,035 feet (8,850 m) above sea level.

GLACIER
Glaciers—"rivers" of ice—such as Alaska's Hubbard (above), move slowly from mountains to the sea. Global warming may be shrinking them.

VALLEY
Valleys, cut by running water or moving ice, may be broad and flat or narrow and steep, such as the Indus River Valley in Ladakh, India (above).

WATERFALL
Waterfalls form when a river reaches an abrupt change in elevation. Above, Kaieteur Falls, in Guyana, descends 800 feet (244 m).

World Climate

Weather is the condition of the atmosphere—temperature, precipitation, humidity, wind—at a given place at a given time. Climate, however, is the average weather for a particular place over a long period of time. Different places on Earth have different climates, but climate is not a random occurrence. It is a pattern that is controlled by factors such as latitude, elevation, prevailing winds, temperature of ocean currents, and location on land relative to water. Climate is generally constant, but many are concerned that human activity may be causing a change in the patterns of climate.

THE BASICS

According to the National Oceanic and Atmospheric Administration (NOAA), 2010 ranks first as the hottest year on record, followed by 1998. The global annual temperature for combined land and ocean surfaces was 1°F (.6°C) above the average established between 1880 and 2004.

Ice cores taken from Antarctica and Greenland have enabled scientists to gain detailed information about the history of Earth's climate and its atmosphere—especially the presence of greenhouse gases—dating back thousands of years.

Data collected by satellite imagery suggest that the Sahara, Earth's largest desert, had a wet climate that supported vast forests some 12,000 years ago. Extremely dry conditions did not begin until about 5,000 years ago.

According to climatologists, Earth had what is called the Little Ice Age, which lasted from the 17th century to the late 19th century. During that time, temperatures were cold enough to cause glaciers to advance.

CLIMATE GRAPHS.
Temperature and precipitation data provide a snapshot of the climate at a particular place. This information can be shown in a special type of graph called a climate graph (see below). Average monthly temperatures (scale on the left side of the graphs) are represented by the lines at the tops of the colored areas, while average monthly precipitation totals (scale on the right side of the graphs) are reflected in the bars. For example, the graph for Belém, Brazil, shows a constant warm temperature with abundant rainfall year-round. In contrast, the graph for Fairbanks, Alaska, shows a cool, variable temperature with only limited precipitation.

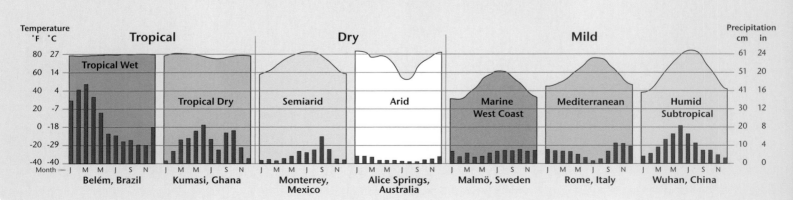

Tropical — Tropical Wet — Belém, Brazil — Tropical Dry — Kumasi, Ghana
Dry — Semiarid — Monterrey, Mexico — Arid — Alice Springs, Australia
Mild — Marine West Coast — Malmö, Sweden — Mediterranean — Rome, Italy — Humid Subtropical — Wuhan, China

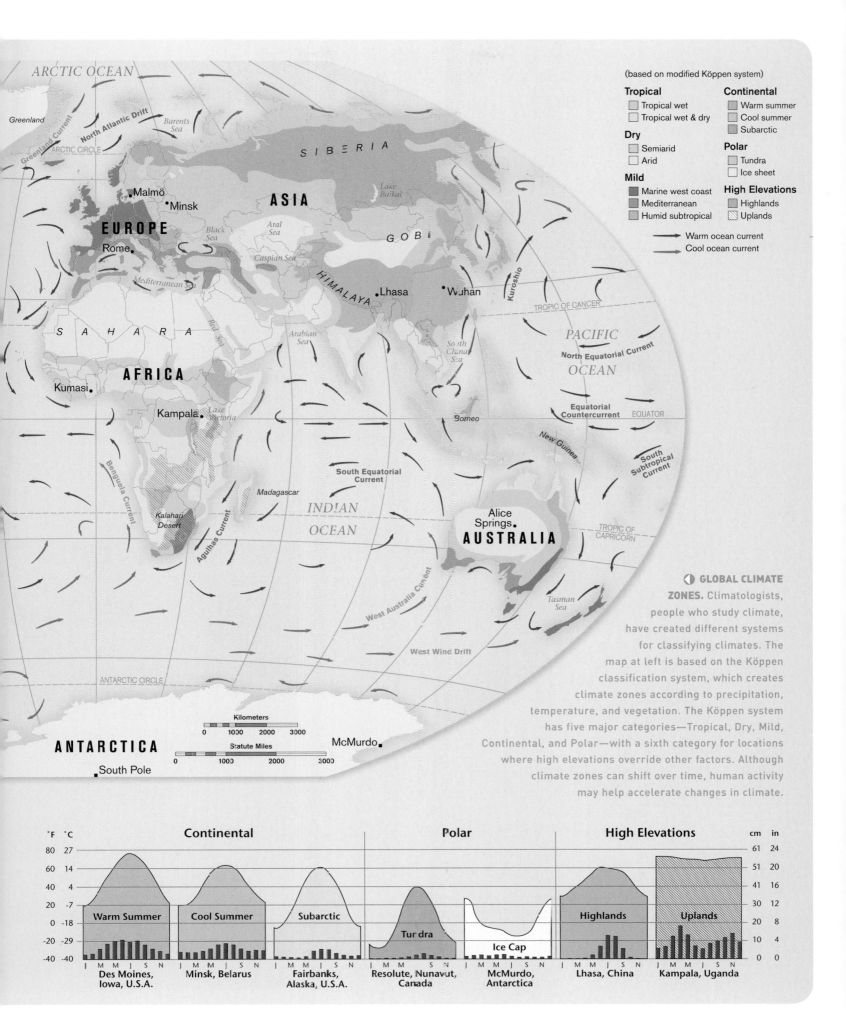

ARCTIC OCEAN

Greenland

Barents Sea

ARCTIC CIRCLE

SIBERIA

ASIA

Lake Baikal

•Malmö
•Minsk

EUROPE

Black Sea

Aral Sea

Rome•

Caspian Sea

GOBI

HIMALAYA

•Lhasa   •Wuhan

Mediterranean Sea

Kuroshio

TROPIC OF CANCER

SAHARA

Arabian Sea

South China Sea

PACIFIC

North Equatorial Current

OCEAN

Kumasi•

AFRICA

Kampala•   Lake Victoria

Borneo

Equatorial Countercurrent   EQUATOR

New Guinea

South Subtropical Current

Benguela Current

Madagascar

South Equatorial Current

INDIAN

Kalahari Desert

Agulhas Current

OCEAN

Alice Springs•

AUSTRALIA

TROPIC OF CAPRICORN

West Australia Current

Tasman Sea

ANTARCTIC CIRCLE

West Wind Drift

ANTARCTICA

Kilometers
0 1000 2000 3000

Statute Miles
0 1000 2000 3000

McMurdo•

•South Pole

Legend (based on modified Köppen system)

Tropical
- Tropical wet
- Tropical wet & dry

Dry
- Semiarid
- Arid

Mild
- Marine west coast
- Mediterranean
- Humid subtropical

Continental
- Warm summer
- Cool summer
- Subarctic

Polar
- Tundra
- Ice sheet

High Elevations
- Highlands
- Uplands

→ Warm ocean current
→ Cool ocean current

GLOBAL CLIMATE ZONES. Climatologists, people who study climate, have created different systems for classifying climates. The map at left is based on the Köppen classification system, which creates climate zones according to precipitation, temperature, and vegetation. The Köppen system has five major categories—Tropical, Dry, Mild, Continental, and Polar—with a sixth category for locations where high elevations override other factors. Although climate zones can shift over time, human activity may help accelerate changes in climate.

°F	°C	Continental			Polar		High Elevations		cm	in
80	27								61	24
60	14								51	20
40	4								41	16
20	-7	Warm Summer	Cool Summer	Subarctic			Highlands	Uplands	30	12
0	-18				Tundra				20	8
-20	-29					Ice Cap			10	4
-40	-40								0	0

Des Moines, Iowa, U.S.A. | Minsk, Belarus | Fairbanks, Alaska, U.S.A. | Resolute, Nunavut, Canada | McMurdo, Antarctica | Lhasa, China | Kampala, Uganda

Factors Influencing Climate

Earth's climate is a bit like a big jigsaw puzzle. To understand it, you need to fit all the pieces together, because climate is influenced by a number of different, but interrelated factors. These include latitude, topography (shape of the land), elevation above sea level, wind systems, ocean currents, and distance from large bodies of water. Climate has always affected the way we live, but scientists now believe that the way we live may also be affecting climate. Pollution from industries and motor vehicles may be contributing to global warming. And this could be causing Earth's climate to change.

WINDWARD

TOPOGRAPHY. Mountain ranges are natural barriers to the movement of air. In North America, prevailing westerly winds carry air full of moisture from the Pacific Ocean to the West Coast. As air rises over the Coast Ranges, light precipitation falls. Farther inland, the much taller Sierra Nevada range triggers heavy precipitation as air rises higher. On the leeward side of the Sierra Nevada, sinking air warms, clouds evaporate, and dry "rain shadow" conditions prevail. As winds continue across the interior plateau, the air remains dry because there is no significant source of moisture.

Windward (wet)   Leeward (dry)

Wind

Pacific Ocean

Coast Ranges   Sierra Nevada

Cool   Warm   Temperature changes as air moves over mountains

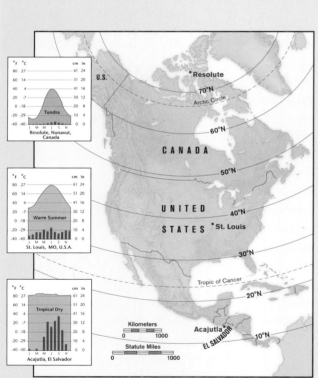

LATITUDE. Energy from the sun drives global climates. Latitude—distance north or south of the Equator—affects the amount of solar energy received. Places near the Equator (see Acajutla, El Salvador, above) have warm temperatures year-round. As distance from the Equator increases (see St. Louis, U.S.A., and Resolute, Canada, above), average temperatures decline, and cold winters become more pronounced.

ELEVATION. In general, climate conditions become cooler as elevation increases. Since cooler air holds less moisture, less precipitation falls. As temperature and moisture conditions change, vegetation also changes. In the mountain diagram (right), dense mixed forest grows near the base of the mountain on the windward side. As elevation increases and temperatures decline, the mixed forest changes to all evergreen, followed by alpine meadows, until finally the mountain's rocky peaks are covered by snow and ice. As air moves down the leeward slope of the mountain, it warms and evaporates moisture, causing the leeward side to be drier and have less vegetation.

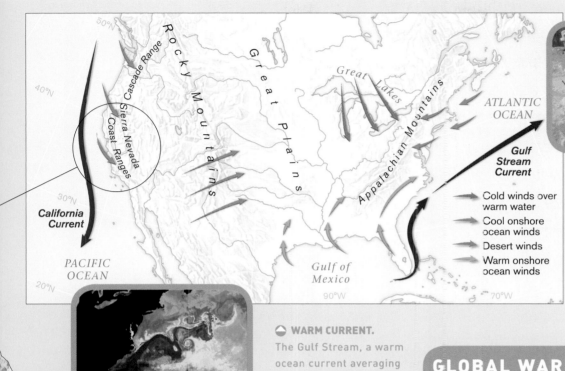

⬤ **DIGGING OUT.** Arctic winds roar across Canada, picking up moisture from the Great Lakes (see purple arrows on map, left). As the moisture-laden air crosses over the frozen land, temperatures fall and heavy precipitation—called lake effect snow—buries cars and roads, as shown here in Oswego, New York, U.S.A.

⬤ **WARM CURRENT.**
The Gulf Stream, a warm ocean current averaging 50–93 miles (80–150 km) wide, sweeps up the East Coast of North America (see red arrow on map above). One branch continues across the North Atlantic Ocean and above the Arctic Circle. In this color-enhanced satellite image (left), the Gulf Stream looks like a dark red river moving up the coast. This "river" of warm water influences climate along its path, bringing moisture and mild temperatures to the East Coast of the United States and causing ice-free ports above the Arctic Circle in Europe.

LEEWARD

GLOBAL WARMING

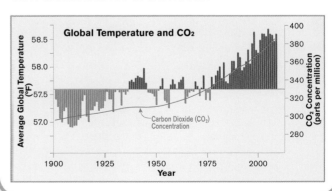

Earth's climate history has been a story of ups and downs, with warm periods followed by periods of bitter cold. The early part of the 20th century was marked by colder than average temperatures (see graph below), followed by a period of gradual and then steady increase in temperature. Scientists are concerned that the current warming trend may be more than a natural cycle. Evidence indicates that human activity is adding to the warming. One sign of change is melting glaciers in Greenland and Antarctica. If glaciers continue to melt, areas of Florida (shown above in red) and other coastal land will be underwater.

Global Temperature and CO₂

Average Global Temperature (°F) — 58.5, 58.0, 57.5, 57.0

CO₂ Concentration (parts per million) — 400, 380, 360, 340, 320, 300, 280

Carbon Dioxide (CO₂) Concentration

Year — 1900, 1925, 1950, 1975, 2000

World Vegetation

Natural vegetation—plants that would grow under ideal circumstances at a particular place—depends on several factors. The climate is very important, as is the quality and type of soil that is available. Therefore, vegetation often reflects patterns of climate. (Compare the vegetation map at right with the world climate map on pages 22–23.) Forests thrive in places with ample precipitation; grasses are found in places with less precipitation or with only seasonal rainfall; and xerophytes—plants able to survive lengthy periods with little or no water—are found in arid areas that receive very little precipitation on a yearly basis. Grasses and shrubs cover almost half of Earth's land.

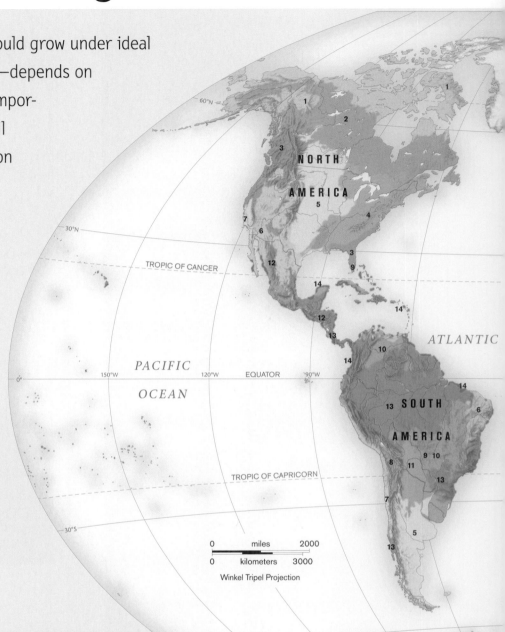

NORTH AMERICA

60°N

30°N

TROPIC OF CANCER

PACIFIC OCEAN

150°W   120°W   EQUATOR   90°W

ATLANTIC

SOUTH AMERICA

TROPIC OF CAPRICORN

30°S

| 0 | miles | 2000 |
| 0 | kilometers | 3000 |

Winkel Tripel Projection

4

TEMPERATE BROADLEAF FOREST

Broadleaf trees that grow in mid-latitude areas with mild temperatures, such as this one in Shenandoah National Park in Virginia, U.S.A., are deciduous, meaning they lose their leaves in winter. Many such forests have been cleared for cropland.

6

DESERT AND DRY SHRUB

Deserts, areas that receive less than 10 inches (25 cm) of rainfall a year, have vegetation that is specially adapted to survive under dry conditions, such as these dry shrubs and cacti growing in the Sonora Desert in Arizona, U.S.A.

1

TUNDRA

With only two to three months of temperatures above freezing, tundra plants are mostly dwarf shrubs, short grasses, mosses, and lichens. Much of Canada's Yukon has tundra vegetation, which turns red as winter approaches.

3

CONIFEROUS FOREST

Needleleaf trees with cones to protect their seeds from bitter winters grow in cold climates with short summers, such as British Columbia, Canada. These trees are important in lumber and papermaking industries.

ARCTIC OCEAN

ARCTIC CIRCLE

EUROPE

ASIA

AFRICA

PACIFIC OCEAN

OCEAN

INDIAN

OCEAN

EQUATOR

AUSTRALIA

Vegetation Zones

1	Tundra
2	Northern coniferous forest (also called boreal forest or taiga)
3	Temperate coniferous forest
4	Temperate broadleaf forest
5	Temperate grassland
6	Desert and dry shrub
7	Mediterranean shrub
8	Mountain grassland
9	Flooded grassland and savanna
10	Tropical grassland and savanna
11	Tropical dry forest
12	Tropical coniferous forest
13	Tropical moist broadleaf (includes rain forest)
14	Mangrove
15	Permanent ice cover

5 TEMPERATE GRASSLAND

Grasslands, such as this tall-grass prairie in south-western Missouri, U.S.A., are found in areas where precipitation is too low to support forests. Many temperate grasslands have been converted to cropland for grain production.

10 TROPICAL GRASSLAND

Tall grasses and scattered trees that can survive a hot, dry season dominate low latitude grasslands, also called savannas. Africa's grasslands are home to game animals, such as this male lion crossing the savanna in Botswana.

13 RAIN FOREST

A waterfall tumbles over a cliff in the Costa Rican rain forest. Rain forest trees can grow to be as much as 200 feet (61 m) above the forest floor. The overlapping branches of the tallest trees keep sunlight from reaching the forest floor.

CROPLAND

People remove natural vegetation in many places to create fields to grow crops to feed both people and animals. Here, a farmer in the Catskill Mountains of New York uses a mechanized harvester to cut corn to feed his dairy cattle.

Environmental Hot Spots

Around the world, people are putting more and more pressure on the environment by dumping pollutants into the air and water and by removing natural vegetation to extract mineral resources or to turn the land into cropland for farming. In more developed countries, industries create waste and pollution; farmers use fertilizers and pesticides that run off into water supplies; and motor vehicles release exhaust fumes into the air. In less developed countries, forests are cut down for fuel or to clear land for farming; grasslands are turned into deserts as farmers and herders overuse the land; and expanding urban areas face problems of water quality and sanitation.

NORTH AMERICA
Toronto
Chicago
New York
Philadelphia
Los Angeles
Miami
México

ATLANTIC OCEAN

PACIFIC OCEAN

Bogotá
SOUTH AMERICA
Lima
Belo Horizonte
São Paulo
Rio de Janeiro
Santiago
Buenos Aires

Cities
- Megacity, over 10 million
- 5 to 10 million

Pollution
- Areas most sensitive to acid rain
- Frequent pollution from shipping

Desertification
- Areas at highest risk of desertification

Deforestation
- Intact forests
- Other forests
- Former forest

ENDANGERED

Human activity poses the greatest threat to Earth's biodiversity— its rich variety of species. Loss of habitat puts many species, including those at right, at great risk. Experts estimate that species are becoming extinct at a rate 100 to 1,000 times higher than would be caused by natural loss.

Monarch Butterfly

Giant Tree Frog

California Condor

Asian Elephant

Rafflesia Flower

Napoleon Wrasse Fish

POLLUTION

Poor air quality is a serious environmental problem. Industrial plants are a major source of pollution. Smoke containing particles that contribute to acid rain is released from a factory in Poland (above).

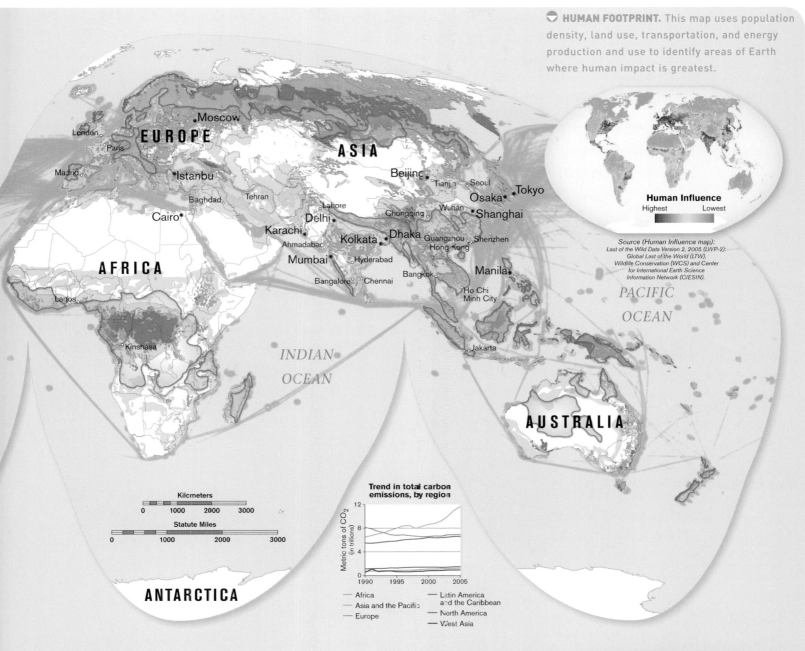

⬇ **HUMAN FOOTPRINT.** This map uses population density, land use, transportation, and energy production and use to identify areas of Earth where human impact is greatest.

Human Influence
Highest — Lowest

Source (Human Influence map):
Last of the Wild Data Version 2, 2005 (LWP-2);
Global Last of the World (LTW).
Wildlife Conservation (WCS) and Center
for International Earth Science
Information Network (CIESIN).

Kilometers
0   1000   2000   3000

Statute Miles
0   1000   2000   3000

Trend in total carbon emissions, by region

Metric tons of CO₂ (in trillions)

— Africa
— Asia and the Pacific
— Europe
— Latin America and the Caribbean
— North America
— West Asia

DEFORESTATION

Loss of forest cover, such as on this hillside in Malaysia, contributes to a buildup of carbon dioxide in the atmosphere, as well as to a loss of biodiversity. This is a frequent problem in the tropics.

DESERTIFICATION

Villagers in Mauritania, Africa, shovel sand away from their schoolhouse. In semiarid areas, which receive limited and often unreliable rainfall, land that is overgrazed or overcultivated can become desertlike.

DAMAGED REEFS

Coral reefs, such as this one in the Indian Ocean near the Maldives, can be damaged by increases in ocean temperatures. If a reef dies, a habitat for the many marine creatures that live there is lost.

PHYSICAL WORLD

Natural Disasters

Every world region has its share of natural disasters—the menacing mix just varies from place to place. The Ring of Fire—grinding tectonic plate boundaries that follow the coasts of the Pacific Ocean—shakes with volcanic eruptions and earthquakes. Coastal lives and livelihoods can be swept away by quake-caused tsunamis. The U.S. heartland endures blizzards in winter and dangerous tornadoes that can strike in spring, summer, or fall. Tropical cyclones batter many coastal areas with ripping winds, torrents of rain, and huge storm surges along their deadly paths.

KINDS OF DISASTERS

Earthquake
A shaking of Earth's crust caused by a volcanic eruption or by the release of energy along a fault in the crust

Tornado
A violently rotating column of air that touches Earth's surface during intense thunderstorm activity

Tropical Cyclone
A huge weather system, fueled by warm water, that can become a rotating storm packing winds of at least 74 miles per hour (119 kph); called hurricanes in the Atlantic Ocean and eastern Pacific, cyclones in the Bay of Bengal and Indian Ocean, and typhoons in the western Pacific

Tsunami
Ocean waves caused by an undersea earthquake or by a volcanic eruption

Volcanic Eruption
The upward movement and usually forceful release of molten material and gases from Earth's interior onto the surface

TORNADO. A funnel cloud roars across open country near Campo, Colorado, U.S.A. More of these storms occur in "Tornado Alley" (see map) than anywhere else on Earth.

TROPICAL CYCLONE. In late October 2012, "Superstorm" Sandy slammed into the U.S. East Coast, bringing widespread destruction and flooding that forced some people to evacuate their home in rafts.

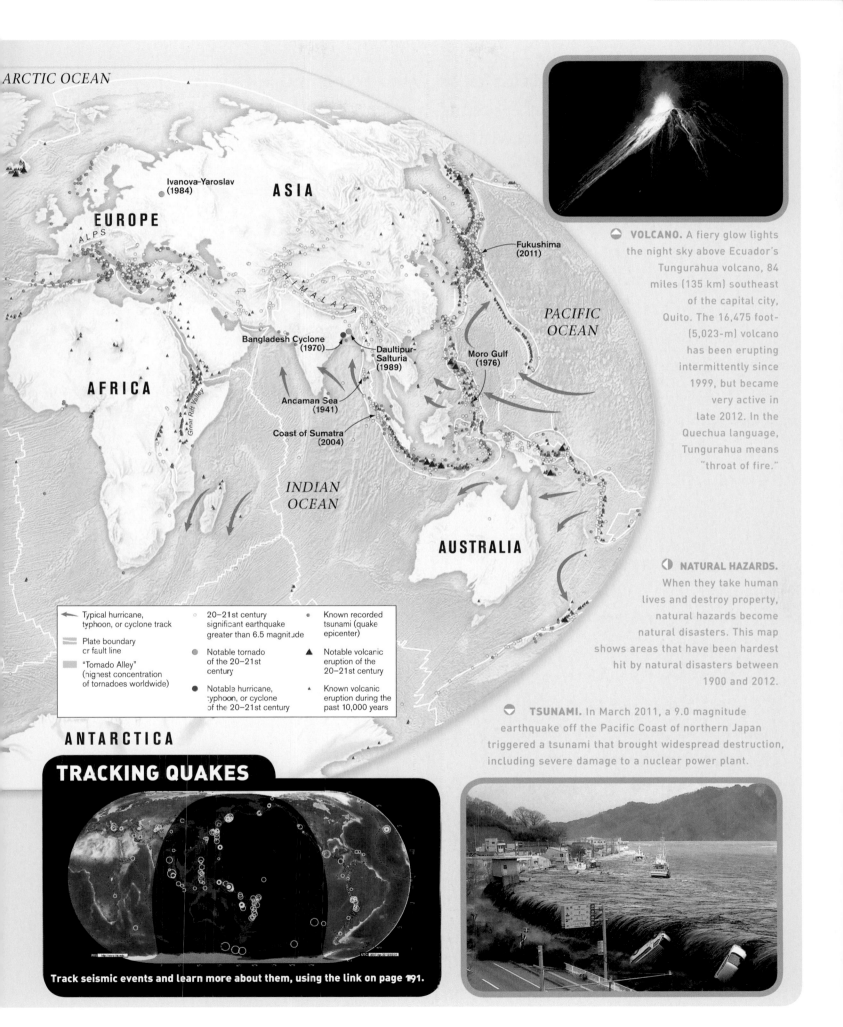

ARCTIC OCEAN

EUROPE

ASIA

ALPS

Ivanova-Yaroslav
(1984)

H I M A L A Y A

Fukushima
(2011)

PACIFIC
OCEAN

AFRICA

Great Rift Valley

Bangladesh Cyclone
(1970)

Daultipur-
Salturia
(1989)

Moro Gulf
(1976)

Ancaman Sea
(1941)

Coast of Sumatra
(2004)

INDIAN
OCEAN

AUSTRALIA

ANTARCTICA

- → Typical hurricane, typhoon, or cyclone track
- Plate boundary cr fault line
- "Tornado Alley" (highest concentration of tornadoes worldwide)
- ○ 20−21st century significant earthquake greater than 6.5 magnitude
- ● Notable tornado of the 20−21st century
- ● Notable hurricane, typhoon, or cyclone of the 20−21st century
- ● Known recorded tsunami (quake epicenter)
- ▲ Notable volcanic eruption of the 20−21st century
- ▲ Known volcanic eruption during the past 10,000 years

VOLCANO. A fiery glow lights the night sky above Ecuador's Tungurahua volcano, 84 miles (135 km) southeast of the capital city, Quito. The 16,475 foot- (5,023-m) volcano has been erupting intermittently since 1999, but became very active in late 2012. In the Quechua language, Tungurahua means "throat of fire."

NATURAL HAZARDS. When they take human lives and destroy property, natural hazards become natural disasters. This map shows areas that have been hardest hit by natural disasters between 1900 and 2012.

TSUNAMI. In March 2011, a 9.0 magnitude earthquake off the Pacific Coast of northern Japan triggered a tsunami that brought widespread destruction, including severe damage to a nuclear power plant.

TRACKING QUAKES

Track seismic events and learn more about them, using the link on page 191.

The Political World

Earth's land area is mainly made up of seven giant continents, but people have divided much of the land into smaller political units called countries. Australia is a continent with a single country, and Antarctica is set aside for scientific research. But the other five continents include almost 200 independent countries. The political map (right) shows boundaries—imaginary lines agreed to by treaties—that separate countries. Some boundaries, such as the one between the United States and Canada, are very stable and have been recognized for many years. Other boundaries, such as the one between Ethiopia and Eritrea in northeast Africa, are relatively new and still disputed. Countries come in all shapes and sizes. Russia and Canada are giants. Other countries, such as Luxembourg in western Europe, are small. Some countries are long and skinny—look at Chile in South America! Still other countries—like Indonesia and Japan in Asia—are made up of groups of islands. The political map is a clue to the diversity that makes Earth so fascinating.

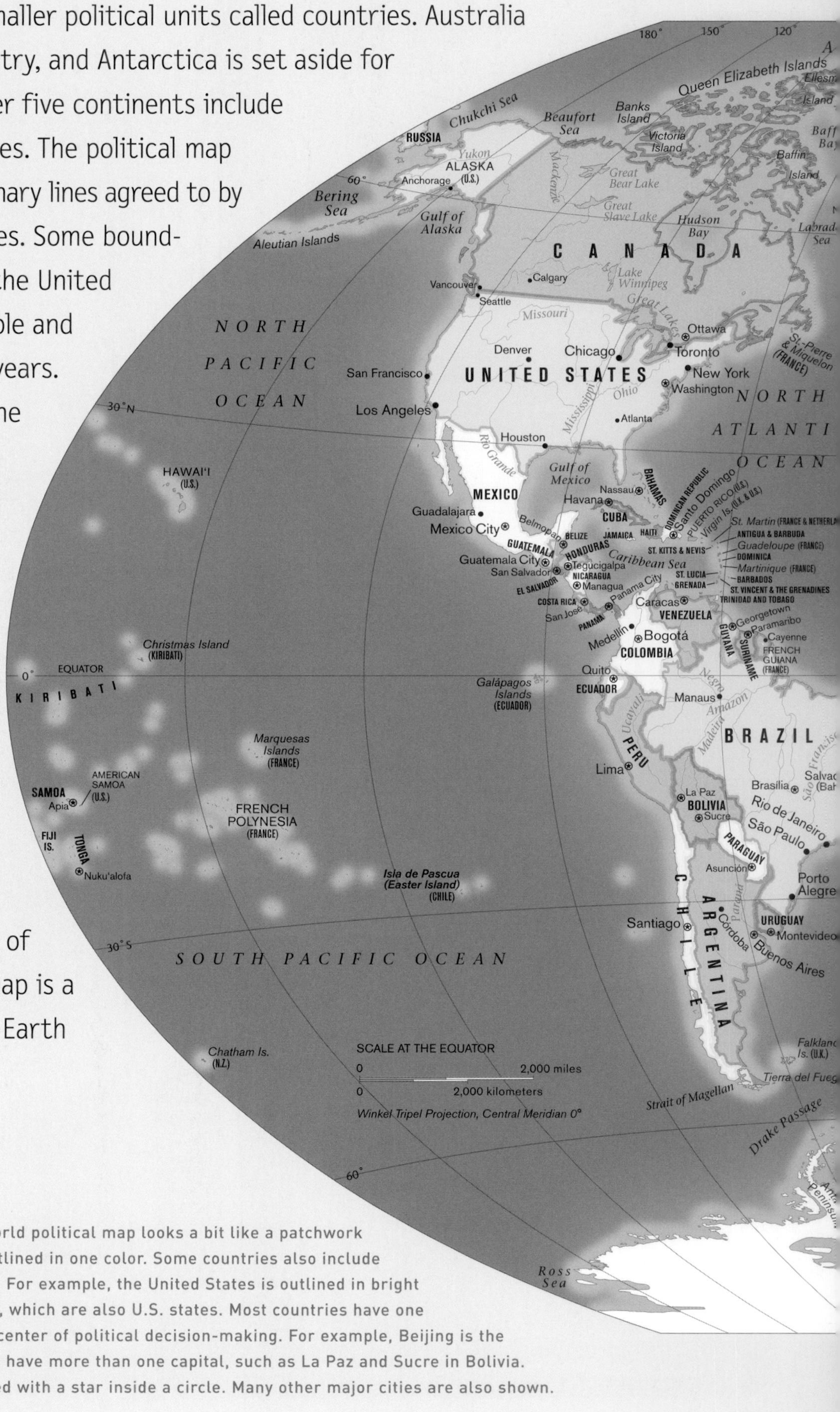

○ **COUNTRIES AND CAPITALS.** The world political map looks a bit like a patchwork quilt. Each country's boundary is outlined in one color. Some countries also include territory beyond the main land area. For example, the United States is outlined in bright green, but so are Alaska and Hawaii, which are also U.S. states. Most countries have one city—called the capital—that is the center of political decision-making. For example, Beijing is the capital of China. But a few countries have more than one capital, such as La Paz and Sucre in Bolivia. The capital of each country is marked with a star inside a circle. Many other major cities are also shown.

SCALE AT THE EQUATOR
0 — 2,000 miles
0 — 2,000 kilometers
Winkel Tripel Projection, Central Meridian 0°

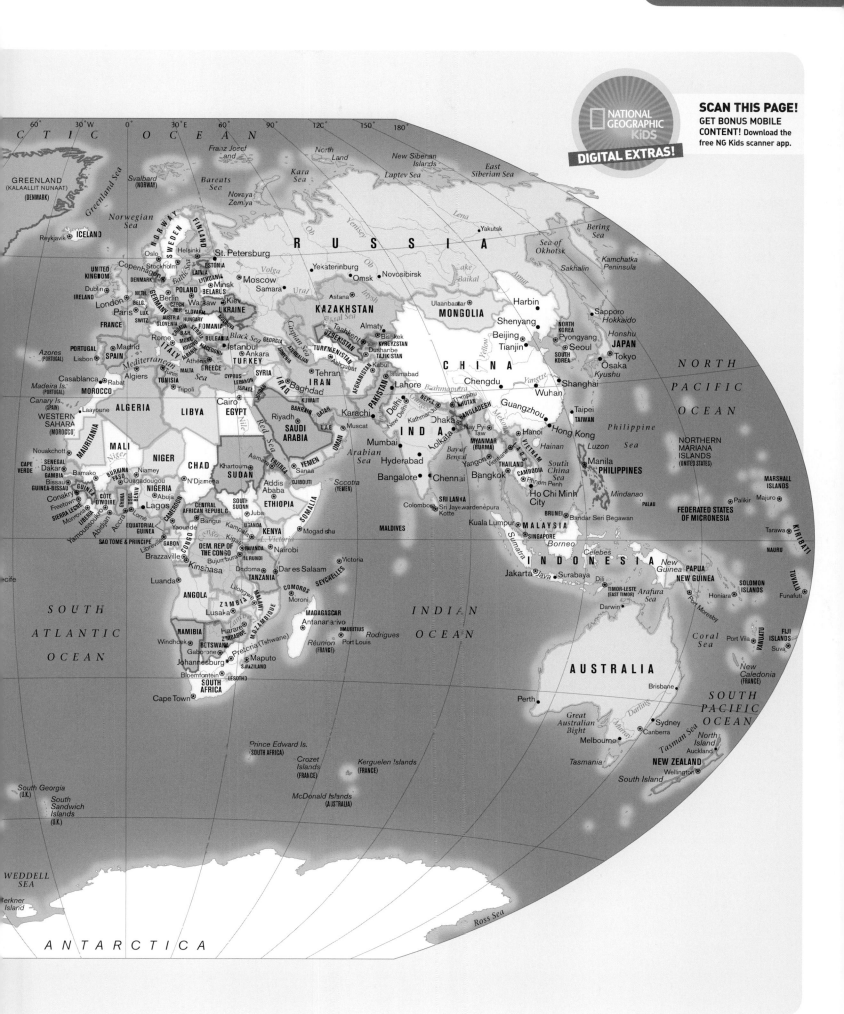

World Population

How big is a billion? It's hard to imagine. But Earth's population is 7.1 billion and rising, with more than a billion living in both China and India. And more than 60 million people are added to the world each year. Most population growth occurs in the less developed countries of Asia, Africa, and Latin America, while some countries in Europe are hardly increasing at all. Population changes can create challenges for countries. Fast-growing countries with young populations need food, housing, and schools. Countries with low growth rates and older populations need workers to sustain their economies.

MOST POPULOUS COUNTRIES

(mid-2012 data)

1.	China	1,350,378,000
2.	India	1,259,721,000
3.	United States	313,858,000
4.	Indonesia	240,990,000
5.	Brazil	194,334,000
6.	Pakistan	180,428,000
7.	Nigeria	170,124,000
8.	Bangladesh	152,875,000

MOST CROWDED COUNTRIES

Population Density (People per sq mi/sq km; 2010 data)

1.	Monaco	45,000 / 18,000
2.	Singapore	19,288 / 7,447
3.	Bahrain	4,709 / 1,818
4.	Malta	3,414 / 1,318
5.	Maldives	2,745 / 1,060
6.	Vatican City	4,180 / 2,090
7.	Bangladesh	2,673 / 1,032
8.	Mauritius	1,650 / 637

DENSITY. Demographers, people who study population, use density to measure how concentrated population is. For example, the population density of Egypt is almost 200 people per square mile (77 per sq km). This assumes that the population is evenly spread throughout the country, but this is not the case in Egypt. Almost all of the people live along the banks of the Nile River. Likewise, Earth's population is not evenly spread across the land. Some places, like central Australia, are almost empty, whereas others, such as Europe or India, are very crowded.

CITY DWELLERS. More than half the world's people have shifted from rural areas to urban centers, with some countries adding more than 100 million to their urban populations between 1950 and 2015 (see map, right). In more developed countries, about 75 percent of the population is urban, compared with just 46 percent in less developed countries. But the fastest growing urban areas are in less developed countries, where thousands flock to cities, such as Dhaka, Bangladesh (photo, far right), in search of a better life. By 2015 there could be as many as 22 cities with populations of 10 million or more.

Los Angeles-Long Beach-Santa Ana

Dallas-Fort Worth

Mexico City

PACIFIC OCEAN

Delhi
28,568,000
22,157,000
1,369,000

Beijing
15,018,000
12,385,000
1,671,000

Shanghai
20,017,000
16,575,000
4,301,000

Moscow
10,663,000
10,550,000
5,356,000

Paris
10,884,000
10,550,000
10,485,000
6,522,000

Dhaka
20,936,000
14,648,000
336,000

Tokyo
37,088,000
36,669,000
11,275,000

Los Angeles
13,677,000
12,762,000
4,046,000

New York
20,636,000
19,425,000
12,338,000

Karachi
18,725,000
13,125,000
1,055,000

Osaka
11,368,000
11,337,000
4,147,000

Istanbul
12,108,000
10,525,000
967,000

Cairo
13,531,000
11,001,000
2,494,000

Mumbai
25,810,000
20,041,000
2,857,000

Manila
14,916,000
11,628,000
1,544,000

Mexico City
20,713,000
19,460,000
2,883,000

Urban Population Growth, 1950–2015 (in millions)

- Over 100
- 20–100
- Under 20

Lagos
15,810,000
10,578,000
325,000

Kolkata
20,112,000
15,552,000
4,513,000

Jakarta
10,850,000
9,210,000
1,452,000

Population growth for largest cities (populations shown for years 1950, 2010, and 2025)

- 2025 (projected)
- 2010
- 1950

São Paulo
21,651,000
20,262,000
2,384,800

Rio de Janeiro
12,650,000
11,950,000
2,950,000

Buenos Aires
13,708,000
13,074,000
5,098,000

Sydney
4,852,000
4,429,000
1,690,000

| 50 | 100 | 150 | 200 | 250 | 300 | 350 | 400 | 450 | 500 | 550 | 600 | 650 | 700 | 750 | 800 | 850 | 900 | 950 | 1 |

Year

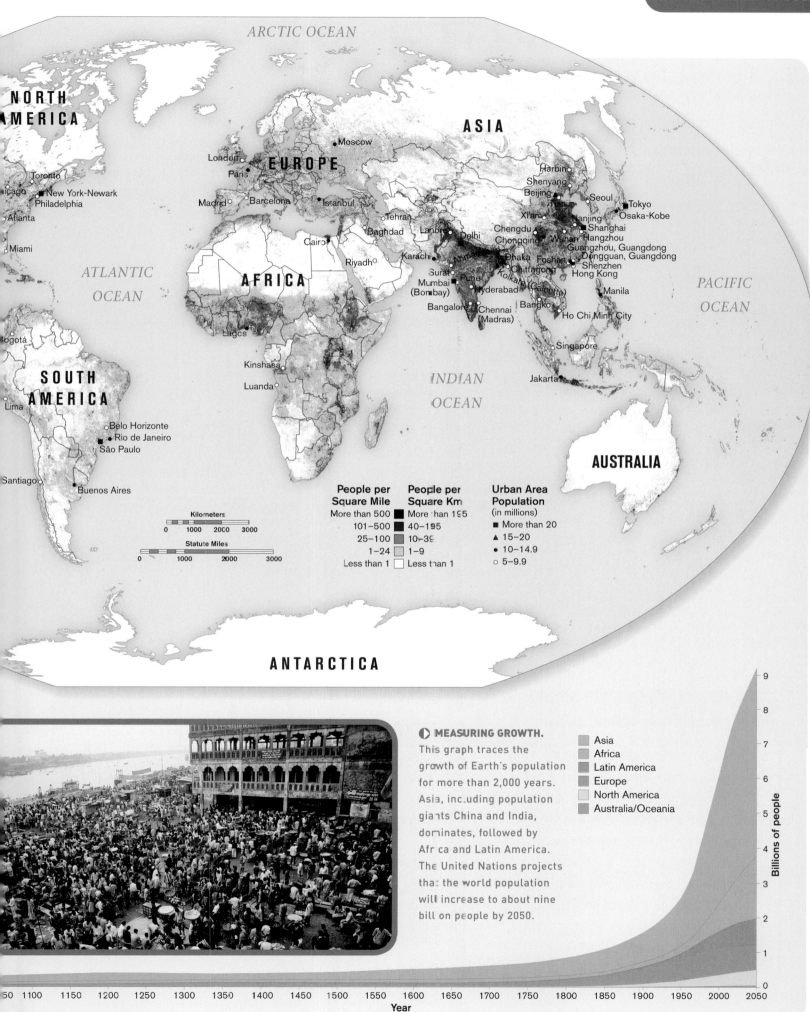

ARCTIC OCEAN

NORTH AMERICA

EUROPE

ASIA

Moscow

London
Paris

Harbin
Shenyang
Beijing
Seoul
Tokyo
Osaka-Kobe

Toronto
Chicago
New York-Newark
Philadelphia
Atlanta

Madrid
Barcelona
Istanbul

Tehran
Baghdad

Xi'an
Tianjin
Nanjing
Shanghai
Chengdu
Chongqing
Wuhan Hangzhou
Guangzhou, Guangdong
Dongguan, Guangdong
Shenzhen
Hong Kong

Miami

ATLANTIC
OCEAN

Cairo

AFRICA

Riyadh

Karachi
Lahore
Delhi
Dhaka
Foshan
Chittagong

Surat
Ahme
Kolkata
(Calcutta)

Mumbai
(Bombay)
Pune
Hyderabad

Manila

PACIFIC
OCEAN

Bangalore
Chennai
(Madras)
Bangko
Ho Chi Minh City

Bogotá

Lima

SOUTH
AMERICA

Lagos

Kinshasa
Luanda

INDIAN
OCEAN

Jakarta

Singapore

Belo Horizonte
Rio de Janeiro
São Paulo

AUSTRALIA

Santiago
Buenos Aires

Kilometers
0   1000   2000   3000

Statute Miles
0   1000   2000   3000

People per Square Mile
More than 500
101–500
25–100
1–24
Less than 1

People per Square Km
More than 195
40–195
10–39
1–9
Less than 1

Urban Area Population
(in millions)
■ More than 20
▲ 15–20
● 10–14.9
○ 5–9.9

ANTARCTICA

⏵ **MEASURING GROWTH.**
This graph traces the growth of Earth's population for more than 2,000 years. Asia, including population giants China and India, dominates, followed by Africa and Latin America. The United Nations projects that the world population will increase to about nine billion people by 2050.

Asia
Africa
Latin America
Europe
North America
Australia/Oceania

9
8
7
6
5
4
3
2
1
0

Billions of people

50 1100 1150 1200 1250 1300 1350 1400 1450 1500 1550 1600 1650 1700 1750 1800 1850 1900 1950 2000 2050

Year

Population Trends

Population growth rates are slowing, total fertility rates are declining, and populations are aging. Nevertheless, world population will continue to increase for many years to come because the base population is so large. Almost 60 million people are added, on average, to the world's population each year, 90 percent of whom are born in less developed countries where poverty is greatest. In more affluent countries, life expectancy is higher and populations are aging. By 2050, almost one-quarter of the world's population will be 60 years of age or older.

HIGHEST FERTILITY RATE

(average number of children born to a woman in her lifetime, 2012 data)

1. Niger	7.1
2. Somalia	6.4
3. Burundi	6.4
4. Mali	6.3
5. Angola	6.3
6. Dem. Rep. of the Congo	6.3
7. Zambia	6.3
8. Afghanistan	6.2

LOWEST FERTILITY RATE

(2012 data)

1. Latvia	1.1
2. Singapore	1.2
3. Andorra	1.2
4. Bosnia and Herzegovina	1.2
5. San Marino	1.2
6. South Korea	1.2
7. Hungary	1.2
8. Moldova	1.3

LONGEST LIFE EXPECTANCY

(average expected life span, both sexes, in years 2011 data)

1. Japan	83
2. San Marino	83
3. Australia	82
4. Spain	82
5. Israel	82
6. France	82
7. Switzerland	82
8. Sweden	82

SHORTEST LIFE EXPECTANCY

(2011 data)

1. Afghanistan	44
2. Zimbabwe	46
3. Guinea-Bissau	48
4. Swaziland	49
5. Zambia	49
6. Dem. Rep. of the Congo	49
7. Lesotho	49
8. Central African Republic	50

◗ **POPULATION GROWTH.**
This map shows projected population change (%) over the next 40 years. Much of Europe, Russia, and Japan face a decline in population due to low birth rates and women waiting longer to have children. Countries in Africa can expect to see an opposite trend as fertility rates remain high.

United States
78 years
1.9
6.1

PACIFIC OCEAN

Brazil
74 years
1.9
20

UNITED STATES

Map Symbols

■ **Life expectancy** (symbol equals 10 years, both sexes)

🛉 **Infant mortality** (symbol equals 10 deaths per 1,000 live births)

🛉 **Fertility rate** (average number of children born to women in a given population; symbol equals 1 child)

POPULATION PYRAMIDS

The population of a country can be shown in a bar graph in which age and sex groups are stacked up (males, left; females, right). This creates a country profile that helps predict future trends. Countries with high birth rates and high percentages of young people, such as Nigeria, are shaped like pyramids, which suggests continued growth. Countries, such as Italy, whose birth rates are below the replacement fertility rate of 2.1 children per couple, show bulges in the higher age brackets, but a narrow base, which indicates population decline.

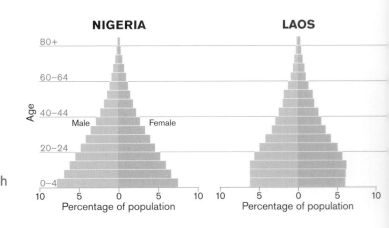

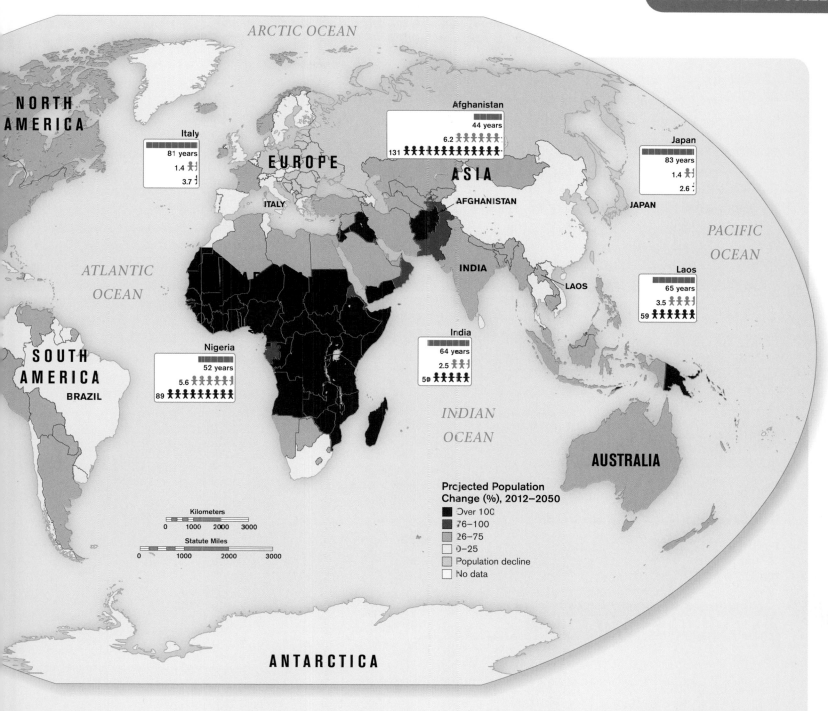

ARCTIC OCEAN

NORTH AMERICA

EUROPE

ASIA

ATLANTIC OCEAN

PACIFIC OCEAN

Italy
81 years
1.4
3.7

Afghanistan
44 years
6.2
131

Japan
83 years
1.4
2.6

ITALY

AFGHANISTAN

INDIA

LAOS

JAPAN

Laos
65 years
3.5
59

SOUTH AMERICA

BRAZIL

Nigeria
52 years
5.6
89

India
64 years
2.5
50

INDIAN OCEAN

AUSTRALIA

Kilometers
0   1000   2000   3000

Statute Miles
0   1000   2000   3000

Projected Population Change (%), 2012–2050
- Over 100
- 76–100
- 26–75
- 0–25
- Population decline
- No data

ANTARCTICA

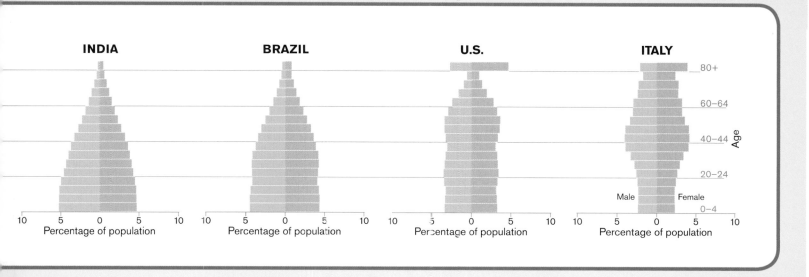

INDIA

BRAZIL

U.S.

ITALY

80+

60–64

40–44

Age

20–24

Male   Female

0–4

10   5   0   5   10
Percentage of population

10   5   0   5   10
Percentage of population

10   5   0   5   10
Percentage of population

10   5   0   5   10
Percentage of population

World Languages & Literacy

Earth's 7.1 billion people live in 195 independent countries, but they speak more than 5,000 languages. Some countries, such as Japan, have one official language. Other countries have many languages, such as India, where 23 are official. Experts believe that humans may once have spoken as many as 10,000 languages, but that number has dropped by one-half and is still declining.

Literacy is the ability to read and write in one's native language. High literacy rates are associated with more developed countries. But literacy is also a gender issue, since women in less developed countries often lack access to education (see pages 42–43).

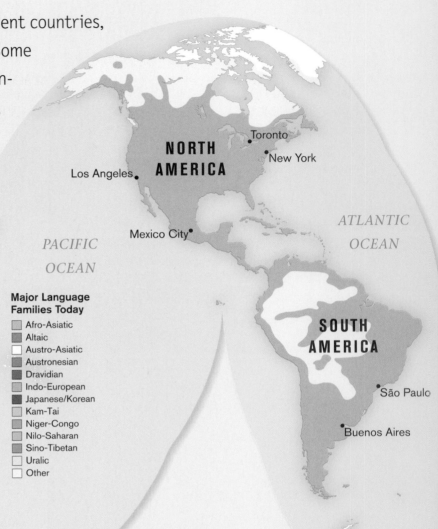

Major Language Families Today

- Afro-Asiatic
- Altaic
- Austro-Asiatic
- Austronesian
- Dravidian
- Indo-European
- Japanese/Korean
- Kam-Tai
- Niger-Congo
- Nilo-Saharan
- Sino-Tibetan
- Uralic
- Other

NORTH AMERICA

Toronto
New York
Los Angeles
Mexico City

SOUTH AMERICA

São Paulo
Buenos Aires

PACIFIC OCEAN

ATLANTIC OCEAN

LEADING LANGUAGES

Some languages have only a few hundred speakers, but 23 languages stand out with more than 50 million speakers each. Earth's population giant, China, has 845 million speakers of Mandarin, more than double the next largest group of language speakers. Colonial expansion, trade, and migration account for the spread of the other most widely spoken languages. With growing use of the Internet, English is becoming the language of the technology age.

Population of first language speakers (in millions)

Language	Speakers
Chinese (Mandarin)	845
Spanish	329
English	328
Arabic	221
Hindi	182
Bengali	181
Portuguese	178
Russian	144
Japanese	122
German	90

Languages

⬤ **EDUCATION AND LITERACY.** These Nenet boys in Siberia spend hours learning the national language—Russian—but this may result in the loss of their native language. Literacy can lead to good jobs in the future for these boys and improved economic success for their country.

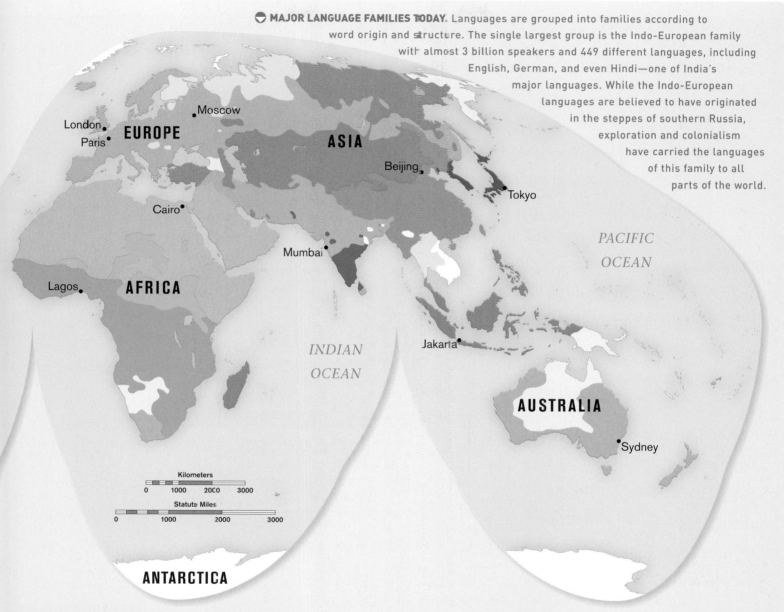

⬤ **MAJOR LANGUAGE FAMILIES TODAY.** Languages are grouped into families according to word origin and structure. The single largest group is the Indo-European family with almost 3 billion speakers and 449 different languages, including English, German, and even Hindi—one of India's major languages. While the Indo-European languages are believed to have originated in the steppes of southern Russia, exploration and colonialism have carried the languages of this family to all parts of the world.

London
Paris
Moscow
EUROPE
ASIA
Beijing
Tokyo
Cairo
Mumbai
PACIFIC OCEAN
Lagos
AFRICA
INDIAN OCEAN
Jakarta
AUSTRALIA
Sydney

Kilometers
0   1000   2000   3000

Statute Miles
0   1000   2000   3000

ANTARCTICA

⬤ **ONE LANGUAGE, TWO FORMS.** Some languages, including Chinese, use characters instead of letters. The Golden Arches provide a clue to the meaning of the characters on the restaurant sign. Many signs, such as the one in the foreground, also show words in pinyin, a spelling system that uses the Western alphabet.

⬤ **UNIVERSAL LANGUAGE.** The widespread use of technology—for example, the electronic games that hold the attention of these children in France—has crossed the language barrier. Computers, the Internet, and electronic communication devices use a universal language that knows no national borders.

World Religions

Rooted in people's attempts to explain the unknown, religion takes many forms. Some belief systems, such as Christianity, Islam, and Judaism, are monotheistic, meaning that followers believe in just one supreme being. Others, like Hinduism, Shintoism, and most native belief systems, are polytheistic, believing in many gods.

All of the major religions have their origins in Asia, but they have spread around the world. Christianity, with the largest number of followers, has three divisions—Roman Catholic, Eastern Orthodox, and Protestant. Islam, with about one-fifth of all believers, has two main divisions—Sunni and Shia. Hinduism and Buddhism together account for almost another one-fifth of believers. Judaism, dating back some 4,000 years, is the oldest of all the major monotheistic religions.

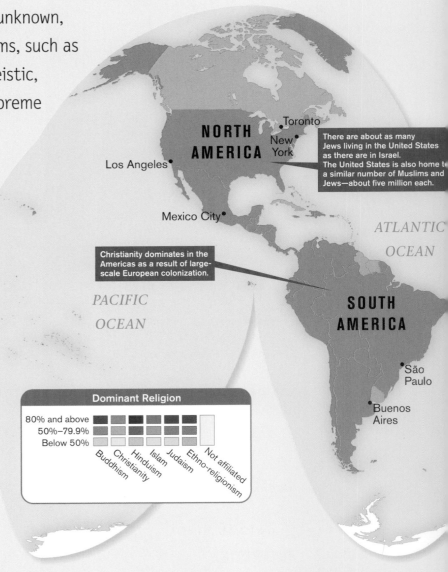

There are about as many Jews living in the United States as there are in Israel. The United States is also home to a similar number of Muslims and Jews—about five million each.

Christianity dominates in the Americas as a result of large-scale European colonization.

Dominant Religion

80% and above	
50%–79.9%	
Below 50%	

Buddhism · Christianity · Hinduism · Islam · Judaism · Ethno-religionism · Not affiliated

BUDDHISM

Founded about 2,500 years ago in northern India by a Hindu prince named Gautama Buddha, Buddhism spread throughout East and Southeast Asia. Buddhist temples house statues, such as the Mihintale Buddha (above) in Sri Lanka.

CHRISTIANITY

Based on the teachings of Jesus Christ, a Jew born some 2,000 years ago in the area of modern-day Israel, Christianity has spread worldwide and actively seeks converts. Followers in Switzerland (above) participate in a procession with lanterns and crosses.

HINDUISM

Dating back more than 4,000 years, Hinduism is practiced mainly in India. Hindus follow sacred texts known as the Vedas and believe in reincarnation. During the festival of Diwali, Hindus light candles (above) to symbolize the victory of good over evil.

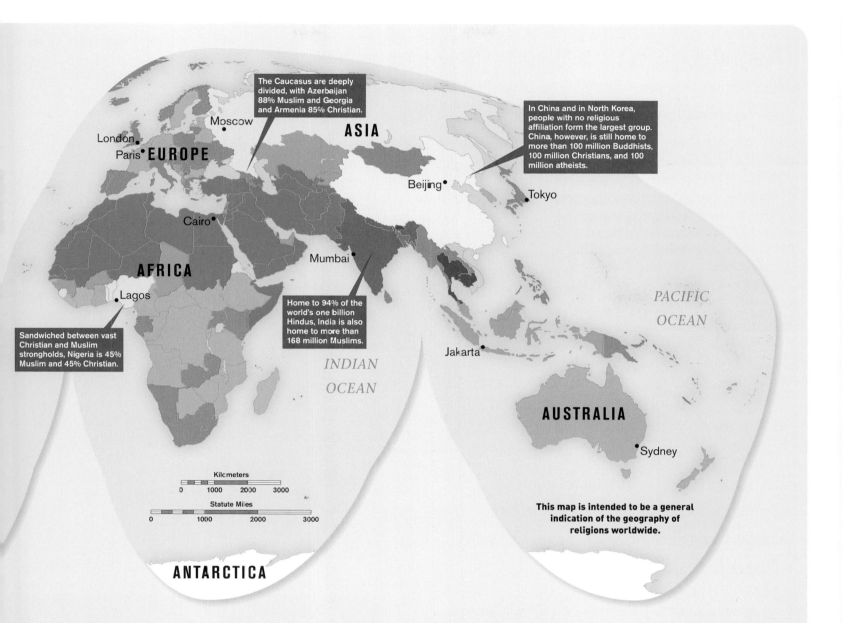

The Caucasus are deeply divided, with Azerbaijan 88% Muslim and Georgia and Armenia 85% Christian.

In China and in North Korea, people with no religious affiliation form the largest group. China, however, is still home to more than 100 million Buddhists, 100 million Christians, and 100 million atheists.

Moscow

London
Paris •EUROPE

ASIA

Beijing•

Tokyo

Cairo•

AFRICA

Mumbai•

PACIFIC OCEAN

Lagos

Home to 94% of the world's one billion Hindus, India is also home to more than 168 million Muslims.

Sandwiched between vast Christian and Muslim strongholds, Nigeria is 45% Muslim and 45% Christian.

INDIAN OCEAN

Jakarta•

AUSTRALIA

•Sydney

Kilometers
0   1000   2000   3000

Statute Miles
0   1000   2000   3000

This map is intended to be a general indication of the geography of religions worldwide.

ANTARCTICA

ISLAM

Muslims believe that the Koran, Islam's sacred book, records the words of Allah (God) as revealed to the Prophet Muhammad around A.D. 610. Believers (above) circle the Kabah in the Haram Mosque in Mecca, the spiritual center of the faith.

JUDAISM

The traditions, laws, and beliefs of Judaism date back to Abraham, its founder, and to the Torah, the first five books of the Old Testament. Followers (above) pray before the Western Wall, which stands below Islam's Dome of the Rock in Jerusalem.

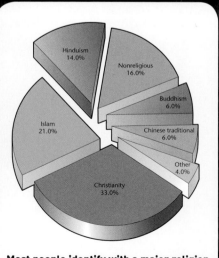

RELIGIOUS FOLLOWERS

Hinduism 14.0%
Nonreligious 16.0%
Buddhism 6.0%
Chinese traditional 6.0%
Islam 21.0%
Other 4.0%
Christianity 33.0%

Most people identify with a major religion. Some are nonreligious.

World Economies

A country's economy can be divided into three parts, or sectors—agriculture, industry, and services. Sometimes a fourth sector dealing with information and knowledge is added. The map shows that the economies of the United States and Western Europe are dominated by the service sector. These economies enjoy a high GDP (Gross Domestic Product) per capita—the value of goods and services produced each year, averaged per person in each country. In contrast, some economies in Africa and Asia still depend mostly on agriculture, which generates a low GDP per capita.

HIGHEST GDP PER CAPITA*	
1. Luxembourg	$104,196
2. Norway	$102,249
3. Qatar	$99,839
4. Switzerland	$76,598
5. Australia	$69,582
6. United Arab Emirates	$65,755
7. Sweden	$55,969
8. Denmark	$55,150
9. United States	$52,805
10. Canada	$52,088

LOWEST GDP PER CAPITA*	
1. Democratic Republic of the Congo	$251
2. Malawi	$262
3. Burundi	$317
4. Niger	$434
5. Central African Republic	$451
6. Madagascar	$458
7. Liberia	$470
8. Ethiopia	$518
9. Guinea-Bissau	$529

*All data as of 2013.

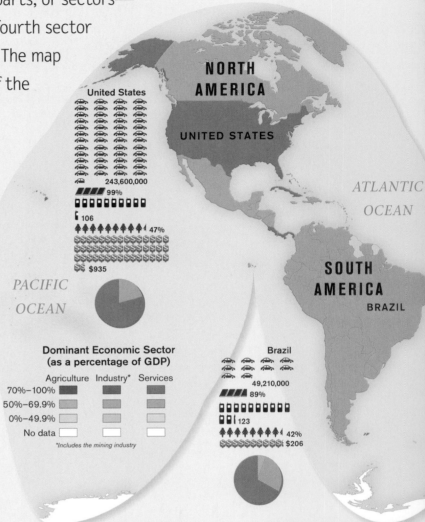

Dominant Economic Sector (as a percentage of GDP)

	Agriculture	Industry*	Services
70%–100%			
50%–69.9%			
0%–49.9%			
No data			

*Includes the mining industry

United States
243,600,000
99%
106
47%
$935

Brazil
49,210,000
89%
123
42%
$206

🌑 **INFORMATION.** Computers and other technologies have opened employment opportunities dealing with information and knowledge creation. These college students in the United Kingdom learn skills in an Information Technology lab that will prepare them for 21st-century jobs.

🌑 **INDUSTRY.** A man assembles a hybrid Prius car on an automated assembly line in a Toyota factory in Japan. Manufacture of cars is an important industrial activity and a key part of the global economy.

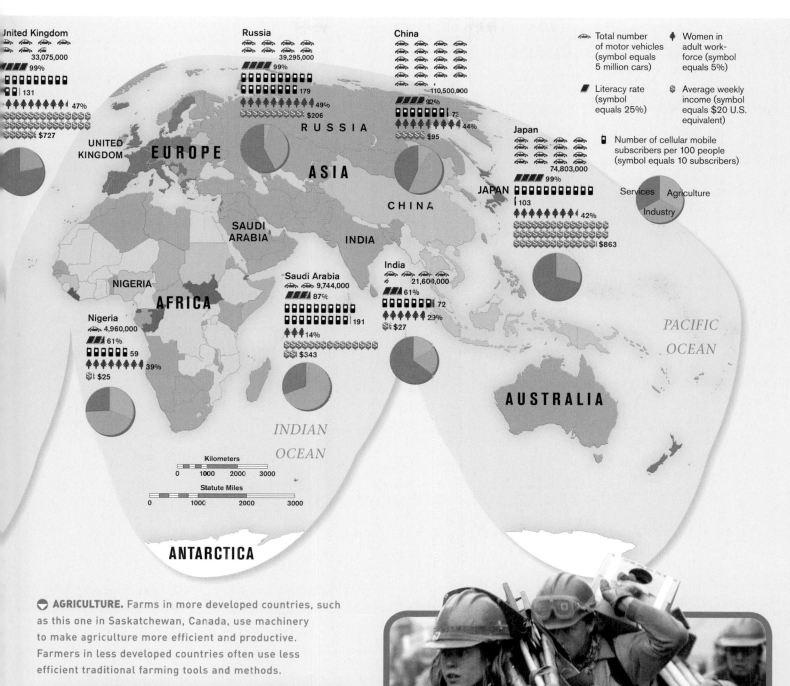

United Kingdom
33,075,000
99%
131
47%
$727

UNITED KINGDOM

EUROPE

Russia
39,295,000
99%
179
49%
$206
95

RUSSIA

ASIA

China
110,500,000
92%
73
44%
$95

CHINA

INDIA

SAUDI ARABIA

Japan
74,803,000
99%
103
42%
$863

JAPAN

Services   Agriculture

Industry

Total number of motor vehicles (symbol equals 5 million cars)

Women in adult work-force (symbol equals 5%)

Literacy rate (symbol equals 25%)

Average weekly income (symbol equals $20 U.S. equivalent)

Number of cellular mobile subscribers per 100 people (symbol equals 10 subscribers)

NIGERIA

AFRICA

Nigeria
4,960,000
61%
59
39%
$25

Saudi Arabia
9,744,000
87%
191
14%
$343

India
21,600,000
61%
72
23%
$27

PACIFIC OCEAN

AUSTRALIA

INDIAN OCEAN

Kilometers
0   1000   2000   3000

Statute Miles
0   1000   2000   3000

ANTARCTICA

⬤ **AGRICULTURE.** Farms in more developed countries, such as this one in Saskatchewan, Canada, use machinery to make agriculture more efficient and productive. Farmers in less developed countries often use less efficient traditional farming tools and methods.

⬤ **SERVICES.** People employed in the service sector, such as these national forest firefighters in Washington State, U.S.A., use their skills and training to provide services rather than products. Teachers, lawyers, and store clerks, among others, are also part of the service sector.

World Trade

World trade has expanded at a rapid rate in the decades since the end of World War II in 1945. In fact, trade has grown much faster than world production. Some countries, such as the United States, have complex economies that involve trading many different products, especially manufactured goods. But many less developed countries (see map at right) rely on only a few products—sometimes even just one product—to generate trade income. In recent years, commercial services, such as financial and information management, have expanded and become an important part of world trade.

◖ **TRADE.** The map (right) shows the richest and poorest economies around the world. The wealth of economies can be measured in terms of Gross National Income (GNI) per person—that is, income derived from economic activity. The arrows on the map show the movement and volume of trade among different world regions.

TOP MERCHANDISE EXPORTERS

(2011 data, billion U.S. $)	
1. China	$1,898
2. United States	$1,480
3. Germany	$1,472
4. Japan	$823
5. Netherlands	$661
6. France	$596
7. South Korea	$555
8. Italy	$523
9. Russia	$522

TOP MERCHANDISE IMPORTERS

(2011 data, billion U.S. $)	
1. United States	$2,266
2. China	$1,743
3. Germany	$1,254
4. Japan	$855
5. France	$714
6. United Kingdom	$638
7. Netherlands	$599
8. Italy	$557
9. South Korea	$524

TOP COMMERCIAL SERVICE EXPORTERS

(2011 data, billion U.S. $)	
1. United States	$581
2. United Kingdom	$274
3. Germany	$253
4. China	$182
5. France	$167
6. Japan	$142
7. Spain	$140
8. India	$137
9. Netherlands	$134

TOP COMMERCIAL SERVICE IMPORTERS

(2011 data, billion U.S. $)	
1. United States	$395
2. Germany	$289
3. China	$237
4. United Kingdom	$170
5. Japan	$166
6. France	$143
7. India	$124
8. Netherlands	$118
9. Ireland	$114

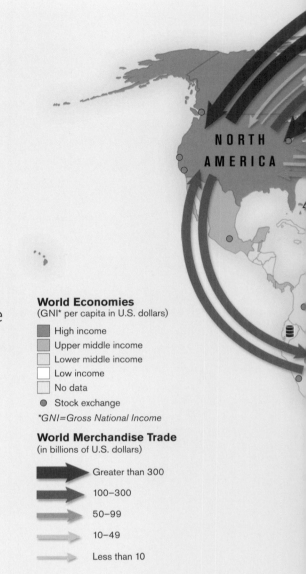

NORTH AMERICA

World Economies
(GNI* per capita in U.S. dollars)

- High income
- Upper middle income
- Lower middle income
- Low income
- No data
- ● Stock exchange

*GNI=Gross National Income

World Merchandise Trade
(in billions of U.S. dollars)

- Greater than 300
- 100–300
- 50–99
- 10–49
- Less than 10

MAIN TRADING NATIONS

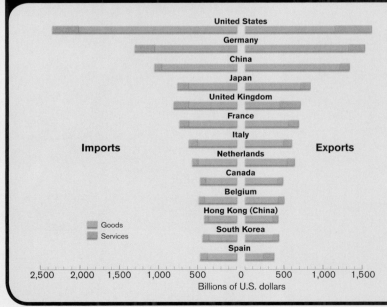

United States
Germany
China
Japan
United Kingdom
France
Italy
Netherlands
Canada
Belgium
Hong Kong (China)
South Korea
Spain

Imports   Exports

■ Goods
■ Services

2,500 2,000 1,500 1,000 500 0 500 1,000 1,500
Billions of U.S. dollars

The United States, Germany, and China dominate world trade. They protect their economies by imposing quotas and taxes that limit trade in products, such as agriculture and textiles, from other countries. Member countries of the World Trade Organization are negotiating to reduce trade barriers so that all countries can compete in the world economy.

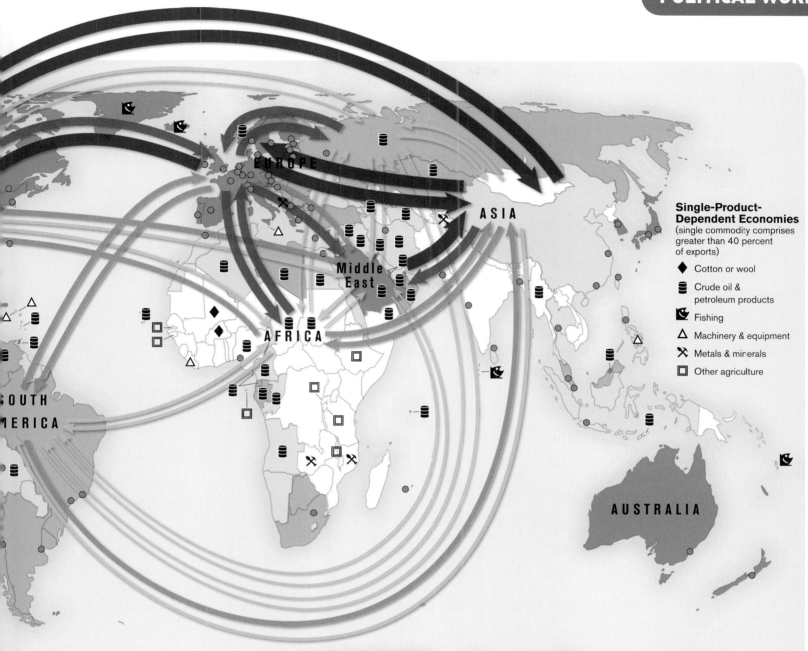

Single-Product-Dependent Economies
(single commodity comprises greater than 40 percent of exports)

- ◆ Cotton or wool
- 🛢 Crude oil & petroleum products
- 🐟 Fishing
- △ Machinery & equipment
- ✖ Metals & minerals
- ☐ Other agriculture

▶ TRADE AGREEMENTS.

Trade within regions is increasing. Neighboring countries, such as the countries of the European Union, agree to offer each other trade benefits that can improve the economy of the whole region. Such agreements allow products, workers, and money to move more easily among member countries. However, these agreements may also prevent trade with nonmember countries that may be able to provide products at a lower cost.

Major Regional Trade Agreements

- **APEC** - Asia-Pacific Economic Cooperation
- **ASEAN** - Association of Southeast Asian Nations
- **APEC & ASEAN**
- **COMESA** - Common Market for Eastern and Southern Africa
- **ECOWAS** - Economic Community of West African States
- **EU** - European Union
- **MERCOSUR** - Southern Common Market
- **NAFTA & APEC** - North American Free Trade Agreement
- **SAPTA** - South Asian Preferential Trade Arrangement

World Water

Water is Earth's most precious resource. Although more than two-thirds of the planet is covered by water, fresh water, which is needed by plants and animals—including humans—is only about 2.5 percent of all the water on Earth. Much of this is trapped deep underground or frozen in ice sheets and glaciers. Of the small amount of water that is fresh, less than one percent is available for human use.

The map at right shows each country's access to renewable freshwater supplies. Watersheds are large areas that drain into a particular river or lake.

Unfortunately, human activity often puts great stress on watersheds. For example, in Brazil, plans are being made to build large dams on the Amazon. This will alter the natural flow of water in this giant watershed. In the United States, heavy use of chemical fertilizers and pesticides has created toxic runoff that threatens the health of the Mississippi watershed.

Access to clean fresh water is critical for human health. But in many places, safe water is scarce due to population pressure and pollution.

WATER FACTS

Rivers that have been dammed to generate electricity are the source of almost 90 percent of Earth's renewable energy resources.

North America's Great Lakes hold about 20 percent of Earth's available fresh water.

If all the glaciers and ice sheets on Earth's surface melted, they would raise the level of Earth's oceans by about 230 feet (70 m). It is estimated that during the last ice age, when glaciers covered about one-third of the land, sea level was 400 feet (122 m) lower than it is today.

Desalination is the process of removing salt from ocean water so that it can be used for irrigation, water for livestock, and for drinking. Most of the world's desalination plants are in the arid countries of the Arabian Peninsula.

Because of the water cycle, Earth has roughly the same amount of water now as it has had for two billion years.

If all the world's water were placed in a gallon jug, the fresh water available for humans to use would equal only about one tablespoon.

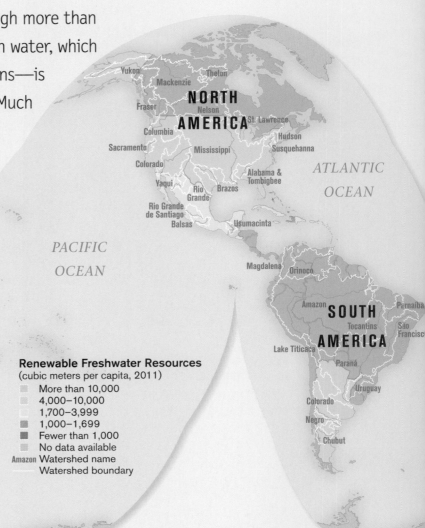

Renewable Freshwater Resources
(cubic meters per capita, 2011)
- More than 10,000
- 4,000–10,000
- 1,700–3,999
- 1,000–1,699
- Fewer than 1,000
- No data available
- Amazon Watershed name
- Watershed boundary

◗ **BIG SPLASH!** Water sports are a favorite recreational activity, especially in hot places such as Albuquerque, New Mexico, U.S.A., where these young people cool down in a giant wave pool.

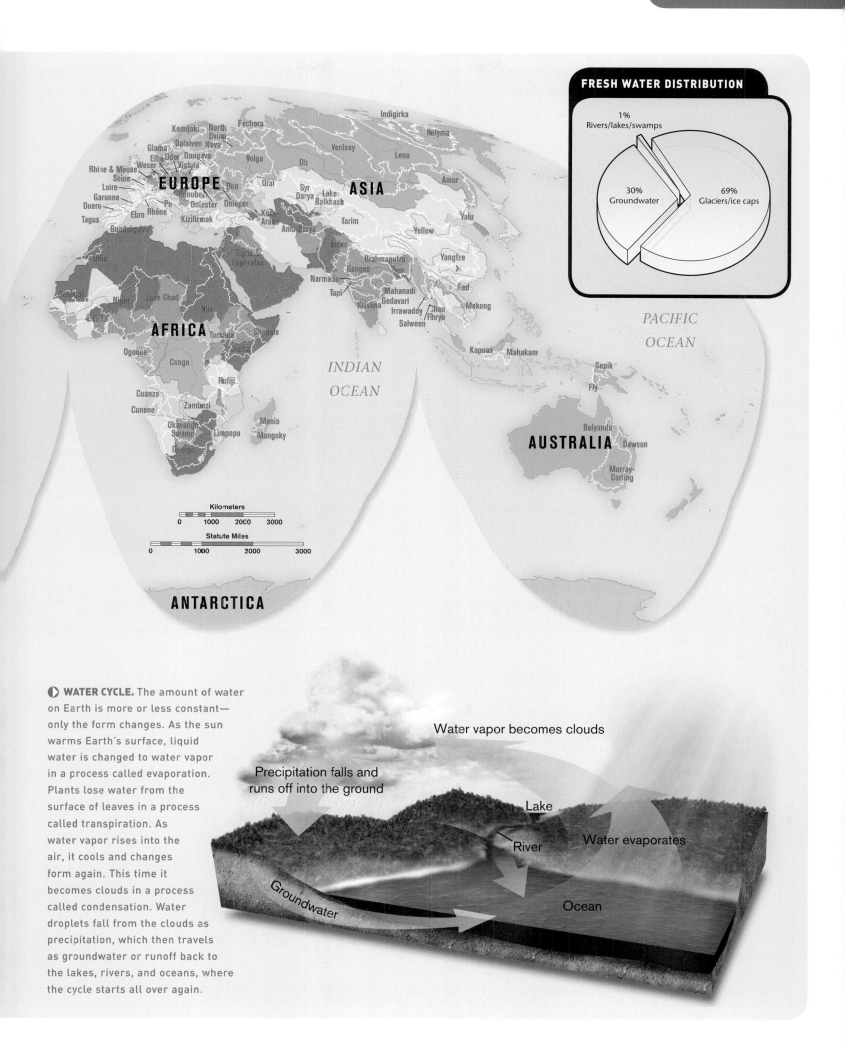

FRESH WATER DISTRIBUTION

1%
Rivers/lakes/swamps

30%
Groundwater

69%
Glaciers/ice caps

EUROPE

ASIA

AFRICA

AUSTRALIA

ANTARCTICA

INDIAN OCEAN

PACIFIC OCEAN

Kilometers
0   1000   2000   3000

Statute Miles
0   1000   2000   3000

Kemijoki   North Dvina   Fechora   Indigirka   Kolyma
Glama   Dalälven   Neva   Yenisey   Lena
Elbe   Oder   Daugava   Volga   Ob   Amur
Rhine & Meuse   Weser   Vistula   Ural   Syr Darya   Lake Balkhash   Yalu
Seine   Loire   Danube   Dniester   Dnieper   Kura-Araks   Tarim   Yellow
Garonne   Po   Rhône   Amu Darya   Yangtze
Duero   Ebro   Kizilirmak   Indus   Brahmaputra   Red
Tagus   Guadalquivir   Tigris & Euphrates   Ganges   Mahanadi   Mekong
Ural   Narmada   Tapi   Krishna   Godavari   Chao Phrya
Senegal   Niger   Lake Chad   Nile   Irrawaddy   Salween
Volta   Turkana   Shebele   Kapuas   Mahakam
Ogooué   Congo   Juba   Sepik
Cuanza   Rufiji   Fly
Cunene   Zambezi   Mania   Belyando   Dawson
Okavango Swamp   Limpopo   Mangoky   Murray-Darling
Orange

WATER CYCLE. The amount of water on Earth is more or less constant—only the form changes. As the sun warms Earth's surface, liquid water is changed to water vapor in a process called evaporation. Plants lose water from the surface of leaves in a process called transpiration. As water vapor rises into the air, it cools and changes form again. This time it becomes clouds in a process called condensation. Water droplets fall from the clouds as precipitation, which then travels as groundwater or runoff back to the lakes, rivers, and oceans, where the cycle starts all over again.

Water vapor becomes clouds

Precipitation falls and runs off into the ground

Lake

River

Water evaporates

Groundwater

Ocean

World Food

Earth produces enough food for all its inhabitants but not everyone gets enough to eat. It's a matter of distribution. Agricultural regions, shown in the map at right, are unevenly spread around the world, and it is sometimes difficult to move food supplies from areas of surplus to areas of great need. Africa, in particular, has regions where hunger and malnourishment rob people of healthy, productive lives.

In recent decades, food production has increased, especially production of meat and cereals, such as corn, wheat, and rice. They dominate the calorie supply of people, especially in Africa and Asia. But increased yields of grain require intensive use of fertilizers and irrigation, which are not only expensive but also possibly a threat to the environment.

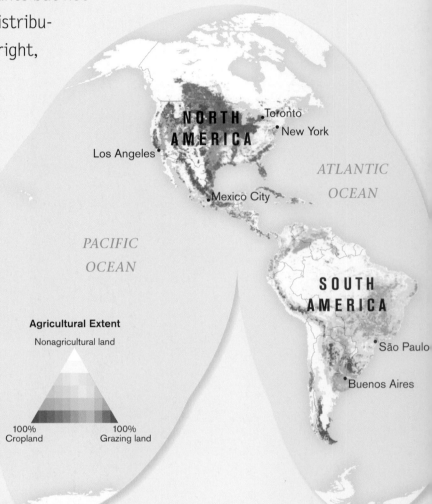

Agricultural Extent

Nonagricultural land

100% Cropland   100% Grazing land

HARVEST BY FISHING COUNTRY

The world's yearly catch of ocean fish is more than four times what it was in 1950. The most heavily harvested areas are in the North Atlantic and western Pacific Oceans. Overfishing is becoming a serious problem. At least seven of the most-fished species are considered to be at their limit. Aquaculture—raising fish and seaweed in controlled ponds—accounts for 40 percent of the fish people eat. This practice began some 4,000 years ago in China, where it continues today, accounting for about two-thirds of the country's total output. Fish are among the most widely traded food products, with 75 percent of the total catch sold on the international market each year.

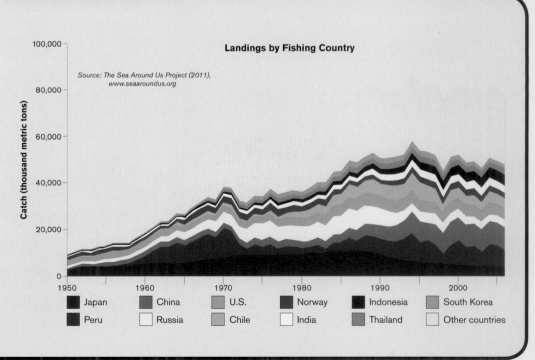

Landings by Fishing Country

Source: The Sea Around Us Project (2011), www.seaaroundus.org

Catch (thousand metric tons)

Legend:
- Japan
- Peru
- China
- Russia
- U.S.
- Chile
- Norway
- India
- Indonesia
- Thailand
- South Korea
- Other countries

ASIA

Moscow

London
Paris EUROPE

Beijing

Tokyo

Cairo

*PACIFIC
OCEAN*

AFRICA

Mumbai

Lagos

*INDIAN
OCEAN*

Jakarta

AUSTRALIA

Sydney

Kilometers
0   1000   2000   3000

Statute Miles
0   1000   2000   3000

ANTARCTICA

⬥ **CASTING NETS.** Fishermen in Orissa, India, cast their nets on the Birupa River. Fish is an important source of protein in their diets. Any surplus catch can be sold in the local market.

STAPLE GRAINS

CORN. A staple in prehistoric Mexico and Peru, corn (or maize) is native to the New World. By the time Columbus's crew first tasted it, corn was already a hardy crop in much of North and South America.

WHEAT. One of the two oldest grains (barley is the other), wheat was important in ancient Mediterranean civilizations. Today, it is the most widely cultivated grain. Wheat grows best in temperate climates.

RICE. Originating in Asia many millennia ago, rice is the staple grain for about half the world's people. It is a labor-intensive plant that grows primarily in paddies (flooded fields) and thrives in the hot, humid tropics.

POLITICAL WORLD

World Energy & Minerals

Almost everything people do—from cooking to powering an airplane—requires energy. But energy comes in different forms. Traditional energy sources, still used by many people in the developing world, include burning dried animal dung and wood. Industrialized countries and urban centers around the world rely on coal, oil, and natural gas—called fossil fuels because they formed from decayed plant and animal material accumulated from long ago. Fossil fuel deposits, either in the ground or under the ocean floor, are unevenly distributed on Earth (see map, right), and many countries frequently cannot afford them.

Carbon dioxide from the burning of fossil fuels as well as other emissions may be contributing to global warming. Concerned scientists are looking at new ways to harness renewable sources of energy, such as water, wind, and sun.

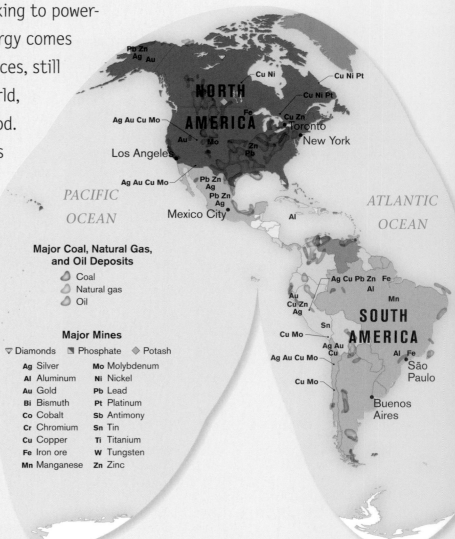

Major Coal, Natural Gas, and Oil Deposits
- Coal
- Natural gas
- Oil

Major Mines
▽ Diamonds   ▧ Phosphate   ◇ Potash

Ag Silver	**Mo** Molybdenum
Al Aluminum	**Ni** Nickel
Au Gold	**Pb** Lead
Bi Bismuth	**Pt** Platinum
Co Cobalt	**Sb** Antimony
Cr Chromium	**Sn** Tin
Cu Copper	**Ti** Titanium
Fe Iron ore	**W** Tungsten
Mn Manganese	**Zn** Zinc

OIL, GAS, AND COAL

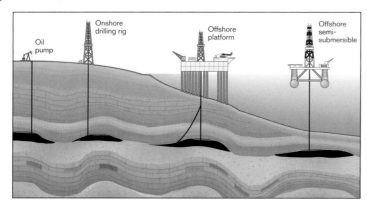

⬭ **DRILLING FOR OIL AND GAS.** The type of equipment used depends on whether the oil or natural gas is in the ground or under the ocean. This illustration shows some of the different kinds of onshore and offshore drilling equipment.

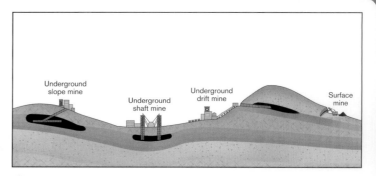

⬭ **COAL MINING.** The mining of coal made the industrial revolution possible, and coal still remains a major energy source. Work that was once done by people using picks and shovels now relies heavily on mechanized equipment. This diagram shows some of the various kinds of mines currently in use.

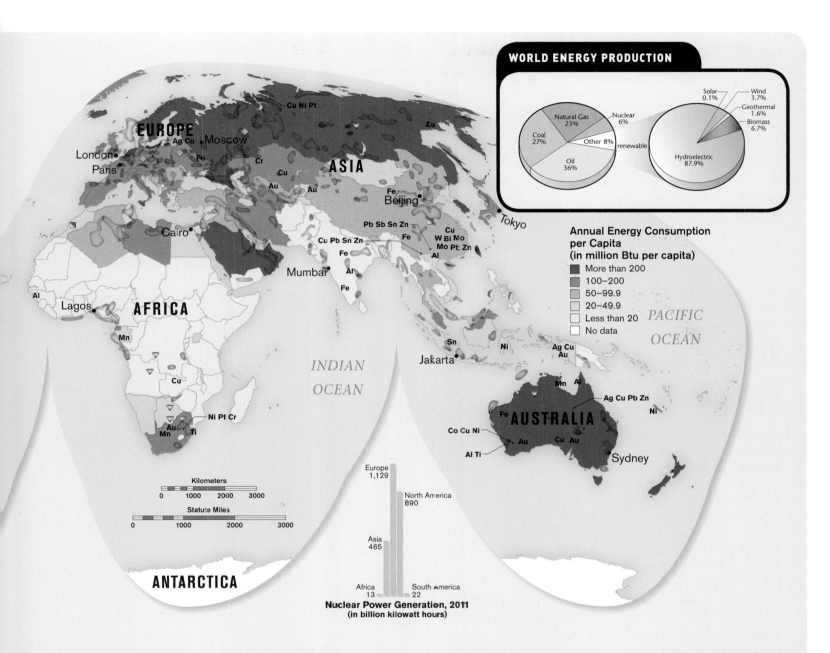

WORLD ENERGY PRODUCTION

Coal 27%
Natural Gas 23%
Nuclear 6%
Other 8% renewable
Oil 36%

Solar 0.1%
Wind 3.7%
Geothermal 1.6%
Biomass 6.7%
Hydroelectric 87.9%

EUROPE
London
Paris
ASIA
Moscow
Ag Cu
Fe
Cr
Cu
Au
Au
Cu Ni Pt
Au
Fe
Beijing
Tokyo
Cairo
Pb Sb Sn Zn
Fe
Cu Pb Sn Zn
Fe
Cu
W Bi Mo
Mo Pt Zn
Al
Mumbai
Al
Fe
Al
Lagos
AFRICA
Mn
Cu
Cu
Ni Pt Cr
Au
Mn
Ti

INDIAN OCEAN

Sn
Jakarta
Ni
Ag Cu
Au
PACIFIC OCEAN

Mn Al
Fe AUSTRALIA
Ag Cu Pb Zn
Ni
Co Cu Ni
Au
Cu Au
Al Ti
Sydney

Annual Energy Consumption per Capita (in million Btu per capita)
More than 200
100–200
50–99.9
20–49.9
Less than 20
No data

Kilometers
0   1000   2000   3000

Statute Miles
0   1000   2000   3000

ANTARCTICA

Europe 1,129
North America 890
Asia 465
Africa 13
South America 22

Nuclear Power Generation, 2011 (in billion kilowatt hours)

HYDROELECTRIC POWER

Hydroelectric plants, such as Santiago del Estero in Argentina (above), use dams to harness running water to generate clean, renewable energy.

GEOTHERMAL POWER

Geothermal power, originating from groundwater heated by magma, provides energy for this power plant in Iceland. Swimmers enjoy the warm, mineral-rich waters of a lake created by the power plant.

SOLAR POWER

Solar panels on Samso Island in Denmark capture and store energy from the sun, an environmentally friendly alternative to the use of fossil fuels.

WIND POWER

Strong winds blowing through California's, U.S.A., mountain passes spin the blades of windmills on an energy farm, powering giant turbines that generate electricity for the state.

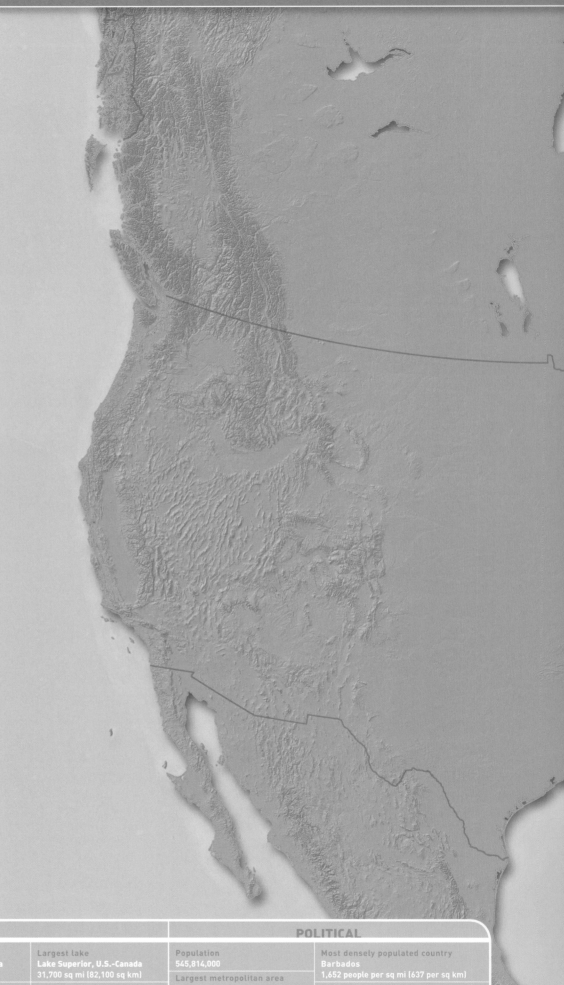

PHYSICAL			POLITICAL	
Land area 9,449,000 sq mi (24,474,000 sq km)	**Lowest point** **Death Valley, California** -282 ft (-86 m)	**Largest lake** **Lake Superior, U.S.-Canada** 31,700 sq mi (82,100 sq km)	**Population** 545,814,000	**Most densely populated country** **Barbados** 1,652 people per sq mi (637 per sq km)
Highest point **Mount McKinley (Denali), Alaska** 20,320 ft (6,194 m)	**Longest river** **Mississippi-Missouri,** **United States** 3,710 mi (5,971 km)		**Largest metropolitan area** **Mexico City, Mexico** Pop. 19,319,000	**Economy** **Farming: cattle, grains, cotton, sugar** **Industry: machinery, metals, mining** **Services**
			Largest country **Canada** 3,855,101 sq mi (9,984,670 sq km)	

North America

North America

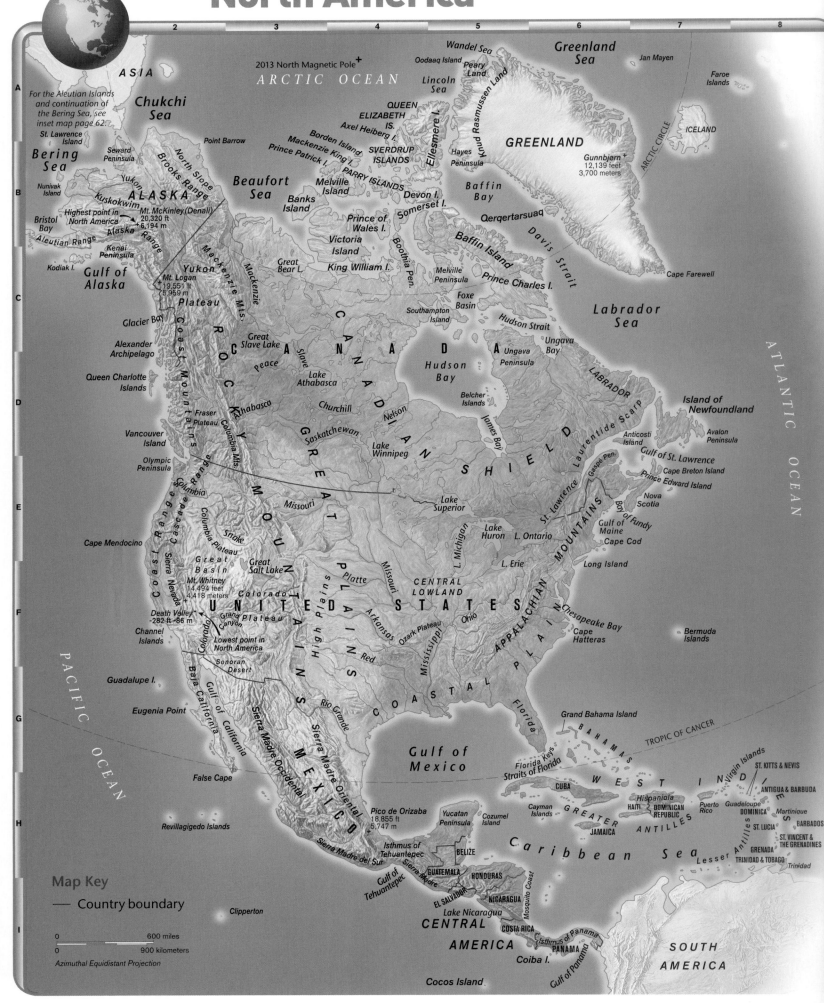

2   3   4   5   6   7   8

ASIA

Chukchi Sea

For the Aleutian Islands and continuation of the Bering Sea, see inset map page 62.

2013 North Magnetic Pole +

ARCTIC OCEAN

Wandel Sea

Oodaaq Island   Peary Land

Greenland Sea

Jan Mayen

Lincoln Sea

Faroe Islands

ICELAND

ARCTIC CIRCLE

Point Barrow

St. Lawrence Island

Bering Sea

Seward Peninsula

North Slope

Brooks Range

QUEEN ELIZABETH IS.

Axel Heiberg I.

Borden Island

Mackenzie King I.

Prince Patrick I.

SVERDRUP ISLANDS

PARRY ISLANDS

Ellesmere I.

Knud Rasmussen Land

Hayes Peninsula

GREENLAND

Gunnbjørn + 12,139 feet 3,700 meters

Nunivak Island

ALASKA

Yukon

Kuskokwim

Mt. McKinley (Denali) 20,320 ft + 6,194 m

Beaufort Sea

Melville Island

Banks Island

Devon I.

Somerset I.

Baffin Bay

Qeqertarsuaq

Davis Strait

Bristol Bay

Highest point in North America

Alaska Range

Mackenzie Mts.

Victoria Island

Prince of Wales I.

King William I.

Boothia Pen.

Baffin Island

Prince Charles I.

Cape Farewell

Aleutian Range

Kenai Peninsula

Kodiak I.

Gulf of Alaska

Mt. Logan 19,551 ft + 5,959 m

Yukon Plateau

Mackenzie

Great Bear L.

Melville Peninsula

Foxe Basin

Labrador Sea

Glacier Bay

Coast Mountains

ROCKY

Great Slave Lake

CANADA

Southampton Island

Hudson Strait

Ungava Bay

Alexander Archipelago

Peace

Slave

Athabasca

CANADIAN

Hudson Bay

Ungava Peninsula

LABRADOR

Queen Charlotte Islands

Lake Athabasca

Churchill

Nelson

Belcher Islands

Laurentide Scarp

Island of Newfoundland

Vancouver Island

Fraser Plateau

Athabasca

Columbia Mts.

Saskatchewan

GREAT

James Bay

Anticosti Island

Avalon Peninsula

Olympic Peninsula

Columbia Range

Lake Winnipeg

SHIELD

Gulf of St. Lawrence

Cape Breton Island

Prince Edward Island

Cascade Range

Columbia Plateau

Missouri

Lake Superior

St. Lawrence

Gaspé Pen.

Nova Scotia

Cape Mendocino

Coast Ranges

Sierra Nevada

Snake

Great Basin

MOUNTAINS

Lake Huron

L. Ontario

MOUNTAINS

Gulf of Maine

Bay of Fundy

Cape Cod

Great Salt Lake

PLAINS

Platte

Missouri

L. Michigan

L. Erie

APPALACHIAN

Long Island

Mt. Whitney 14,494 feet 4,418 meters

Colorado Plateau

UNITED

High Plains

CENTRAL LOWLAND

Chesapeake Bay

Death Valley -282 ft -86 m

Grand Canyon

STATES

Arkansas

Ozark Plateau

Ohio

COASTAL PLAIN

Cape Hatteras

Channel Islands

Colorado

Lowest point in North America

Mississippi

Red

Bermuda Islands

Guadalupe I.

Sonoran Desert

Rio Grande

Florida

Eugenia Point

Baja California

Gulf of California

Grand Bahama Island

TROPIC OF CANCER

PACIFIC OCEAN

False Cape

Sierra Madre Occidental

Sierra Madre Oriental

MEXICO

Gulf of Mexico

Florida Keys

Straits of Florida

BAHAMAS

WEST

CUBA

Cayman Islands

GREATER

Hispaniola

HAITI

DOMINICAN REPUBLIC

Puerto Rico

Virgin Islands

INDIES

ST. KITTS & NEVIS

ANTIGUA & BARBUDA

Revillagigedo Islands

Pico de Orizaba 18,855 ft + 5,747 m

Yucatan Peninsula

Cozumel Island

JAMAICA

ANTILLES

Guadeloupe

DOMINICA

ST. LUCIA

Martinique

BARBADOS

Sierra Madre del Sur

Isthmus of Tehuantepec

BELIZE

GUATEMALA

Caribbean Sea

Lesser Antilles

ST. VINCENT & THE GRENADINES

GRENADA

TRINIDAD & TOBAGO

Trinidad

Gulf of Tehuantepec

Sierra Madre

HONDURAS

Mosquito Coast

EL SALVADOR

NICARAGUA

Clipperton

Lake Nicaragua

CENTRAL

COSTA RICA

Isthmus of Panama

PANAMA

Gulf of Panama

SOUTH AMERICA

AMERICA

Coiba I.

Cocos Island

ATLANTIC OCEAN

Map Key

—— Country boundary

0   600 miles

0   900 kilometers

Azimuthal Equidistant Projection

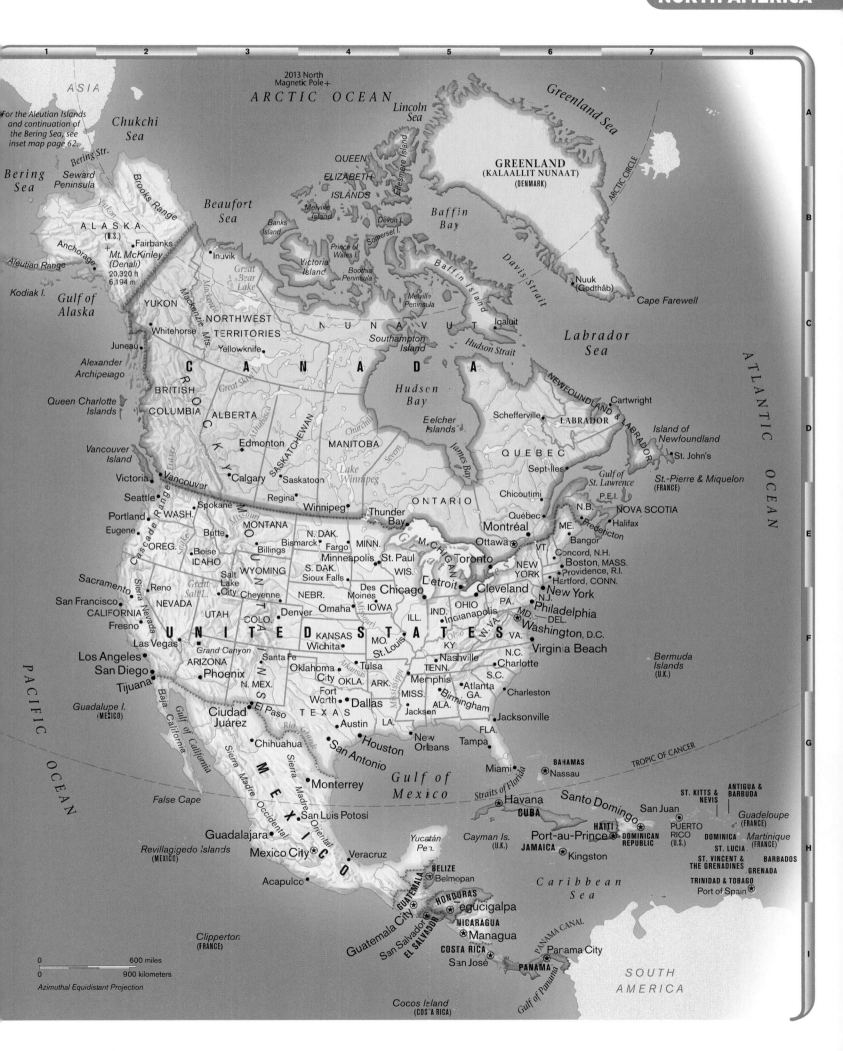

ASIA

ARCTIC OCEAN

2013 North Magnetic Pole +

Lincoln Sea

Greenland Sea

Chukchi Sea

For the Aleutian Islands and continuation of the Bering Sea, see inset map page 62.

Bering Str.

Beaufort Sea

QUEEN ELIZABETH ISLANDS

Banks Island

Melville Island

Devon I.

Prince of Wales I.

Somerset I.

Boothia Peninsula

Baffin Bay

Ellesmere Island

ARCTIC CIRCLE

GREENLAND (KALAALLIT NUNAAT) (DENMARK)

Bering Sea

Seward Peninsula

Brooks Range

Yukon

ALASKA (U.S.)

Anchorage

Fairbanks

Mt. McKinley (Denali) 20,320 ft 6,194 m

Inuvik

Great Bear Lake

Victoria Island

Baffin Island

Davis Strait

Nuuk (Godthåb)

Cape Farewell

Aleutian Range

Kodiak I.

Gulf of Alaska

YUKON

Mackenzie Mts.

NORTHWEST TERRITORIES

NUNAVUT

Southampton Island

Hudson Strait

Iqaluit

Labrador Sea

ATLANTIC OCEAN

Whitehorse

Yellowknife

Great Slave

C A N A D A

Juneau

Alexander Archipelago

BRITISH COLUMBIA

R O C K Y

Athabasca

Churchill

Eelcher Islands

NEWFOUNDLAND & LABRADOR

Cartwright

Queen Charlotte Islands

Vancouver Island

ALBERTA

SASKATCHEWAN

MANITOBA

Hudson Bay

James Bay

Seven

Scheffferville

LABRADOR

Island of Newfoundland

Victoria

Vancouver

Edmonton

Fraser

Calgary

Saskatoon

Lake Winnipeg

ONTARIO

QUEBEC

Sept-Îles

Gulf of St. Lawrence

St-Pierre & Miquelon (FRANCE)

St. John's

Seattle

Portland

WASH.

Spokane

Regina

Winnipeg

Thunder Bay

Chicoutimi

P.E.I.

N.B.

NOVA SCOTIA

Cascade Range

Snake

Missouri

MONTANA

N. DAK.

MINN.

M I C H I G A N

Québec

Fredericton

Halifax

Eugene

OREG.

Butte

Billings

Bismarck

Fargo

Montréal

ME.

Bangor

Boise

IDAHO

WYOMING

S. DAK.

Minneapolis

St. Paul

WIS.

Ottawa

Toronto

VT.

Concord, N.H.

Boston, MASS.

Sacramento

Sierra Nevada

Reno

Great Salt L.

Salt Lake City

Cheyenne

NEBR.

Sioux Falls

Des Moines

IOWA

Chicago

Detroit

Cleveland

NEW YORK

New York

Providence, R.I.

Hartford, CONN.

N.J.

San Francisco

CALIFORNIA

NEVADA

UTAH

COLO.

Denver

Omaha

Missouri

ILL.

IND.

Indianapolis

OHIO

PA.

Philadelphia

MD.

DEL.

Fresno

U N I T E D

S T A T E S

KANSAS

MO.

St. Louis

KY.

W. VA.

VA.

Washington, D.C.

Las Vegas

Grand Canyon

Wichita

Arkansas

Nashville

TENN.

N.C.

Virginia Beach

Bermuda Islands (U.K.)

Los Angeles

San Diego

Tijuana

ARIZONA

Phoenix

N. MEX.

Santa Fe

Oklahoma City

OKLA.

ARK.

Memphis

MISS.

Birmingham

ALA.

Atlanta

GA.

S.C.

Charlotte

Charleston

Guadalupe I. (MEXICO)

Baja California

Gulf of California

El Paso

Ciudad Juárez

Rio Grande

Fort Worth

Dallas

T E X A S

Austin

LA.

Jackson

New Orleans

Tampa

FLA.

Jacksonville

PACIFIC OCEAN

Chihuahua

Sierra Madre Occidental

San Antonio

Houston

Gulf of Mexico

Miami

BAHAMAS

Nassau

TROPIC OF CANCER

False Cape

M E X I C O

Monterrey

Sierra Madre Oriental

San Luis Potosí

Straits of Florida

Havana

CUBA

Santo Domingo

San Juan

ST. KITTS & NEVIS

ANTIGUA & BARBUDA

Guadalajara

Revillagigedo Islands (MEXICO)

Mexico City

Veracruz

Yucatán Pen.

Cayman Is. (U.K.)

JAMAICA

Port-au-Prince

HAITI

Kingston

DOMINICAN REPUBLIC

PUERTO RICO (U.S.)

DOMINICA

ST. LUCIA

Guadeloupe (FRANCE)

Martinique (FRANCE)

BARBADOS

Acapulco

BELIZE

Belmopan

Caribbean Sea

ST. VINCENT & THE GRENADINES

GRENADA

TRINIDAD & TOBAGO

Port of Spain

Clipperton (FRANCE)

Guatemala City

GUATEMALA

San Salvador

EL SALVADOR

HONDURAS

Tegucigalpa

NICARAGUA

Managua

COSTA RICA

San José

PANAMA

PANAMA CANAL

Panama City

SOUTH AMERICA

Cocos Island (COSTA RICA)

Gulf of Panama

0   600 miles
0   900 kilometers

Azimuthal Equidistant Projection

North America

LAND OF CONTRASTS

From the windswept tundra of Alaska, U.S.A., to the rain forest of Panama, the third largest continent stretches 5,500 miles (8,850 km), spanning natural environments that support wildlife from polar bears to jaguars. Over thousands of years, Native American groups spread across these varied landscapes. But this rich mosaic of cultures largely disappeared with the onslaught of European fortune hunters and land seekers. While abundant resources and fast-changing technology have brought prosperity to Canada and the United States, other countries wrestle with the most basic needs. Promise and problems abound across this contrasting realm of 23 countries and 546 million people.

◐ **STORY IN THE ROCKS.** Slanting sun rays reveal layers in the rocks of the Grand Canyon. Each rock layer—oldest on the canyon floor, youngest at the canyon's rim—tells us about Earth's changing history.

◐ **DRESSED TO CELEBRATE.** This boy in Mexico's southern state of Chiapas wears traditional clothing, including a brightly colored string tie and a broad-brimmed sombrero with elaborate stitching around the edge.

● **HOLD TIGHT.** These daring rafters are running the roaring rapids of the Kicking Horse River in Br tish Columbia, Canada's westernmost province. Rivers tumbling down the steep slopes of the Rocky Mountains provide many recreational opportunities.

◀ **STREET MUSIC.** People from around the world visit New Orleans, Louisiana, U.S.A., to hear jazz musicians fill the air with their music.

◀ **NIGHT SONG.** This coyote sends his mournful howl into the dark Montana night. Members of the dog fami_y, coyotes originated in the southwestern United States but are now found through-out North America—even in urban areas.

more about
North America

⬤ **DWELLINGS FROM THE PAST.** Between A.D. 1000 and A.D. 1300 native people known as Ancestral Puebloans built cliff dwellings called pueblos, such as this one in Mesa Verde, Colorado, U.S.A.

⬤ **MAYA TREASURE.** The Pyramid of the Magician marks the ruins of Uxmal on the Yucatán Peninsula. Nearly four million people of Maya descent still live in southern Mexico and Central America.

◑ **FROZEN SUMMER.** Because it lies so far north, even summers are cold in Greenland. Here, local people navigate their boat among icebergs in waters off the village of Augpilagtoq.

◀ **HIGH FLYER.** A young Kutchin boy sails off a snowbank on snowshoes in Canada's Yukon. The Kutchin, an Athabascan tribe, live in the forested lands of eastern Alaska and western Canada. The name Kutchin means "people."

◔ **SWIMMING FREE.** A variety of fish swim among colorful corals in the clear blue waters of the Caribbean Sea. Tropical waters are the habitat for many species of fish.

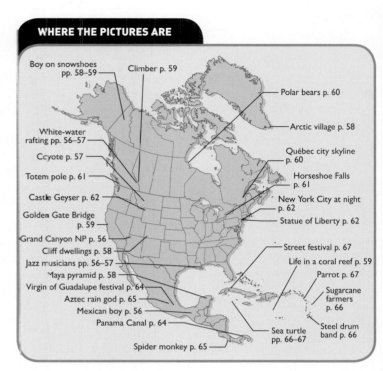

WHERE THE PICTURES ARE

Boy on snowshoes pp. 58–59
Climber p. 59
Polar bears p. 60
Arctic village p. 58
White-water rafting pp. 56–57
Québec city skyline p. 60
Coyote p. 57
Horseshoe Falls p. 61
Totem pole p. 61
New York City at night p. 62
Castle Geyser p. 62
Statue of Liberty p. 62
Golden Gate Bridge p. 59
Grand Canyon NP p. 56
Street festival p. 67
Cliff dwellings p. 58
Life in a coral reef p. 59
Jazz musicians pp. 56–57
Parrot p. 67
Maya pyramid p. 58
Sugarcane farmers p. 66
Virgin of Guadalupe festival p. 64
Aztec rain god p. 65
Mexican boy p. 56
Steel drum band p. 66
Panama Canal p. 64
Sea turtle pp. 66–67
Spider monkey p. 65

◔ **DON'T LOOK DOWN.** Clinging to a sheer rock face, a young woman demonstrates great skill as she scales a steep cliff in Banff National Park in Canada. Covering more than 2,500 square miles (6,475 sq km) in the Canadian Rockies, Banff is a major tourist attraction.

◔ **WESTERN GATEWAY.** The Golden Gate Bridge marks the entrance to San Francisco Bay. Beyond the bridge, captured above in the warm glow of twilight, is the California port city named after the bay.

Canada

Topped only by Russia in area, Canada has just 35 million people—fewer than live in the U.S. state of California. Ancient rocks yield abundant minerals. Lakes and rivers in Quebec are tapped for hydropower, and wheat farming and cattle ranching thrive across the western Prairie Provinces. Vast forests attract loggers, and mountain slopes provide a playground for nature lovers. Enormous deposits of oil sands lie waiting for technology to find a cheap way to convert them to hundreds of billions of barrels of oil. Most Canadians live within a hundred miles (161 km) of the U.S. border. Here, too, are its leading cities: Asia-focused Vancouver, ethnically diverse Toronto, capital Ottawa, and French-speaking Montreal.

THE BASICS

STATS

Area
3,855,101 sq mi (9,984,670 sq km)

Population
34,860,000

Predominant languages
English, French (both official)

Predominant religion
Christianity (Roman Catholic, Protestant)

GDP per capita
$40,500

Life expectancy
81 years

Literacy rate
99%

GEO WHIZ

Canada ranks second behind Saudi Arabia in largest oil reserves, thanks to the oil contained in the Athabasca tar sands in northern Alberta.

The Inuit territory of Nunavut has issued license plates in the shape of a polar bear for cars, motorcycles, and snowmobiles.

Canada is a constitutional monarchy, with Britain's Queen Elizabeth II as its head of state.

Montreal is the second most populous French-speaking city in the world, after Paris, France.

Canada's many bays, inlets, and islands give it the longest coastline of any country: 151,023 miles (243,042 km).

Geologists believe Réservoir Manicouagan in Quebec may have been created by the impact of a meteorite more than 200 million years ago.

◖ **SILENT WATCHERS.** Polar bears, North America's largest land carnivores, are adapted to the extreme Arctic environment around Cape Churchill in northern Manitoba. It is estimated that as many as 15,000 polar bears live in Canada.

LONGEST COASTLINE

Country	Coastline
Canada	151,023 miles (243,042 km)
Indonesia	33,998 miles (54,716 km)
Russia	23,397 miles (37,653 km)
Philippines	22,549 miles (36,289 km)
Japan	18,486 miles (29,751 km)
Australia	16,006 miles (25,760 km)
Norway	15,626 miles (25,148 km)
United States	12,380 miles (19,924 km)
New Zealand	9,404 miles (15,134 km)
China	9,010 miles (14,500 km)

Canada has the longest coastline in the world, and at more than 150,000 miles (243,000 km) it far surpasses the length of coastline of any other country.

◖ **FRENCH ENCLAVE.** Chateau Frontenac sparkles in Quebec City's nighttime skyline. Settled by the French in the early 1600s, the province of Quebec has maintained close ties to Europe and to its French heritage.

(Map labels)

ARCTIC CIRCLE
Tuktoyak[tuk]
ALASKA (U.S.)
Inuvik
MACKENZIE MOUNTAINS
YUKON
SELWYN MTS.
Mt. Logan 19,551 ft 5,959 m
St. Elias Mts.
Yukon
Haines Junction
Whitehorse
ROCKY
PACIFIC OCEAN
QUEEN CHARLOTTE IS.
Prince Rupert
Dawson Creek
BRITISH
Prince George
Grande Prairi[e]
COLUMBIA
MOUNTAINS
Campbell River
Fraser
BAN[FF] NAT[IONAL] PAR[K]
Vancouver Island
Kamloops
Columbia
Nanaimo
Kelowna
Victoria
Vancouver

● **KNOWING WHO WE ARE.** Native people of the Pacific Northwest pre-serve their family stories and legends in massive carved poles called totems, such as this one in Stanley Park in Vancouver, British Columbia.

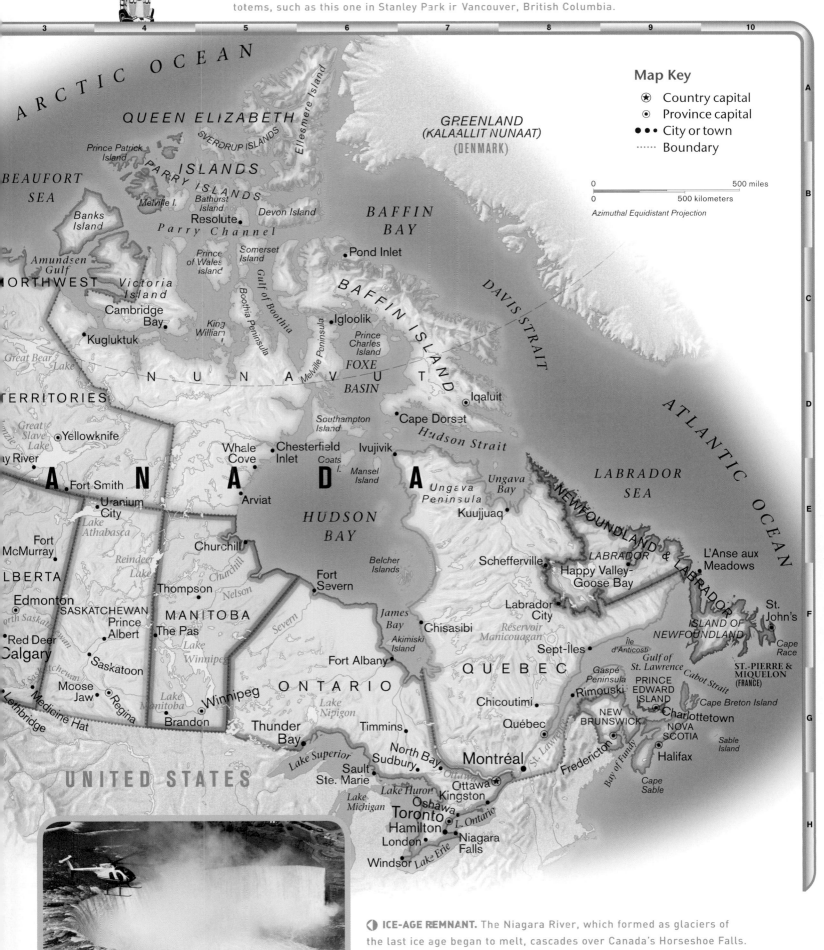

Map Key

⊛ Country capital
◉ Province capital
●●● City or town
······ Boundary

0 _____ 500 miles
0 _____ 500 kilometers
Azimuthal Equidistant Projection

ARCTIC OCEAN

QUEEN ELIZABETH

SVERDRUP ISLANDS

Ellesmere Island

Prince Patrick Island

ISLANDS

PARRY ISLANDS

GREENLAND
(KALAALLIT NUNAAT)
(DENMARK)

BEAUFORT SEA

Melville I.

Bathurst Island

Resolute

Devon Island

BAFFIN BAY

Banks Island

Parry Channel

Pond Inlet

Amundsen Gulf

Prince of Wales Island

Somerset Island

Gulf of Boothia

DAVIS STRAIT

NORTHWEST

Victoria Island

Boothia Peninsula

Igloolik

BAFFIN ISLAND

Cambridge Bay

King William I.

Prince Charles Island

Kugluktuk

Melville Peninsula

FOXE BASIN

Great Bear Lake

N U N A V U T

Iqaluit

ATLANTIC OCEAN

TERRITORIES

Southampton Island

Cape Dorset

Hudson Strait

Great Slave Lake

Yellowknife

Whale Cove

Chesterfield Inlet

Ivujivik

LABRADOR SEA

y River

Coats I.

Mansel Island

C A N A D A

Fort Smith

Arviat

Ungava Peninsula

Ungava Bay

NEWFOUNDLAND & LABRADOR

Uranium City

HUDSON BAY

Kuujjuaq

Lake Athabasca

Churchill

Belcher Islands

Scheffervile

L'Anse aux Meadows

Fort McMurray

Reindeer Lake

LABRADOR

Happy Valley-Goose Bay

LBERTA

Thompson

Churchill

Fort Severn

St. John's

Edmonton

Nelson

Labrador City

SASKATCHEWAN

MANITOBA

James Bay

Chisasibi

Réservoir Manicouagan

ISLAND OF NEWFOUNDLAND

North Saskatchewan

Prince Albert

The Pas

Severn

Akimiski Island

Sept-Îles

Cape Race

Red Deer

Lake Winnipeg

Fort Albany

Île d'Anticosti

Gulf of St. Lawrence

ST.-PIERRE & MIQUELON (FRANCE)

Calgary

Saskatoon

S. Saskatchewan

ONTARIO

QUEBEC

Gaspé Peninsula

Cape Breton Island

Moose Jaw

Lake Manitoba

Chicoutimi

Rimouski

PRINCE EDWARD ISLAND

Medicine Hat

Regina

Brandon

Winnipeg

Lake Nipigon

Québec

NEW BRUNSWICK

Charlottetown

Lethbridge

Thunder Bay

Timmins

NOVA SCOTIA

Sable Island

UNITED STATES

Lake Superior

North Bay

Montréal

Fredericton

Halifax

Sudbury

St. Lawrence

Bay of Fundy

Sault Ste. Marie

Lake Huron

Ottawa

Kingston

Cape Sable

Lake Michigan

Oshawa

Ottawa

Toronto

L. Ontario

Hamilton

Niagara Falls

London

Windsor

Lake Erie

● **ICE-AGE REMNANT.** The Niagara River, which formed as glaciers of the last ice age began to melt, cascades over Canada's Horseshoe Falls. The falls, which stretch across the border between Canada and the United States, are a major tourist attraction.

THE BASICS

STATS

Area
3,794,083 sq mi (9,826,630 sq km)

Population
313,858,000

Predominant languages
English, Spanish

Predominant religion
Christianity (Protestant,
Roman Catholic)

GDP per capita
$48,300

Life expectancy
78 years

Literacy rate
99%

GEO WHIZ

Florida is known as the lightning capital of the United States. Sea breezes from the Gulf of Mexico and the Atlantic Ocean collide over the warm Florida peninsula, producing thunderstorms and the lightning associated with them.

Hawai'i is politically part of the United States but geographically part of the Polynesian cultural region of Oceania.

At 379 feet (115 m), Hyperion, a coast redwood in California's Redwood National Forest, is the world's tallest living tree. It is more than 70 feet (21 m) higher than the Statue of Liberty.

Lake Michigan is the only one of the Great Lakes located entirely within the United States. Each of the other four lakes spans the U.S.-Canada border.

In 2006, 18 whooping crane chicks made a historic migration from Wisconsin to Florida following an ultralight aircraft as part of Operation Migration.

United States

From "sea to shining sea" the United States is blessed with a rich bounty of natural resources. Mineral treasures abound—oil, coal, iron, and gold—and its croplands are among the most productive in the world. Americans have used— and too often overused—this storehouse of raw materials to build an economic base unmatched by any other country. An array of high-tech businesses populate the Sunbelt of the South and West. By combining its natural riches and the creative ideas of its ethnically diverse population, this land of opportunity has become a leading global power.

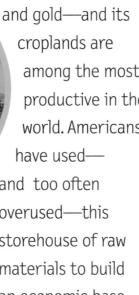

STAPLE CROP.
Approximately 80 million acres (32.4 million ha) are planted in corn in the U.S. Most of the crop is used as livestock feed.

WORLD CITY. The lights of Manhattan glitter around New York City's Chrysler Building. The city's influence as a financial and cultural center extends across the United States and around the world.

LETTING OFF STEAM. Castle Geyser is just one of many active geological features in Yellowstone National Park in Wyoming. The park is part of a region that sits on top of a major tectonic hot spot.

LADY LIBERTY. The Statue of Liberty, a gift from France, stands in New York City's harbor. The statue has become a symbol of hope for millions of immigrants coming to the United States in search of a better life.

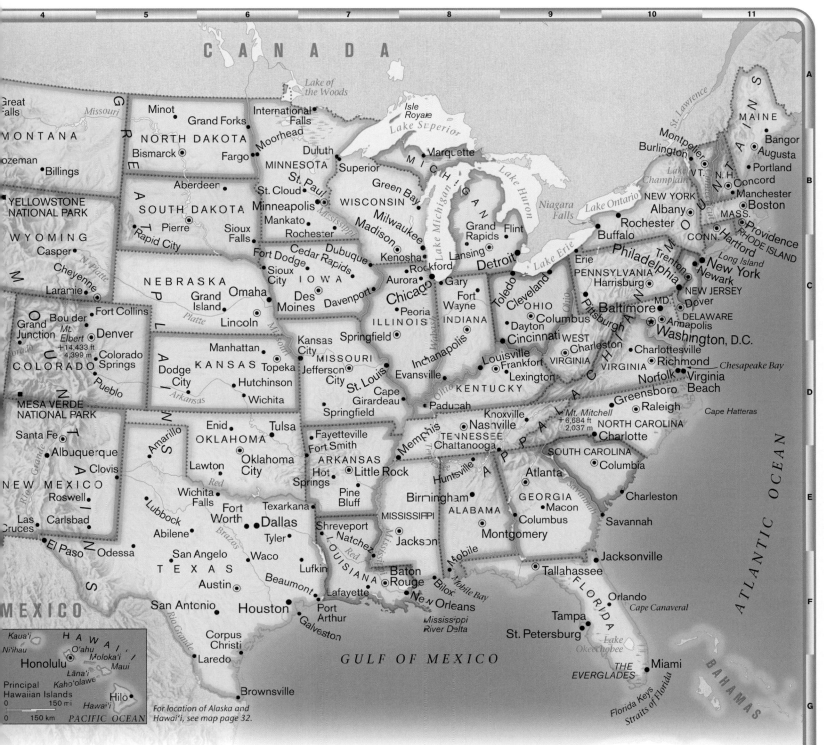

CANADA

MEXICO

GULF OF MEXICO

ATLANTIC OCEAN

PACIFIC OCEAN

Map Key

⊛ Country capital
⊙ State capital
••• City or town
······ Boundary

0   200 miles
0   200 kilometers

Albers Conic Equal-Area Projection

For location of Alaska and Hawai'i, see map page 32.

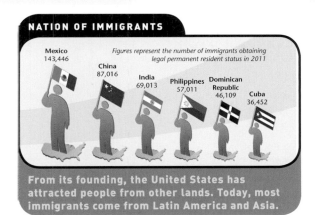

NATION OF IMMIGRANTS

| Mexico 143,446 | China 87,016 | India 69,013 | Philippines 57,011 | Dominican Republic 46,109 | Cuba 36,452 |

Figures represent the number of immigrants obtaining legal permanent resident status in 2011

From its founding, the United States has attracted people from other lands. Today, most immigrants come from Latin America and Asia.

THE BASICS

STATS

Largest country
Mexico
758,449 sq mi (1,964,375 sq km)

Smallest country
El Salvador
8,124 sq mi (21,041 sq km)

Most populous country
Mexico
116,100,000

Least populous country
Belize
326,000

Predominant languages
English, Spanish, Mayan, various Amerindian languages

Predominant religion
Christianity (Roman Catholic, Protestant)

Highest GDP per capita
Mexico
$14,700

Lowest GDP per capita
Nicaragua
$3,200

Highest life expectancy
Costa Rica, Panama
78 years

Highest literacy rate
Costa Rica
95%

GEO WHIZ

Mexico takes its name from the word *Mexica*, another name for the Aztec, the last of the indigenous cultures to rule Mexico before it fell to Spanish conquerors in 1521.

Scientists believe that the crater of the comet that struck Earth 65 million years ago, causing the dramatic climate changes that led to the extinction of the dinosaurs, is at Chicxulub, on the Yucatán Peninsula.

Coral colonies growing along much of the coast of Belize form the longest barrier reef in the Western Hemisphere and the second longest in the world, after Australia's Great Barrier Reef.

Vampire bats, which are only about the size of an adult person's thumb, drink the blood of other animals to survive. They are found throughout Central America.

A new set of locks on the Panama Canal will allow ships with 2.5 times the cargo capacity of ships now traveling the canal to take this shortcut between the Atlantic and Pacific Oceans.

CELEBRATION.
Traditional costumes and musical instruments combine with Christian beliefs during the annual Virgin of Guadalupe festival, observed throughout Mexico. The festival marks the appearance of the Virgin Mary to a peasant in 1531.

Mexico & Central America

VITAL LINK. As many as 14,000 vessels, 5 percent of global trade, use the Panama Canal each year to pass between the Atlantic and Pacific Oceans.

Mexico and most Central American countries share a backbone of mountains, a legacy of powerful Native American empires, and a largely Spanish colonial history. Once-abundant rain forests now are largely gone. Mexico dwarfs its seven Central American neighbors in area, population, and natural resources. Its economy boasts a rich diversity of agricultural crops, highly productive oil fields, a growing manufacturing base, as well as strong trade with the United States and Canada. Overall, Central American countries rely on agricultural products such as bananas and coffee, though tourism is increasing. Modern-day Mexico and Central America struggle to fulfill the hopes of growing populations, some of whom search for better lives by migrating—both legally and illegally—north to the United States.

Tijuana
Ensenada
Mexicali
BAJA CALIFORNIA
Gulf of California
Nogales
Hermosillo
Guaymas
Yaqui
Ciudad Obregón
Los Mochis
La Paz
False Cape

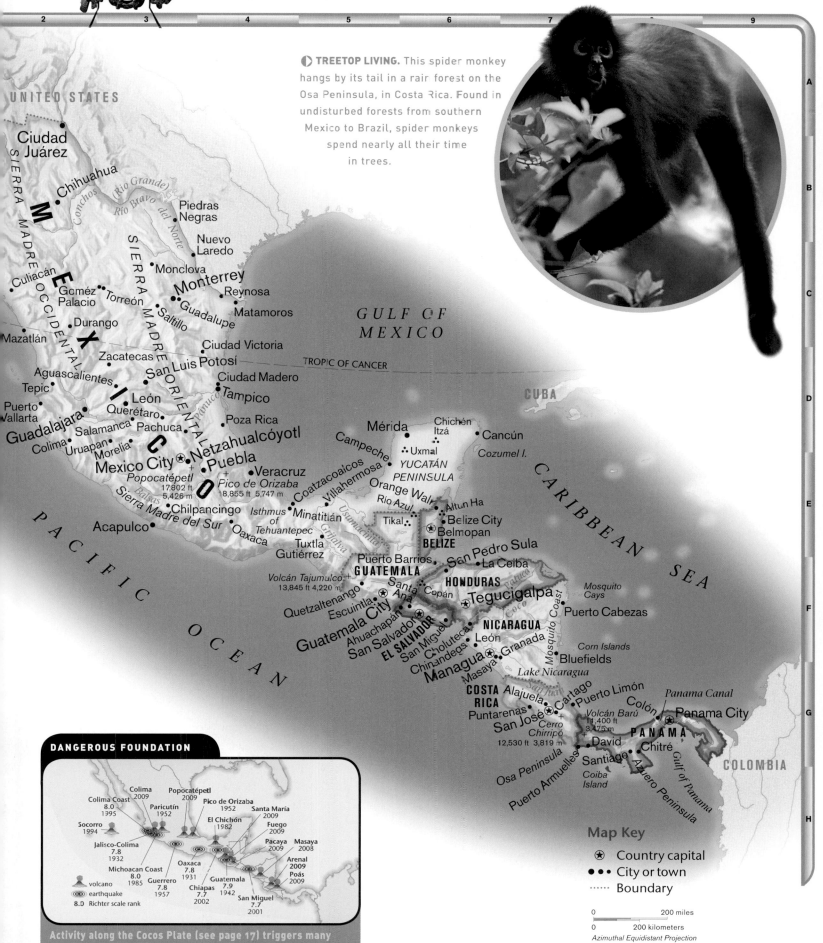

◑ **MYTHS AND LEGENDS.** The powerful Aztec Empire dominated much of Mexico and Central America from 1427 to 1521. The Aztecs worshipped many gods, including Tlaloc (shown here), the god of rain and fertility.

◑ **TREETOP LIVING.** This spider monkey hangs by its tail in a rain forest on the Osa Peninsula, in Costa Rica. Found in undisturbed forests from southern Mexico to Brazil, spider monkeys spend nearly all their time in trees.

DANGEROUS FOUNDATION

Activity along the Cocos Plate (see page 17) triggers many earthquakes and volcanoes in Mexico and Central America. The strongest in the last 100 years are shown here.

Map Key
⊛ Country capital
•●• City or town
······· Boundary

0   200 miles
0   200 kilometers
Azimuthal Equidistant Projection

West Indies & the Bahamas

WEST INDIES & THE BAHAMAS

THE BASICS

STATS

Largest country
Cuba
42,803 sq mi (110,860 sq km)

Smallest country
St. Kitts and Nevis
104 sq mi (269 sq km)

Most populous country
Cuba
11,200,000

Least populous country
St. Kitts and Nevis
54,000

Predominant languages
Spanish, English, French, French patois

Predominant religion
Christian (Roman Catholic, Protestant, and others)

Highest GDP per capita
Bahamas
$30,400

Lowest GDP per capita
Haiti
$1,200

Highest life expectancy
Cuba
78 years

Highest literacy rate
Cuba, Barbados
100%

GEO WHIZ

Voodoo, a religion that combines elements of West African spiritualism and the worship of Roman Catholic saints, is common in Haiti, the Dominican Republic, Cuba, Jamaica, and the Bahamas.

On the seafloor just off San Salvador, in the Bahamas, there is a bronze monument marking the site where Christopher Columbus is believed to have anchored his ship in 1492.

Pico Duarte (10,417 ft/3,175 m), on the island of Hispaniola, is the highest peak in the Caribbean.

Boiling Lake, in Morne Trois Pitons National Park on Dominica, is one of the world's largest thermal lakes.

Grenada, which is nicknamed the Spice Island, is one of the world's chief sources of nutmeg, mace, and other spices.

🜂 **RHYTHM OF THE TROPICS.** When traditional drums were banned in Trinidad in 1884, plantation workers looked for new instruments, including 55-gallon (208-L) oil drums, which were the origin of today's steel drums or "pans."

This region of tropical islands stretches from the Bahamas, off the eastern coast of Florida, to Trinidad and Tobago, off the northern coast of South America. The Greater Antilles—Cuba, Jamaica, Hispaniola, and U.S. territory Puerto Rico—account for nearly 90 percent of the region's land area and most of its 42 million people. A necklace of smaller islands called the Lesser Antilles plus the Bahamas make up most of the rest of this region. Lush vegetation, warm waters, and scenic beaches attract tourists from across the globe. While these visitors bring much needed income, most people in this region remain poor.

◖ **WHITE GOLD.** Sugarcane is an important economic resource throughout the Caribbean. This woman carries freshly cut cane on her head in a field in Barbados.

FUN IN THE SUN

*Figures represent tourist arrivals, 2011

- 4,306,000* — Dominican Republic
- 2,688,000 — Cuba
- 1,952,000 — Jamaica
- 1,344,000 — Bahamas
- 871,000 — Aruba
- 568,000 — Barbados
- 536,000 — U.S. Virgin Islands
- 495,000 — Martinique
- 424,000 — St. Maarten
- 390,000 — Curaçao

These island countries are the region's most popular destinations for tourists seeking sandy beaches, blue waters, and warm breezes.

RARE BIRD. The red-necked Amazon, or Jaco, parrot is found only on the Caribbean island of Dominica, where it lives on flowers, seeds, and fruits native to the island's forests. A Jaco pair typically raises two chicks each year.

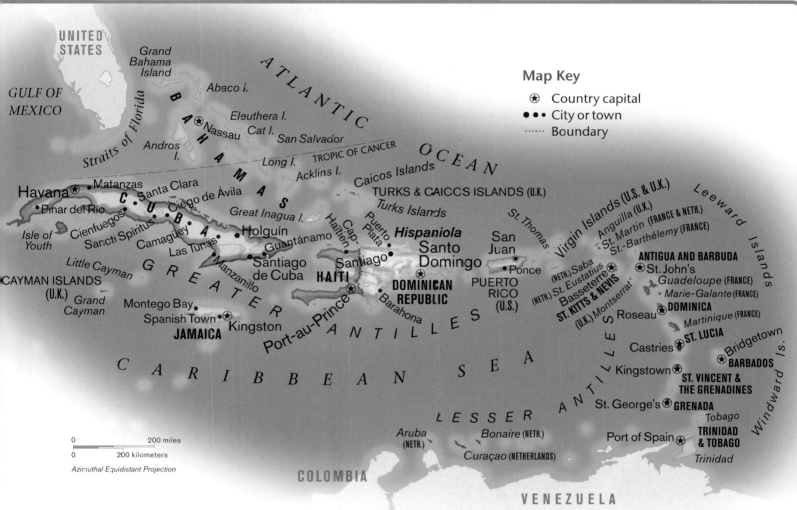

Map Key
⊛ Country capital
●●● City or town
······ Boundary

UNITED STATES
GULF OF MEXICO
Grand Bahama Island
Abaco I.
Eleuthera I.
Cat I.
San Salvador
Nassau
Andros I.
Straits of Florida
Long I.
Acklins I.
TROPIC OF CANCER
Caicos Islands
TURKS & CAICOS ISLANDS (U.K.)
Turks Islands
ATLANTIC OCEAN
St. Thomas
Virgin Islands (U.S. & U.K.)
Anguilla (U.K.)
St. Martin (FRANCE & NETH.)
St.-Barthélemy (FRANCE)
Leeward Islands

Havana ⊛ • Matanzas
• Pinar del Río
Santa Clara
Ciego de Ávila
C U B A
Cienfuegos
Sancti Spíritus
Camagüey
Las Tunas
Holguín
Guantánamo
Great Inagua I.
Cap-Haïtien
Puerto Plata
Hispaniola
Santo Domingo
San Juan
• Ponce
(NETH.) Saba
(NETH.) St. Eustatius ⊛
Basseterre
ST. KITTS & NEVIS
ANTIGUA AND BARBUDA
⊛ St. John's
Guadeloupe (FRANCE)
• Marie-Galante (FRANCE)

Isle of Youth
CAYMAN ISLANDS (U.K.)
Little Cayman
Grand Cayman
Santiago de Cuba
Manzanillo
G R E A T E R
Santiago
HAITI
Barahona
DOMINICAN REPUBLIC
PUERTO RICO (U.S.)
(U.K.) Montserrat
Roseau ⊛
DOMINICA
Martinique (FRANCE)

Montego Bay
Spanish Town
JAMAICA
Kingston
Port-au-Prince
A N T I L L E S
Castries ⊛ ST. LUCIA
Bridgetown
⊛ BARBADOS
Windward Is.

C A R I B B E A N
S E A
Kingstown ⊛
ST. VINCENT & THE GRENADINES
St. George's ⊛ GRENADA
Tobago

L E S S E R
A N T I L L E S
Aruba (NETH.)
Bonaire (NETH.)
Curaçao (NETHERLANDS)
Port of Spain ⊛
TRINIDAD & TOBAGO
Trinidad

0   200 miles
0   200 kilometers
Azimuthal Equidistant Projection

COLOMBIA
VENEZUELA

WATER WORLD. The clear waters of the Caribbean allow face-to-face interaction with sea life, such as this green sea turtle. Adult sea turtles can remain underwater for two hours without breathing.

CELEBRATION. Stilt walkers in brightly colored costumes tower above this street in Old Havana, Cuba, during the annual celebration of Carnival. Introduced by Catholic colonizers from Spain, this festival occurs prior to the beginning of the religious season of Lent.

PHYSICAL			POLITICAL		
Land area 6,880,000 sq mi (17,819,000 sq km)	**Lowest point** Laguna del Carbón, Argentina -344 ft (-105 m)	**Largest lake** Lake Titicaca, Bolivia-Peru 3,200 sq mi (8,290 sq km)	**Population** 396,938,000 **Largest metropolitan area** São Paulo, Brazil: Pop. 19,960,000	**Largest country** Brazil 3,300,169 sq mi (8,547,403 sq km) **Most densely populated country** Ecuador 137 people per sq mi (52 per sq km)	**Economy** **Farming:** cattle, coffee, fruit **Industry:** mining, oil, manufacturing **Services**
Highest point Cerro Aconcagua, Argentina 22,831 ft (6,959 m)	**Longest river** Amazon 4,000 mi (6,437 km)				

South America

South America

CARIBBEAN SEA

NORTH
AMERICA

Lake
Maracaibo

Total drop
3,212 ft 979 m

Orinoco

VENEZUELA

Angel Falls

GUYANA

LLANOS

COLOMBIA

GUYANA HIGHLANDS

SURINAME

FRENCH
GUIANA
(FRANCE)

Malpelo
Island

EQUATOR

Galápagos
Islands

ECUADOR

A M A Z O N

Negro

Amazon

Marajó
Island

Marañón

Amazon

Madeira

Tapajós

Xingu

São Francisco

S e l v a s

Purus

Teles Pires

B A S I N

Tocantins

B R A Z I L

Ucayali

P E R U

B R A Z I L I A N

PACIFIC

OCEAN

Lake
Titicaca

BOLIVIA

H I G H L A N D S

Altiplano

Salar de Uyuni

Pantanal

Paraguay

Atacama Desert

PARAGUAY

Gran Chaco

Iguazú
Falls

TROPIC OF CAPRICORN

San Félix Island

San Ambrosio Island

Paraná

Uruguay

A T L A N T I C   O C E A N

Cerro
Aconcagua
22,831 ft
6,959 m

A R G E N T I N A

C H I L E

Juan Fernández Islands

Highest point in
South America

PAMPAS

URUGUAY

River Plate

Valdés Peninsula

Isla Grande
de Chiloé

Negro

P A T A G O N I A

Gulf of
San Jorge

Taitao
Peninsula

Lowest point in
South America

Wellington Island

Laguna del Carbón
-344 ft -105 m

FALKLAND ISLANDS
(ISLAS MALVINAS)

Strait of Magellan
TIERRA DEL FUEGO

Cape Horn

South Georgia

Map Key

— Country boundary

0		600 miles
0		900 kilometers

Azimuthal Equidistant Projection

CARIBBEAN SEA

NORTH
AMERICA

Santa Marta
Barranquilla
Cartagena
Maracaibo
Lake
Maracaibo
Barquisimeto
Caracas
Valencia
Maracay
Ciudad Guayana
Cúcuta
Bucaramanga
San Cristóbal
VENEZUELA
Georgetown
GUYANA
Paramaribo
SURINAME
Cayenne
FRENCH GUIANA
(FRANCE)
Medellín
Manizales
Ibagué
Bogotá
COLOMBIA
Angel Falls
GUIANA HIGHLANDS
Orinoco
Cali
Boa Vista
Amapá
Boundary claimed
by Suriname
Malpelo Island
(COLOMBIA)
Esmeraldas
Pasto
EQUATOR
Quito
ECUADOR
Galápagos
Islands
(ECUADOR)
Guayaquil
Cuenca
Negro
AMAZON
Manaus
Amazon
Marajó
Island
Belém
São Luís
Parnaíba
Santarém
Iquitos
Marañón
Amazon (Solimões)
S e l v a s
Madeira
Tapajós
Fortaleza
Teresina
Piura
Chiclayo
PERU
B A S I N
Porto Velho
Rio
Branco
Marabá
Xingu
Natal
João Pessoa
Campina Grande
Recife
Trujillo
Chimbote
Ucayali
Purus
Teles Pires
Tocantins
Maceió
Callao
Lima
Ayacucho
Machu Picchu
Cusco
Titicaca
Trinidad
La Paz
BOLIVIA
Santa Cruz
B R A Z I L
BRAZILIAN
Aracaju
Feira de Santana
Salvador
(Bahia)
São Francisco
Arequipa
Cochabamba
Oruro
Sucre
Goiânia
Brasília
HIGHLANDS
Ilhéus
Arica
Salar
de Uyuni
Altiplano
Campo
Grande
Uberlândia
Uberaba
Governador Valadares
Iquique
Tarija
PARAGUAY
Paraguay
Pantanal
São José do
Rio Preto
Ribeirão Preto
Belo Horizonte
TROPIC OF CAPRICORN
Antofagasta
Salta
Gran Chaco
Londrina
Campinas
Nova Iguaçu
São Paulo
Santos
Rio de Janeiro
San Félix Island
(CHILE)
San Ambrosio Island
San Miguel
de Tucumán
Asunción
Iguazú Falls
Curitiba
Resistencia
Corrientes
Passo
Fundo
Florianópolis
La Serena
Cerro
Aconcagua
22,831 ft
6,959 m
Córdoba
Paraná
Uruguaiana
Santa
Maria
Porto Alegre
Valparaíso
Santiago
Mendoza
P A M P A S
Santa Fe
Rosario
URUGUAY
Juan Fernández Islands
(CHILE)
Talca
ARGENTINA
ANDES
Buenos
Aires
La Plata
Montevideo
River Plate
Concepción
Mar del Plata
Temuco
Negro
Bahía Blanca
Puerto Montt
Viedma
Isla Grande
de Chiloé
PATAGONIA
Valdés Peninsula
Taitao
Peninsula
Comodoro Rivadavia
Gulf of San Jorge
Wellington I.
Laguna del Carbón
-344 ft -105 m
Stanley
FALKLAND ISLANDS (ISLAS MALVINAS)
(UNITED KINGDOM)
Río Gallegos
Strait of Magellan
Punta Arenas
TIERRA DEL FUEGO
Ushuaia
Cape Horn
South Georgia
(U.K.)

PACIFIC OCEAN

ATLANTIC OCEAN

0   600 miles
0   900 kilometers
Azimuthal Equidistant Projection

South America

A MIX OF OLD AND NEW

South America stretches from the warm waters of the Caribbean to the frigid ocean around Antarctica. Draining a third of the continent, the mighty Amazon carries more water than the world's next ten biggest rivers combined. Its basin contains the planet's largest rain forest. The Andes tower along the continent's western edge from Colombia to southern Chile. The Amerindian peoples who lived in the Andes were no match for the gold-seeking Spanish who arrived in 1532. The Spanish, along with the Portuguese, ruled most of the continent for almost 300 years. Centuries of ethnic blending have woven Amerindian, European, African, and Asian heritage into South America's rich cultural fabric.

⊜ SILENT STALKER. The jaguar is the largest member of the cat family native to the Americas. The largest populations of this at-risk species are found in the southern Amazon basin.

◖ ROYAL CITY. Built by an Inca ruler between 1460 and 1470, Machu Picchu reveals the Inca's skill as stone masons. Massive blocks of granite were carved so carefully that all seams fit tightly without the use of mortar.

◑ **SOUTHERN METROPOLIS.** A 1,300-foot (396-m)-high block of gran te called Sugar Loaf dominates the harbor of Brazil's second largest city, Rio de Janeiro. Rio was Brazil's capital until 1960 and remains the country's most popular tourist destination.

◖ **NATURAL HERITAGE.** Extending 2.5 miles (4 km) along the border between Brazil and Argentina, Iguazú Falls, which means "great water" in the local Guarani language, is clouded in mist as the water drops 296 feet (90 m) into the Iguazú River.

◖ **MOUNTAIN BUDDIES.** An Aymara woman, with her llama, follows a traditional mountain lifestyle in the Andes of Peru.

more about
South America

🌐 **GLEAMING SANDS.** The white sands of Rio de Janeiro's 2.5-mile (4-km)-long Copacabana and Leme Beaches are among the most famous in the world, attracting tourists year-round. The beaches, which are now lined with upscale hotels that overlook Guanabara Bay, were once the site of thriving fishing villages.

🌐 **ICY COLD.** Rising to an elevation of almost 11,000 feet (3,353 m), Mount Fitz Roy in southern Argentina's Patagonia region presents major challenges to adventurous climbers who must contend with strong winds and bitter cold.

🌐 **QUIET VIGIL.** A young Pinare Indian sits beside a rushing stream in Venezuela, holding his traditional spear ready to catch a fish. Many groups of native people live in relative isolation from the modern world.

JUICY HARVEST. Grapes hang in heavy clusters ready for picking in a vineyard near Santiago, Chile. Second only to Italy, Chile produces almost one-quarter of the world's supply of fresh grapes. Grapes are Chile's leading fresh-fruit export.

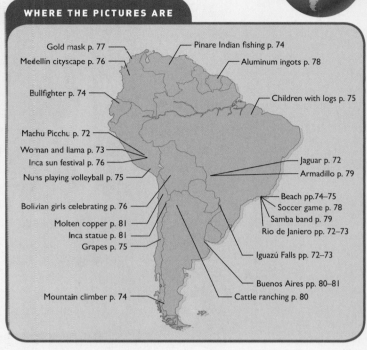

WHERE THE PICTURES ARE

Gold mask p. 77
Medellín cityscape p. 76
Pinare Indian fishing p. 74
Aluminum ingots p. 78
Bullfighter p. 74
Children with logs p. 75
Machu Picchu p. 72
Woman and llama p. 73
Inca sun festival p. 76
Nuns playing volleyball p. 75
Jaguar p. 72
Armadillo p. 79
Bolivian girls celebrating p. 76
Beach pp.74–75
Soccer game p. 78
Samba band p. 79
Rio de Janiero pp. 72–73
Molten copper p. 81
Inca statue p. 81
Grapes p. 75
Iguazú Falls pp. 72–73
Buenos Aires pp. 80–81
Cattle ranching p. 80
Mountain climber p. 74

ENVIRONMENTAL TRAGEDY. These giants of the rain forest dwarf two children in the Amazon village of Paragominas in Brazil. Harvesting such trees provides income for villagers but poses a serious long-term threat to the environment.

EL TORRO! Introduced to South America during the Spanish colonization, bullfighting is a popular sport and the focus of many festivals. Here, in Cayambe, Ecuador, a matador flashes his red cape before the bull.

BREAK TIME. Colonization of South America by Spain and Portugal in the 16th century brought a new religion—Roman Catholicism—to the region. Here, Catholic nuns in Arequipa, Peru, take a break from prayers to engage in a game of volleyball.

THE BASICS

STATS

Largest country
Peru
496,224 sq mi (1,285,216 sq km)

Smallest country
Ecuador
109,483 sq mi (283,560 sq km)

Most populous country
Colombia
47,415,000

Least populous country
Bolivia
10,836,000

Predominant languages
Spanish, Amerindian languages and dialects, English

Predominant religion
Christianity (Roman Catholic)

Highest GDP per capita
Venezuela
$12,600

Lowest GDP per capita
Bolivia
$4,800

Highest life expectancy
Ecuador
76 years

Highest literacy rate
Peru, Venezuela
93%

GEO WHIZ

On the llanos of Venezuela, capybaras, the world's largest rodents, are stalked and killed by anacondas, snakes weighing as much as 550 pounds (250 kg).

Some of the world's finest emeralds come from Colombia. Emeralds were sacred stones to the Inca, and some of the mines that ancient people worked are still a source of quality gemstones.

The world's only marine iguanas are among the unique animal species that live on the Galápagos, a volcanic chain of islands in the Pacific that belongs to Ecuador.

Bolivia's Madidi National Park is home to more plant and animal species than any other preserve in South America.

Northwestern South America

Like a huge letter "C," five countries crest the continent's northwest—Venezuela, Colombia, Ecuador, Peru, and Bolivia. Each has a seacoast, except for landlocked Bolivia. Dominated by the volcano-studded Andes range, the region contains huge rain forests in the upper Amazon and Orinoco River basins. Colombia and Venezuela share an extensive tropical grassland called Los Llanos. Though Spanish conquistador Pizarro defeated the Inca in the 16th century, Quechua, the Inca language, is still spoken by millions of Amerindians living in the altiplanos—high plateaus of

⬤ **HAIL THE SUN.** The ancient Inca celebrated the new year in June with the festival of Inti Raymi. The tradition continues today in Cusco, Peru, with the Festival of the Sun, when the celestial body is honored through music and dance.

the Andes. Rich oil resources are centered around Lake Maracaibo, in Venezuela. Many people in the region are poor, and drug wars have caused political instability, but recent democratic successes offer some hope for the future.

⬤ **FOLKLORE CENTER.** Founded as a mining town, Oruro, Bolivia, is a UNESCO cultural heritage site. Each November a weeklong festival celebrates traditional Andean culture with ancient dances, music, and rituals.

⬤ **OLD MEETS NEW.** Against a backdrop of skyscrapers, a modern urban train speeds past the old government palace in Medellín, Colombia. Known as a center of illegal drug trafficking, the city has worked hard to change its image, introducing economic and social changes that have improved safety.

◗ **ANCIENT ARTISANS.** Early cultures of Colombia left no great stone monuments, but they distinguished themselves with their fine gold work, which may have encouraged Europeans to search for El Dorado, the legendary City of Gold.

Map Key

⊛ Country capital

••• City or town

····· Boundary

0   200 miles
0   300 kilometers
Azimuthal Equidistant Projection

CARIBBEAN SEA

Aruba (Neth.)
Bonaire (Netherlands)
Curaçao (Neth.)
GRENADA

Santa Marta
Barranquilla
Cartagena
Valledupar
Sincelejo
Montería
PANAMA

Gulf of Venezuela
Maracaibo
Cabimas
Ciudad Ojeda
Mérida
Lake Maracaibo
Puerto Cabello
Maracay
Caracas
Los Teques
Valencia
Barcelona
Cumaná
Puerto La Cruz
Maturín
TRINIDAD & TOBAGO

Barquisimeto
Barinas
Pico Bolívar
16,427 ft 5,007 m
VENEZUELA

ATLANTIC OCEAN

Cúcuta
Barrancabermeja
San Cristóbal

Medellín
Manizales
Pereira
Armenia
Tuluá
Buenaventura
Cali
Palmira
Ibagué
Neiva
Popayán
Pasto
Florencia

Bucaramanga
Sogamoso
Tunja
Bogotá
Villavicencio
COLOMBIA
San José del Guaviare

Magdalena
Cauca
Meta

GUIANA HIGHLANDS
Orinoco
Ciudad Bolívar
Ciudad Guayana
Angel Falls
Total drop
3,212 ft 979 m
Mt. Roraima
9,094 ft 2,772 m
GUYANA

EQUATOR

Ibarra
Cayambe
Portoviejo
Quito
Manta
Chimborazo
20,702 ft 6,310 m
Riobamba
ECUADOR
Guayaquil
Milagro
Machala
Cuenca
Loja
Talara
Sullana
Piura

Putumayo
A M A Z O N

Amazon (Solimões)
Negro

B A S I N

B R A Z I L

Iquitos
Amazon

Marañón
Ucayali

Chiclayo
Cajamarca
Trujillo
Chimbote
Nevado Huascarán
22,205 ft 6,768 m
PERU
Huánuco
Pucallpa

Purus
Madeira

PACIFIC OCEAN

Callao
Lima
Huancayo
Machu Picchu
Cusco
Ica

Apurímac
Madre de Dios
Guaporé
Mamoré

Trinidad

Arequipa
Puno
Lake Titicaca
Tacna
Nevado Sajama
21,463 ft 6,542 m
Altiplano

La Paz
(administrative capital)
BOLIVIA
Cochabamba
Santa Cruz
Oruro
Sucre
(constitutional capital)
Potosí
Salar de Uyuni
Tarija

A N D E S

CHILE
ARGENTINA
PARAGUAY
Pantanal

Northeastern South America

⬤ **GOAL!** Maracanã Stadium in Rio de Janeiro is packed with enthusiastic soccer fans. Brazil has a long history of producing world-class soccer players and strong teams—winning the coveted World Cup five times.

Brazil dominates the region as well as the continent in size (it is the world's fifth largest country in area) and population (half of South America's 397 million people live here). Leading cities São Paulo and Rio de Janeiro are among the world's largest, and the country's vast agricultural lands make it a top global exporter of coffee, soybeans, beef, orange juice, and sugar.

The vast Amazon rain forest, once a dense wilderness of unmatched biodiversity, is now threatened by farmers, loggers, and miners. To Brazil's north are lands colonized by the British, Dutch, and French—now sparsely settled Guyana, Suriname, and French Guiana, a French overseas department where the European Space Agency maintains its Spaceport, a launch site for explorations beyond Earth. Formerly known as the Guianas, these lands are populated by a mix of people with African, South Asian, and European heritage.

THE BASICS

STATS

Largest country
Brazil
3,300,169 sq mi (8,547,403 sq km)

Smallest country
Suriname
63,037 sq mi (163,265 sq km)

Most populous country
Brazil
194,334,000

Least populous country
Suriname
542,000

Predominant languages
Portuguese, English, Dutch, Hindi

Predominant religions
Christianity (Roman Catholic, Protestant), Hindu, Islam

Highest GDP per capita
Brazil, Suriname
$11,800

Lowest GDP per capita
Guyana
$7,600

Highest life expectancy
Brazil
73 years

Highest literacy rate
Guyana
92%

GEO WHIZ

Guyana has as many as 300 species of catfish, roughly a quarter of the total number living in South America. Locals hunt them and other fish for the international aquarium trade by probing hollow tree trunks submerged on river bottoms.

Paramaribo, Suriname's capital, is a melting pot of Dutch, Chinese, Hindu, East Indian, and Javanese cultures. Dutch is the only official language.

Brazil covers almost half of South America's land area. It is the world's largest Portuguese-speaking country and the largest Catholic country.

The Pantanal, the world's largest freshwater wetland, is almost ten times the size of the Florida Everglades. It is formed by the seasonal flooding of several rivers in southwestern Brazil.

⬤ **BAUXITE TO ALUMINUM.** By exploiting rich deposits of bauxite, the ore from which aluminum is made, and inexpensive hydropower, the small country of Suriname produces aluminum ingots for export, such as these headed for global markets.

VAST WATERSHED

The United States at the same scale as South America

Amazon Basin

South America

The Amazon River basin, which includes more than 2.6 million square miles (6.7 million sq km), would cover much of the contiguous United States.

◑ **THE SIX-BANDED ARMADILLO,** found throughout the dry grass-land areas of northeastern South America, lives on plants and insects. Also known as the yellow armadillo, it is unlike others of its species in that it remains active during the day.

Map Key
⊛ Country capital
•●• City or town
······ Boundary

0 ———— 400 miles
0 ———— 400 kilometers
Azimuthal Equidistant Projection

ATLANTIC OCEAN

VENEZUELA

GUIANA

HIGHLANDS

Orinoco

Georgetown
GUYANA
Paramaribo
SURINAME
Cayenne
FRENCH GUIANA (FRANCE)

COLOMBIA

Boa Vista

Boundary claimed by Suriname

Pico da Neblina
9,888 ft
3,014 m
Negro
Macapá
EQUATOR

Putumayo

A M A Z O N
Itacoatiara
Amazon
Marajó Island
Belém
São Luís
Parnaíba

Manaus
(Solimões)
Altamira
Paragominas
Codó
Sobral
Fortaleza

Tefé
Coari
Parintins
Santarém
Tucuruí
Caxias
Teresina

Amazon
S e l v a s
Tapajós
Marabá
Imperatriz
Natal

BASIN
Xingu
Araguaína
Crato
João Pessoa
Olinda

Cruzeiro do Sul
Madeira
Purus
B R A Z I L
Palmas
Petrolina
Jaboatão
Recife

Porto Velho
Teles Pires
Gurupi
Barreiras
Arapiraca
Maceió

Rio Branco
Ariquemes
Alvorado
Feira de Santana
Aracaju

ERU
Madre de Dios
Ji-Paraná (Rondônia)
Alta Floresta
Iurueña
B R A Z I L I A N
Jequié
Alagoinhas

Guaporé
Várzea Grande
Cuiabá
Brasília
São Francisco
Itabuna
Salvador (Bahia)

Mamoré
Rondonópolis
Anápolis
Vitória da Conquista
Ilhéus

Lake Titicaca
BOLIVIA
Goiânia
H I G H L A N D S
Teófilo Otoni

Pantanal
Uberlândia
Governador Valadares

Paraguay
Campo Grande
Belo Horizonte
Linhares

CHILE
São José do Rio Preto
Ribeirão Preto
Juiz de Fora
Vitória

TROPIC OF CAPRICORN
Paraná
São José dos Campos
Nova Iguaçu
Vila Velha

PARAGUAY
São Paulo
Guaratinguetá
Duque de Caxias
Niterói
Rio de Janeiro

Londrina
Santo André
Santos

Iguazú Falls
ARGENTINA
Curitiba
Paranaguá
Joinville

Uruguay
Florianópolis

Caxias do Sul
Criciúma

Santa Maria
Novo Hamburgo
Canoas
Porto Alegre

Paraná
Patos Lagoon
Pelotas

URUGUAY

◑ **NATIONAL RHYTHM.** Samba, often called Brazil's national music, combines the music traditions of the country's popula-tions—Amerindian, Portuguese, and African. Here a samba band practices on Rio de Janeiro's Ipanema Beach.

THE CONTINENT:
SOUTH AMERICA

Southern South America

Four countries make up this region, which is sometimes called the Southern Cone because of its shape. Long north-south distances in Chile and Argentina result in varied environments. Chile's Atacama Desert in the north contrasts with much cooler, moister lands in the country's south, where there are fjords and glaciers. Nine of ten Chileans live in Middle Chile, in and around booming Santiago. Similarly, most neighboring Argentinians live in the central Pampas region, where wheat and cattle flourish on the fertile plains. Farther south lie the arid, windswept plateaus of Patagonia. Landlocked Paraguay is small in comparison, less urbanized, and one of South America's poorest countries. Compact Uruguay is smaller still, but it possesses a strong agricultural economy, including cattle- and sheep-raising.

THE BASICS

STATS

Largest country
Argentina
1,073,518 sq mi (2,780,400 sq km)

Smallest country
Uruguay
68,037 sq mi (176,215 sq km)

Most populous country
Argentina
40,829,000

Least populous country
Uruguay
3,381,000

Predominant languages
Spanish, Guarani, English, Italian, German, French

Predominant religion
Christianity (Roman Catholic, Protestant)

Highest GDP per capita
Argentina
$17,700

Lowest GDP per capita
Paraguay
$6,200

Highest life expectancy
Chile
78 years

Highest literacy rate
Uruguay
98%

GEO WHIZ

Guanacos, a member of the camel family that is most numerous in the Patagonia region of Chile and Argentina, keeps enemies at bay by spitting at them.

The Itaipú Dam, which spans the Paraná River between Brazil and Paraguay, is currently the world's largest operating hydroelectric power plant.

Guarani is the name of a people native to Paraguay, the country's basic unit of money, and one of its two official languages. Spanish is the other.

Argentinians eat 150 pounds (68 kg) of beef per person each year, making the country the world's largest per capita consumer of this meat.

Chile's Chuquicamata mine is among the world's largest open-pit copper mines.

COWBOYS OF THE PAMPAS. Cattle are herded by gauchos, the Argentine term for cowboys. The country's extensive grass-covered plains support grain and cattle production on ranches called estancias.

GATEWAY CITY. Skyscrapers in the modern skyline rise above Buenos Aires, capital of Argentina and second largest metropolitan area in South America. Situated on the Rio de la Plata, the city was established in 1536 by Spanish explorers. Its port is one of the busiest in South America.

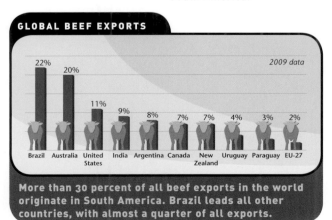

GLOBAL BEEF EXPORTS

2009 data

Brazil	Australia	United States	India	Argentina	Canada	New Zealand	Uruguay	Paraguay	EU-27
22%	20%	11%	9%	8%	7%	7%	4%	3%	2%

More than 30 percent of all beef exports in the world originate in South America. Brazil leads all other countries, with almost a quarter of all exports.

◖ **INCA TREASURE.** Near the frozen summit of Argentina's Cerro Llullaillaco, second highest active volcano in the world, archaeologists excavated Inca ruins and uncovered well-preserved mummies and 20 clothed statues, such as the one at left.

◑ **DESERT RICHES.** Molten copper is poured into molds at a refinery near Chuquicamata, the world's largest copper deposit, located in northern Chile's Atacama Desert. Chile accounts for about 35 percent of the world's copper production.

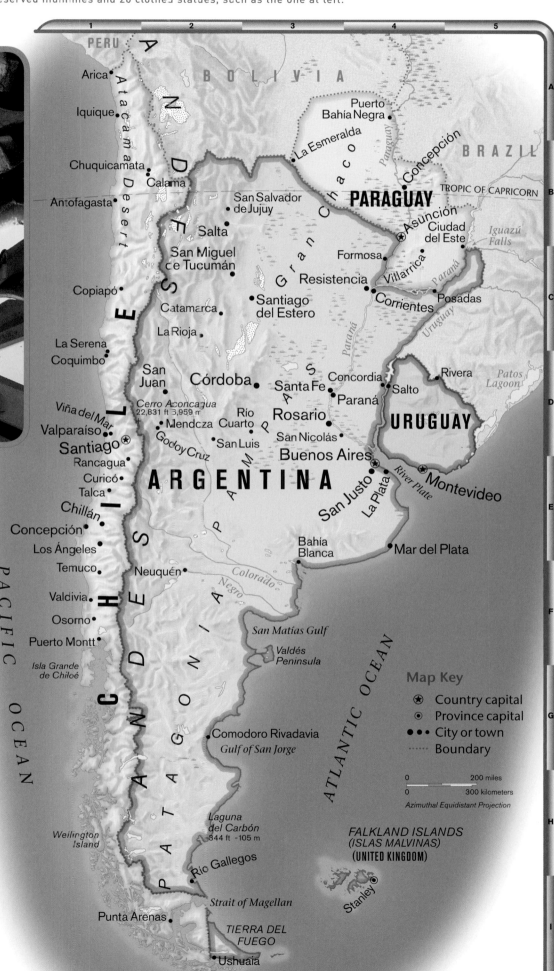

PERU

BOLIVIA

BRAZIL

Arica

Iquique

Chuquicamata
Calama

Antofagasta

Atacama Desert

Puerto
Bahía Negra

La Esmeralda

Concepción

PARAGUAY

Asunción

Ciudad
del Este

Iguazú
Falls

TROPIC OF CAPRICORN

San Salvador
de Jujuy

Salta

San Miguel
de Tucumán

Gran Chaco

Formosa

Villarrica

Resistencia

Corrientes

Posadas

Copiapó

Catamarca

Santiago
del Estero

La Rioja

La Serena

Coquimbo

San
Juan

Córdoba

Santa Fe

Concordia

Paraná

Salto

Rivera

Patos
Lagoon

Viña del Mar

Cerro Aconcagua
22,831 ft 6,959 m

Mendoza

Río
Cuarto

Rosario

URUGUAY

Valparaíso

Santiago

Godoy Cruz

San Luis

San Nicolás

Rancagua

Curicó

Talca

ARGENTINA

Buenos Aires

River Plate

Montevideo

Chillán

Concepción

San Justo

La Plata

Los Ángeles

Bahía
Blanca

Mar del Plata

Temuco

Neuquén

Colorado

Valdivia

Negro

Osorno

Puerto Montt

Isla Grande
de Chiloé

San Matías Gulf

Valdés
Peninsula

ATLANTIC OCEAN

PACIFIC OCEAN

ANDES

CHILE

PAMPAS

PATAGONIA

Map Key
✪ Country capital
◉ Province capital
●●● City or town
⋯⋯ Boundary

Comodoro Rivadavia
Gulf of San Jorge

FALKLAND ISLANDS
(ISLAS MALVINAS)
(UNITED KINGDOM)

0   200 miles
0   300 kilometers
Azimuthal Equidistant Projection

Wellington
Island

Laguna
del Carbón
-344 ft -105 m

Stanley

Río Gallegos

Strait of Magellan

Punta Arenas

TIERRA DEL
FUEGO

Ushuaia

Cape Horn

THE CONTINENT:
EUROPE

PHYSICAL

Land area
3,841,000 sq mi (9,947,000 sq km)

Highest point
El'brus, Russia
18,510 ft (5,642 m)

Lowest point
Caspian Sea
-92 ft (-28 m)

Longest river
Volga, Russia
2,290 mi (3,685 km)

Largest lake entirely in Europe
Ladoga, Russia
6,835 sq mi (17,703 sq km)

POLITICAL

Population
740,965,000

Largest metropolitan area
Moscow, Russia
Pop. 10,523,000

Largest country entirely in Europe
Ukraine
233,090 sq mi (603,700 sq km)

Most densely populated country
Monaco
45,000 people per sq mi
(18,000 per sq km)

Economy
Farming: vegetables, fruit, grains
Industry: chemicals, machinery
Services

Europe

Europe

Europe-Asia Boundary

Ural

KAZAKHSTAN

Caspian Depression

CASPIAN SEA

Caucasus Mountains

AZERBAIJAN

ARMENIA

GEORGIA

Lowest point in Europe
-92 ft · -28 m

El'brus
18,510 ft
5,642 m

Highest point in Europe

SEA OF AZOV

Crimea

BLACK SEA

Bosporus

TURKEY

CYPRUS

U R A L   M O U N T A I N S

Ural

Kama

Volga

Don

Don

Dnieper

Pechora

Northern Dvina

Volga

Oka

CENTRAL RUSSIAN UPLAND

UKRAINE

Volga

Dnieper

MOLDOVA

ROMANIA

Danube

Carpathian Mountains

Balkan Mountains

BULGARIA

ARCTIC OCEAN

BARENTS SEA

WHITE SEA

Kola Peninsula

Lake Ladoga

Lake Region

F I N L A N D

Gulf of Finland

ESTONIA

LATVIA

Western Dvina

LITHUANIA

RUSSIA

BELARUS

N O R T H E R N   E U R O P E A N   P L A I N

Dniester

Tisza

BALKAN PENINSULA

SERBIA

KOSOVO

MACEDONIA

ALBANIA

GREECE

AEGEAN SEA

Dardanelles

Crete

Rhodes

IONIAN SEA

Peloponnesus

North Cape

S C A N D I N A V I A

Gulf of Bothnia

BALTIC SEA

S W E D E N

N O R W A Y

Vistula

POLAND

Oder

Elbe

CZECH REP.

SLOVAKIA

HUNGARY

Danube

Drava

Sava

AUSTRIA

SLOVENIA

CROATIA

BOSNIA & HERZEGOVINA

MONTENEGRO

ADRIATIC SEA

A p e n n i n e s

ITALY

SAN MARINO

VATICAN CITY

TYRRHENIAN SEA

Sicily

Etna
10,876 ft
3,315 m

MALTA

MEDITERRANEAN SEA

NORWEGIAN SEA

Jan Mayen

ICELAND

Vatnajökull

ARCTIC CIRCLE

Faroe Islands

Shetland Islands

Orkney Islands

Outer Hebrides

Highlands

Great Britain

The Pennines

UNITED KINGDOM

IRISH SEA

Ireland

BRITISH ISLES

NORTH SEA

Jutland

DENMARK

Sjælland

NETHERLANDS

GERMANY

BELGIUM

LUX.

Rhine

Seine

FRANCE

Loire

Brittany

Bay of Biscay

English Channel

Massif Central

Mont Blanc
15,781 ft
4,810 m

SWITZ.

LIECH.

A L P S

Rhône

Po

MONACO

Riviera

Corsica

Sardinia

Balearic Islands

Pyrenees

ANDORRA

SPAIN

Ebro

Douro

Tagus

PORTUGAL

IBERIAN PENINSULA

Cantabrian Mountains

Baetic Mountains

Strait of Gibraltar

AFRICA

ATLANTIC OCEAN

Map Key
—— Country boundary

400 miles
600 kilometers

Azimuthal Equidistant Projection

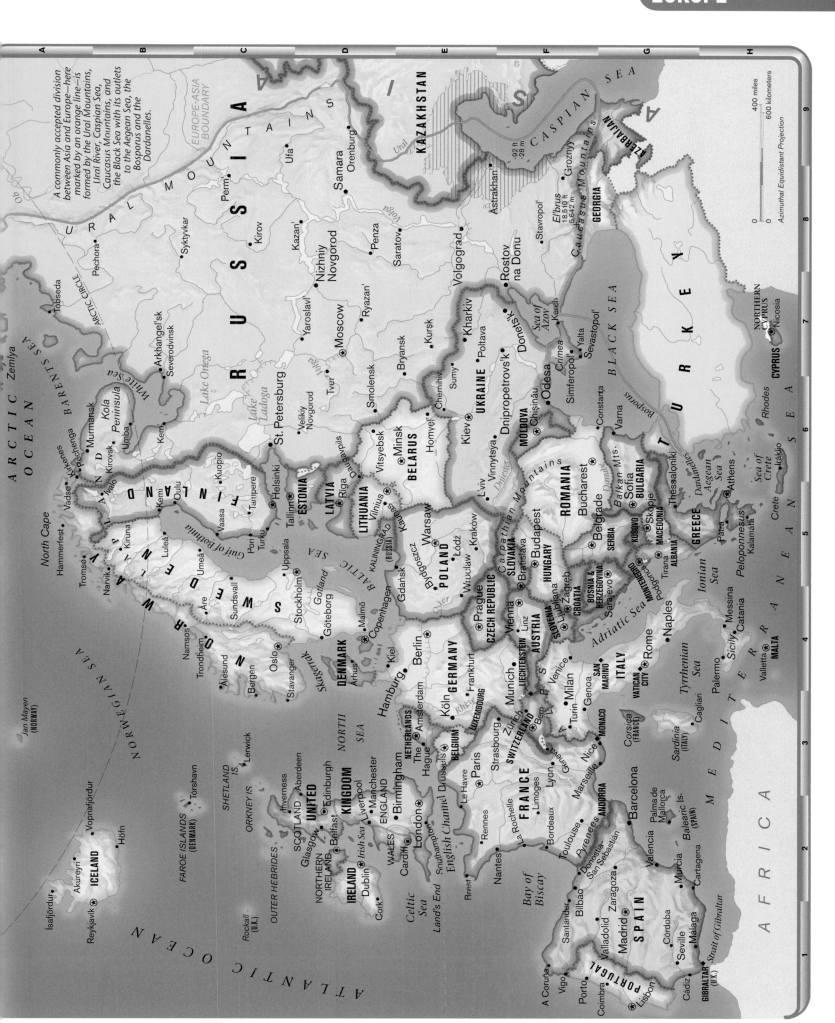

A commonly accepted division between Asia and Europe—here marked by an orange line—is formed by the Ural Mountains, Ural River, Caspian Sea, Caucasus Mountains, and the Black Sea with its outlets to the Aegean Sea, the Bosporus and the Dardanelles.

400 miles
600 kilometers
0
0
Azimuthal Equidistant Projection

KAZAKHSTAN

CASPIAN SEA

AZERBAIJAN

GEORGIA

Elbrus
18,510 ft
5,642 m
Grozny

Astrakhan'
-92 ft
-28 m

Stavropol'

Ural

Orenburg

Ufa

Samara

Perm'

Kirov

Syktyvkar

Kazan'

Penza

Nizhniy Novgorod

Saratov

Volga

Volgograd

Rostov na Donu

R U S S I A

Pechora

Tobseda

ARCTIC CIRCLE

Arkhangel'sk

Severodvinsk

Yaroslavl'

Lake Onega

Lake Ladoga

Tver

Moscow

Ryazan'

Kursk

Kharkiv

Sea of Azov

Kerch

Crimea

Yalta

Sevastopol'

Simferopol'

Donets'k

Poltava

BLACK SEA

T U R K E Y

NORTHERN CYPRUS
Nicosia

CYPRUS

Rhodes

Irakliо

Sea of Crete

Crete

M E D I T E R R A N E A N   S E A

Aegean Sea

Dardanelles

Athens

Pátra

Peloponnesus

Kalamáta

Ionian Sea

GREECE

Thessaloníki

Skopje

MACEDONIA

ALBANIA

Tirana

Pogdorica

KOSOVO

SERBIA

MONTENEGRO

Belgrade

Danube

Balkan Mts.

Sofia

BULGARIA

Varna

Constanţa

Bucharest

ROMANIA

Chişinău

MOLDOVA

Odesa

Vinnytsya

Dnipropetrovs'k

UKRAINE

Kiev

Homyel'

Chernihiv

Sumy

Bryansk

Smolensk

Veliky Novgorod

St. Petersburg

Helsinki

Tampere

Turku

Pori

Vaasa

Kuopio

Oulu

Kemi

Gulf of Bothnia

F I N L A N D

ARCTIC OCEAN

BARENTS SEA

Zemlya

North Cape

Murmansk

Kirovsk

Umba

Pechenga

Kirkenes

Vadsø

Hammerfest

Tromsø

Narvik

Kiruna

Namsos

Trondheim

Ålesund

Bergen

Stavanger

Oslo

Kola Peninsula

White Sea

Kem'

N O R W A Y

S W E D E N

Luleå

Umeå

Are

Sundsvall

Uppsala

Stockholm

Göteborg

Gotland

B A L T I C   S E A

ESTONIA

Tallinn

Riga

LATVIA

Daugavpils

LITHUANIA

Vilnius

KALININGRAD (RUSSIA)

Vitsyebsk

Minsk

BELARUS

L'viv

Warsaw

POLAND

Łódź

Kraków

Wrocław

Bydgoszcz

Gdańsk

Oder

Prague

CZECH REPUBLIC

SLOVAKIA

Bratislava

Vienna

AUSTRIA

HUNGARY

Budapest

SLOVENIA

Ljubljana

Zagreb

CROATIA

BOSNIA & HERZEGOVINA

Sarajevo

Adriatic Sea

Naples

ITALY

Rome

VATICAN CITY

Messina

Sicily

Catania

Palermo

Tyrrhenian Sea

Cagliari

Sardinia (ITALY)

MALTA

Valletta

Copenhagen

DENMARK

Århus

Malmö

Kiel

Hamburg

Berlin

GERMANY

Köln

Frankfurt

Rhine

Munich

LIECHTENSTEIN

SWITZERLAND

Bern

Zürich

AUSTRIA

Linz

Venice

Milan

Turin

Genoa

SAN MARINO

MONACO

Nice

Marseille

Lyon

Limoges

FRANCE

Bordeaux

Toulouse

ANDORRA

Pyrenees

Barcelona

Zaragoza

Valencia

Murcia

Cartagena

Palma de Mallorca

Balearic Is. (SPAIN)

Madrid

Valladolid

Córdoba

Seville

Málaga

GIBRALTAR (U.K.)

Strait of Gibraltar

S P A I N

Cádiz

Lisbon

Coimbra

Porto

A Coruña

Vigo

PORTUGAL

Santander

Bilbao

Donostia-San Sebastián

Bay of Biscay

Nantes

Rennes

La Rochelle

Le Havre

Paris

Strasbourg

LUXEMBOURG

BELGIUM

Brussels

The Hague

Amsterdam

NETHERLANDS

English Channel

Southampton

London

Cardiff

WALES

ENGLAND

Birmingham

Manchester

Liverpool

Irish Sea

Dublin

IRELAND

Cork

Belfast

NORTHERN IRELAND

Glasgow

Edinburgh

SCOTLAND

Aberdeen

Inverness

UNITED KINGDOM

OUTER HEBRIDES

Lerwick

SHETLAND IS.

ORKNEY IS.

Land's End

Celtic Sea

Brest

Rockall (U.K.)

FAROE ISLANDS (DENMARK)

Tórshavn

NORTH SEA

NORWEGIAN SEA

Jan Mayen (NORWAY)

Höfn

Akureyri

Ísafjördur

Vopnafjördur

Reykjavík

ICELAND

A T L A N T I C   O C E A N

A F R I C A

URAL MOUNTAINS

EUROPE-ASIA BOUNDARY

Caucasus Mountains

Carpathian Mountains

A L P S

Europe

SMALL SPACES, DIVERSE PLACES

○ **WIND POWER.**
A traditional windmill stands silent in Spain, calling to mind scenes from the classic Spanish novel *Don Quixote*. Modern windmills are used to generate electricity and pump water.

A cluster of islands and peninsulas jutting west from Asia, Europe is bordered by two oceans and more than a dozen seas, which are linked to inland areas by canals and navigable rivers such as the Rhine and Danube. The continent boasts a bounty of landscapes. Sweeping west from the Urals is the fertile Northern European Plain. Rugged uplands form part of Europe's western coast, while the Alps shield Mediterranean lands from frigid northern winds. Here, first Greek and then Roman civilizations laid Europe's cultural foundation. Its colonial powers built wealth from vast empires, while its inventors and thinkers revolutionized world industry, economy, and politics. Today, the 27-member European Union seeks to unite the continent's diversity.

○ **CHEERY GREETINGS.** Laughing children clown for the camera in Klaipeda, Lithuania. Klaipeda is the northernmost ice-free port on the eastern coast of the Baltic Sea.

◗ **ROCKY SENTINEL.** Towering 14,693 feet (4,478 m) in elevation, the Matterhorn, on the border between Switzerland and Italy, is one of Europe's most famous mountains. Frequent avalanches on its steep slopes pose challenges for mountain climbers.

⬤ **WATCHFUL GUARDIAN.** A gargoyle stares out across the Paris skyline from a ledge of Notre Dame Cathedral. Gargoyles were first used in Gothic architecture as waterspouts but later were decorative additions meant to ward off evil spirits.

⬤ **WINDOW ON THE PAST.** The brightly painted houses of Nyhavn (New Harbor), once the homes and warehouses of wealthy Copenhagen merchants, are now shops and restaurants and one of the city's most popular tourist attractions.

more about
Europe

⬆ **AGELESS TIME.** This famous astronomical clock, built in 1410 in Prague, Czech Republic, has an astronomical dial on top of a calendar dial. Together, they keep track of time as well as the movement of the sun, moon, and stars.

◗ **CLIFF DWELLERS.** The town of Positano clings to the rocky hillside along Italy's Amalfi coast. In the mid-19th century, more than half the town's population emigrated, mainly to the United States. The economy today is based on tourism.

◖ **SEABIRDS OF THE NORTH.** Colorful Atlantic puffins perch on a grass-covered cliff in Iceland, Europe's westernmost country. These unusual birds are skilled fishers but have difficulty becoming airborne and often crash upon landing.

⬆ **CITY AT NIGHT.** A winged victory statue atop the Metropolis Building, a classic example of early 20th–century architecture, appears to watch the evening traffic on the Gran Via in Madrid, Spain.

GLIMPSE OF THE PAST. Rome's Colosseum is a silent reminder of a once powerful empire that stretched from the British Isles to Persia (now Iran). The concrete, stone, and brick structure combined classic Greek and Roman architectural styles and could seat as many as 50,000 people.

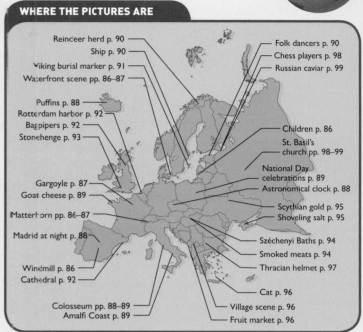

WHERE THE PICTURES ARE

Reindeer herd p. 90
Ship p. 90
Viking burial marker p. 91
Waterfront scene pp. 86–87
Puffins p. 88
Rotterdam harbor p. 92
Bagpipers p. 92
Stonehenge p. 93
Gargoyle p. 87
Goat cheese p. 89
Matterhorn pp. 86–87
Madrid at night p. 88
Windmill p. 86
Cathedral p. 92
Colosseum pp. 88–89
Amalfi Coast p. 89

Folk dancers p. 90
Chess players p. 98
Russian caviar p. 99
Children p. 86
St. Basil's church pp. 98–99
National Day celebrations p. 89
Astronomical clock p. 88
Scythian gold p. 95
Shoveling salt p. 95
Széchenyi Baths p. 94
Smoked meats p. 94
Thracian helmet p. 97
Cat p. 96
Village scene p. 96
Fruit market p. 96

LUNCHTIME! Varieties of creamy, fresh goat cheese are displayed in a market in the Brittany region of northern France.

NATIONAL PRIDE. Young women carry banners in a parade marking Poland's National Day. Celebrated each year on May 3, it is the anniversary of the 1997 proclamation of the Polish Constitution.

THE CONTINENT:
EUROPE

THE BASICS

STATS

Largest country
Sweden 173,732 sq mi (449,964 sq km)

Smallest country
Denmark 16,640 sq mi (43,098 sq km)

Most populous country
Sweden 9,514,000

Least populous country
Iceland 320,000

Predominant languages
Russian, Polish, Swedish, Danish, Finnish, Norwegian, Lithuanian, Latvian, Estonian, Icelandic

Predominant religion
Christianity (Lutheran, Roman Catholic, Orthodox)

Highest GDP per capita
Norway $102,300

Lowest GDP per capita
Latvia $16,800

Highest life expectancy
Iceland, Sweden
81 years

Highest literacy rate
Estonia, Finland, Iceland, Latvia, Lithuania, Norway
100%

GEO WHIZ

Finland has more than 185,000 lakes. In fact, the southeastern part of the country is called the Lake Region.

The national symbol of Denmark is a statue of Hans Christian Andersen's Little Mermaid, in Copenhagen's harbor.

Vatnajökull, in Iceland, is the largest glacier in Europe.

According to Finnish folklore, Father and Mother Christmas live with their helpers on a mountain called Korvatunturi, in the country's Lapland region.

During Iceland's Thorrablot winter festival, locals celebrate by eating a Viking dish of rotten Greenland shark meat.

Legoland theme park, in Billund, Denmark, features miniature cities, models of famous landmarks such as the Taj Mahal, Statue of Liberty, and Mount Rushmore, and more—all made from some 33 million Lego blocks.

Northern Europe

This entire region lies in latitudes similar to Canada's Hudson Bay, but the warm North Atlantic Drift current moderates temperatures in western parts of the region, from volcanically active Iceland to Denmark and Norway. The area's better farmlands lie in southern Sweden and the breezy lowlands of Denmark. Lightly populated but mostly urban, Northern Europe is home to slightly more than 32 million people. Sweden is the largest and most populous country. Forested, lake-dotted Finland shares a long border with Russia. Estonia, Latvia, and Lithuania—the so-called Baltic States—were republics of the Russian-dominated Soviet Union, which ceased to exist in 1991.

NORDIC HERDERS. The Sami, indigenous people of northern Europe, herd their reindeer across the borders of Norway, Sweden, Finland, and Russia. Some use snowmobiles instead of horses.

MIGHTY WARSHIP. In 1628 the warship *Vasa* sank in the cold waters of Stockholm Harbor on its maiden voyage. After 333 years it was raised and reconstructed.

COLORFUL TRADITION.
Costumed folk dancers perform traditional dances at an open-air museum in Tallinn, Estonia.

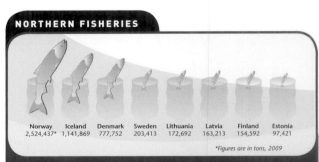

NORTHERN FISHERIES

Norway	Iceland	Denmark	Sweden	Lithuania	Latvia	Finland	Estonia
2,524,437*	1,141,869	777,752	203,413	172,692	163,213	154,592	97,421

*Figures are in tons, 2009

Large schools of fish thrive in the cold waters off northern Europe. Norway harvests the most, bringing in more than 2.5 million tons of fish annually.

◐ **MARKER FROM THE PAST.** A stone memorial marks the burial site of Viking warriors in Sweden. Although their main activities were farming and trade, Vikings are better known for their ships and their fierce raids on towns across Europe.

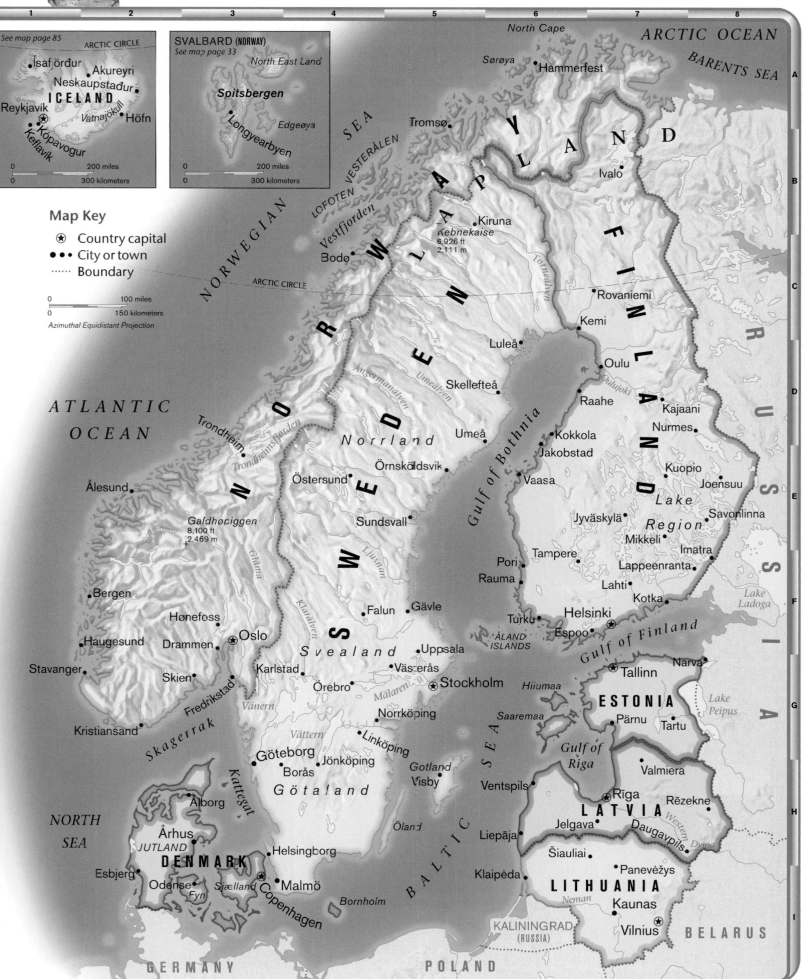

1   2   3   4   5   6   7   8

See map page 85
ARCTIC CIRCLE
Isafjörður
Akureyri
Neskaupstaður
ICELAND
Reykjavik
Vatnajökull   Höfn
Kópavogur
Keflavik
0   200 miles
0   300 kilometers

SVALBARD (NORWAY)
See map page 33
North East Land
Spitsbergen
Longyearbyen   Edgeøya
0   200 miles
0   300 kilometers

North Cape
ARCTIC OCEAN
BARENTS SEA
Søroya   Hammerfest
Tromsø

Map Key
⊛ Country capital
••• City or town
...... Boundary

0   100 miles
0   150 kilometers
Azimuthal Equidistant Projection

L A P L A N D

NORWEGIAN SEA

LOFOTEN VESTERÅLEN
Vestfjorden
Bodø
ARCTIC CIRCLE

Kiruna
Kebnekaise
6,926 ft
2,111 m
Tornealven

F I N L A N D

Ivalo

Rovaniemi

Kemi

Luleå

Oulu
Raahe
Oulujoki

Kajaani
Nurmes
Kuopio
Joensuu

Skellefteå

Umeå

Kokkola
Jakobstad
Vaasa

ATLANTIC OCEAN

Trondheim
Trondheimsfjorden

Ångermanälven
Umeälven

N o r r l a n d

Örnsköldsvik
Östersund

Gulf of Bothnia

Lake
Region

Jyväskylä   Savonlinna
Mikkeli   Imatra

Ålesund

Galdhøpiggen
8,100 ft
2,469 m

Glåma

N O R W A Y

S W E D E N

Sundsvall

Ljusnan

Tampere
Pori
Rauma

Lappeenranta
Lahti
Kotka
Lake
Ladoga

Bergen

Klarälven

Falun   Gävle

Turku
Helsinki
Espoo

ÅLAND
ISLANDS

Gulf of Finland

R U S S I A

Hønefoss
Haugesund   Drammen   Oslo
S v e a l a n d
Uppsala
Karlstad   Västerås
Skien   Örebro   Stockholm
Stavanger   Mälaren
Fredrikstad   Vänern   Norrköping
Vättern   Linköping

Hiiumaa
Saaremaa

Tallinn   Narva

ESTONIA
Pärnu   Tartu

Lake
Peipus

Kristiansand
Skagerrak
Göteborg
Borås   Jönköping
G ö t a l a n d
Gotland
Visby

Gulf of
Riga

Valmiera

B A L T I C   S E A

Ventspils

Rēzekne

Kattegat
Ålborg
**NORTH
SEA**
Århus
JUTLAND
Esbjerg   **DENMARK**
Odense   Helsingborg
Fyn   Malmö
Sjælland   Copenhagen
Bornholm

Öland

Liepāja

Klaipėda

LATVIA
Jelgava
Daugavpils
Western Dvina

Šiauliai

Panevėžys
LITHUANIA
Neman
Kaunas

KALININGRAD
(RUSSIA)

Vilnius

BELARUS

G E R M A N Y   P O L A N D

THE CONTINENT:
EUROPE

THE BASICS

STATS

Largest country
France 210,026 sq mi (543,965 sq km)

Smallest country
Vatican City 0.2 sq mi (0.4 sq km)

Most populous country
Germany 81,825,000

Least populous country
Vatican City 836

Predominant languages
German, French, English, Italian, Spanish, Dutch, Portuguese

Predominant religion
Christianity (Roman Catholic, Protestant)

Highest GDP per capita
Luxembourg $104,200

Lowest GDP per capita
Malta $25,600

Highest life expectancy
Spain, France, Switzerland, Sweden 82 years

Highest literacy rate
Andorra, Liechtenstein, Luxembourg, Vatican City
100%

GEO WHIZ

Fossil hunters discovered a new species of dinosaur in northern Spain in 2006. Measuring up to 120 feet (37 m) and weighing 48 tons (44 t), *Turiasaurus riodevemsis* is the largest dinosaur ever found in Europe.

The catacombs of Paris, which date from Roman times, contain the skeletons of some six million people, including some victims of the French Revolution.

Antwerp, Belgium, is the center of the world's diamond industry.

The ears on several rhinoceros images in France's Chauvet cave look so much like a certain fast-food chain's Golden Arches that researchers have nicknamed them McEars.

Portugal is the world's leading producer of cork.

Mount Etna, on Italy's island of Sicily, is known as the home of Zeus, ruler of all Greek gods. It is also Europe's highest active volcano.

Western Europe

Eighteen countries crowd this diverse region, which has enjoyed a central role in world affairs for centuries while suffering the results of devastating wars. The past half-century has seen bitter rivals become wiser allies, with today's European Union growing out of the need to rebuild economic and political stability after World War II. Fertile soil in the many river valleys across the Northern European Plain and on Mediterranean hillsides gives rise to abundant harvests of a wide variety of crops. France leads in agricultural production and area, while Germany is the most populous country. These and other countries in this region face a population problem unlike that seen in most other regions: a decline in numbers.

⬤ **MONUMENT TO FAITH.** The towering spires of La Sagrada Familia (The Holy Family) rise above Barcelona, Spain. This massive Roman Catholic church has been under construction for more than a century.

⬤ **HIGHLAND TUNE.** Bagpipers in formal dress parade through the streets of Edinburgh, Scotland. Bagpipes may have arrived with Roman invaders, but today they are most associated with the Scottish Highlands.

⬤ **MODERN SPAN.** Tall red arches support the Willem Bridge across the Maas River in Rotterdam, Netherlands. The Maas, which flows into the North Sea, is a major trade and transport artery, linking the Netherlands to the rest of Europe.

HOW BIG IS A COUNTRY?

MONACO
VATICAN CITY
SAN MARINO
LIECHTENSTEIN
MALTA
RHODE ISLAND
ANDORRA

Area of R.I.
1,045 sq mi (2,706 sq km)

Europe's six smallest countries (see pages 169–171 for areas) would fit inside Rhode Island, the smallest U.S. state, with room to spare.

◖ **CELTIC POWER.** These rock pillars are part of Stonehenge, a puzzling arrangement of stones on the plains of southern England. Erected more than 5,000 years ago, Stonehenge is believed to be associated with sun worship.

0 — 200 miles
0 — 300 kilometers
Azimuthal Equidistant Projection

Map Key
★ Country capital
◉ Province capital
••• City or town
⋯⋯ Boundary

FINLAND

ESTONIA

NORWAY

SWEDEN

Shetland Islands

Orkney Islands

BALTIC SEA

POLAND

Rockall (UNITED KINGDOM)

Outer Hebrides

Inner Hebrides

Inverness

SCOTLAND · Aberdeen

Perth · Dundee

Glasgow · Edinburgh

UNITED

Londonderry

NORTHERN IRELAND · Belfast

Isle of Man

Newcastle

Sunderland

Leeds

KINGDOM

Kingston upon Hull

NORTH SEA

DENMARK

Kiel

Rostock

Lübeck

Hamburg

IRELAND

IRISH SEA

Limerick · Dublin ★

Liverpool

Manchester

Sheffield

Nottingham

Frisian Islands

Groningen

Oldenburg

Bremen

Berlin ★

Hannover

Magdeburg

Leipzig

Dresden

Waterford

Cork

Birmingham

WALES

ENGLAND

NETHERLANDS

The Hague

Amsterdam ★

Utrecht

Dortmund

Bielefeld

Erfurt

GERMANY

Chemnitz

Cardiff

London ★

Bristol

Thames

Rotterdam

Brugge

Antwerp

Essen

Köln

Bonn

Frankfurt

CZECH REPUBLIC

SLOVAKIA

CELTIC SEA

Plymouth

Southampton

ENGLISH CHANNEL

Strait of Dover

Brussels ★

BELGIUM

Lille

Charleroi

Luxembourg ★

LUXEMBOURG

Mainz

Mannheim

Nürnberg

Linz

Vienna ★

Channel Islands (U.K.)

Amiens

Rouen

Le Havre

Reims

Metz

Nancy

Karlsruhe

Stuttgart

Augsburg

Salzburg

AUSTRIA

HUNGARY

Brest

Caen

Paris ★

Strasbourg

Freiburg

Munich

Innsbruck

Graz

Rennes

Orléans

Seine

Mulhouse

Basel

Rhine

Besançon

Zürich

LIECHTENSTEIN

Bolzano

Trento

SLOVENIA

Trieste

Angers

Le Mans

Tours

Nantes

Loire

FRANCE

Dijon

Lausanne

Bern ★

SWITZERLAND

ALPS

Verona

Venice

Padova

CROATIA

BAY OF BISCAY

Limoges

Vichy

Lyon

Geneva

Mont Blanc 15,781 ft 4,810 m

Matterhorn 14,691 ft 4,478 m

Milan

Po

Ferrara

Bologna

ADRIATIC SEA

BOSNIA & HERZEGOVINA

SERBIA

Clermont-Ferrand

MASSIF CENTRAL

St.-Étienne

Turin

Modena

APENNINES

Ancona

MONTENEGRO

Bordeaux

Garonne

Nîmes

Avignon

Genoa

Florence

SAN MARINO

Perugia

Pescara

ALBANIA

Donostia-San Sebastián

Santander

Bilbao

Toulouse

Montpellier

Aix-en-Provence

Nice

MONACO

Pisa

Rome ★

ITALY

A Coruña

Gijón

Oviedo

PYRENEES

Marseille

Toulon

LIGURIAN SEA

Bastia

VATICAN CITY ★

Foggia

Bari

Vigo

Santiago de Compostela

León

Vitoria-Gasteiz

Pamplona

ANDORRA ★

Perpignan

CORSICA

Ajaccio

Naples

Vesuvius 4,203 ft 1,281 m

Salerno

Taranto

Braga

Porto

Burgos

Andorra la Vella

Sabadell

Martaró

Lecce

Bragança

Duero

Valladolid

Zaragoza

Lleida

Barcelona

Gulf of Taranto

Viseu

Ebro

Tarragona

Sassari

TYRRHENIAN SEA

Cosenza

IONIAN SEA

Coimbra

Salamanca

Madrid ★

Castelló de la Plana

BALEARIC SEA

Minorca

SARDINIA

PORTUGAL

Tagus

Toledo

Valencia

Majorca

Palma de Mallorca

Cagliari

Messina

Reggio di Calabria

Lisbon ★

SPAIN

Guadiana

Badajoz

Albacete

BALEARIC ISLANDS

Palermo

Taormina

Setúbal

SIERRA MORENA

Murcia

Alicante

Marsala

SICILY

Catania

Córdoba

Jaén

Cartagena

Syracuse

Huelva

Seville

Granada

MEDITERRANEAN

Jerez

Málaga

Almería

Cádiz

GIBRALTAR (U.K.)

Algeciras

Ceuta (SPAIN)

ALBORAN SEA

Valletta

MALTA

Strait of Gibraltar

Melilla (SPAIN)

MOROCCO

ALGERIA

TUNISIA

SEA

ATLANTIC OCEAN

THE BASICS

STATS

Largest country
Ukraine 233,090 sq mi (603,700 sq km)

Smallest country
Moldova 13,050 sq mi (33,800 sq km)

Most populous country
Ukraine 45,556,000

Least populous country
Moldova 4,114,000

Predominant languages
Ukrainian, Russian, Polish, Hungarian, Czech, Belarusian, Slovak, Moldovan

Predominant religions
Christianity (Roman Catholic, Orthodox, Protestant), Judaism, Islam

Highest GDP per capita
Czech Republic $27,100

Lowest GDP per capita
Moldova $3,400

Highest life expectancy
Czech Republic 77 years

Highest literacy rate
Poland, Slovakia, Belarus, Ukraine 100%

GEO WHIZ

The Wieliczka salt mine has been in operation since the 13th century. Known as the underground salt cathedral of Poland, it features historical, religious, and mythical figures, chambers, chapels, and an exhibit about how salt is mined, all carved in salt.

The Pinsk Marshes, one of Europe's largest wetlands, covers thousands of square miles in southern Belarus and northwestern Ukraine. In 1970 the area was chosen as the site of the Chernobyl Nuclear Power Plant, largely because few people lived there and it had ready access to water. An explosion closed the power plant in 1986, and much of the area is still uninhabitable due to radioactive contaminants.

Budapest did not become a united city until 1873. Until that time there were two cities—Buda on the west bank of the Danube and Pest on the east. The first bridge between the cities was built in the mid-1800s by Count Istvan Széchenyi.

The so-called Velvet Revolution was the nonviolent uprising against the Communist government of Czechoslovakia in 1989 that led to the creation of two new countries: the Czech Republic and Slovakia.

Eastern Europe

🔘 **TIME TO EAT.** Smoked sausages and bacon, ready for purchase in the market, are an important part of the diet in the countries of eastern Europe.

Eastern Europe stretches from the Baltic Sea southeast to the Black Sea. Before 1991, Ukraine, Belarus, and Moldova were part of the Soviet Union, with the region's other countries largely under its control. A small, separated segment of Russia is still nearby: Kaliningrad. Much of the region has a continental climate similar to that of the U.S. Midwest. Nearly the size of Texas, Ukraine is the region's largest country in both population and area. Like Poland, it holds rich agricultural and industrial resources. Warsaw is the region's largest city, while the historic charms of Prague and Budapest make them popular tourist stops. With the exceptions of Hungarians and Moldovans, most people in these lands are linked by branches of Slavic language and ethnicity.

◗ **HEALING WATERS.** Budapest's Széchenyi Baths, built between 1909 and 1913, are famous for their medicinal thermal waters, discovered in 1879. A total of 15 baths, as well as saunas and steam rooms, are housed in buildings decorated with sculptures and mosaics by Hungary's leading artists.

◖ **ANCIENT GOLD.** This skillfully crafted gold collar, called a pectoral, was found in a Scythian burial mound in Ukraine. The Scythians occupied the area from modern Ukraine into Russia from the eighth century B.C. to the second century A.D.

LATVIA

LITHUANIA

KALININGRAD (RUSSIA)

Olsztyn

Hrodna

Białystck

Warsaw

Brest

Radom

Lublin

Kielce

Vistula

Rzeszów

Tarnów

L'viv

CARPATHIAN

Košice

Miskolc

Uzhhorod

Nyiregyháza

Debrecen

HUNGARY

ROMANIA

MOUNTAINS

Vitsyebsk

Orsha

Barysaw

Mahilyow

Minsk

Baranavichy

Babruysk

Homyel'

Pinsk

Pinsk Marshes

Mazyr

Western Dvina

BELARUS

Dnieper

Chernihiv

Chernobyl'

Sumy

RUSSIA

Luts'k

Rivne

Zhytomyr

Kiev

Bila Tserkva

Dnieper

Kharkiv

Poltava

Lysychans'k

Ternopil'

UKRAINE

Dniester

Khmel'nyts'kyy

Vinnytsya

Cherkasy

Kremenchuk

Slov''yans'k

Kramators'k

Kostyantynivka

Kadivka

Luhans'k

Ivano-Frankivs'k

Oleksandriya

Alchevs'k

Kam'yanets'-Podil's'kyy

Kirovohrad

Dniprodzerzhyns'k

Horlivka

Krasnyy Luch

Chernivtsi

Kryvyy Rih

Dnipropetrovs'k

Yenakiyeve

Donets'k

Makiyivka

Dniester

Bălţi

Zaporizhzhya

Nikopol'

MOLDOVA

Chişinău

Mykolayiv

Dnieper

Melitopol'

Mariupol'

Berdyans'k

Tiraspol

Kherson

Prut

Odesa

SEA OF AZOV

Danube

Kerch

CRIMEA

Yevpatoriya

Simferopol'

Sevastopol'

Yalta

BLACK SEA

COMMUNICATION CHALLENGE

West Slavic 20%	Polish (40.0 million speakers)
	Czech (9.5 million speakers)
	Slovak (5.0 million speakers)
South Slavic 10%	Bulgarian (9.1 million speakers)
	Bosnian (2.2 million speakers)
	Serbian (7.0 million speakers)
East Slavic 70%	Slovene (2.0 million speakers)
	Macedonian (2.1 million speakers)
	Croatian (5.5 million speakers)
	Belarusian (8.6 million speakers)
	Russian (144.0 million speakers)
	Ukrainian (37.0 million speakers)

Slavic languages of Eastern Europe share a common origin, but they have evolved into a dozen distinctly different languages.

Map Key

⊛ Country capital
••• City or town
···· Boundary

0   200 miles
0   300 kilometers
Azimuthal Equidistant Projection

◖ **MOUNTAIN OF SALT.**
These men shovel salt at a storage depot in Crimea, Ukraine. Salt is a traditional symbol of friendship in Ukraine.

THE BASICS

STATS

Largest country
Romania 92,043 sq mi (238,391 sq km)

Smallest country
Cyprus 3,572 sq mi (9,251 sq km)

Most populous country
Romania 21,408,000

Least populous country
Montenegro 622,000

Predominant languages
Romanian, Greek, Serbian, Croatian, Bulgarian, Albanian, Turkish, English

Predominant religions
Christianity (various Orthodox, Roman Catholic), Islam

Highest GDP per capita
Slovenia $28,800

Lowest GDP per capita
Kosovo $6,500

Highest life expectancy
Greece 80 years

Highest literacy rate
Slovenia
100%

GEO WHIZ

Along the coast of Croatia there are huge fish farms where bluefin tuna are raised, making the country an important supplier of this highly edible, very popular fish.

The Dalmatian, a popular breed of dog, is named for its region of origin: Dalmatia, along the Adriatic coast of the Balkan Peninsula.

Dracula tours abound in Romania, home of Vlad Dracula (also known as Vlad the Impaler), who ruled the region between the Danube and the Transylvanian Alps in the 15th century.

The famous Lipizzan horses of the Spanish Riding School in Vienna, Austria, trace their ancestry and their name back more than 400 years to a horse farm in Lipica, Slovenia.

Nicosia (Lefkosia) is the capital of both the independent Republic of Cyprus and the Rebublic of Northern Cyprus, which is under Turkish control.

Balkans & Cyprus

The Balkans—named for a Bulgarian mountain range—make up a rugged land with a rough history. Ethnic and religious conflict have long troubled the area. Since 1991, seven new countries have emerged from the breakup of Yugoslavia (see inset on page 97). Kosovo is the most recent. The storied Danube River winds east across the Balkans, separating Bulgaria from Romania, the region's largest country in both area and population. Rimmed by four seas—the Black, Aegean, Ionian, and Adriatic—the Balkans, particularly Greece, have a long maritime history. With more than 3.7 million people, Greece's capital, Athens, is the largest city in the region. In 2004, Cyprus, which has been uneasily divided for three decades into Turkish and Greek sections, joined the European Union along with Greece.

⬤ **TRADITIONAL LIFE.** Villagers walk down a cobbled street in Gusinje, a rural town in northeastern Montenegro. A place of rugged mountains, Montenegro is one of the countries that emerged from the former Yugoslavia.

⬤ **LAZY DAYS.** A cat stretches out along a whitewashed wall on the Greek island of Thíra. The blue dome in the background is part of a Greek Orthodox church.

⬤ **COLORFUL BOUNTY.** An open-air fruit market overflows with grapes, plums, apples, and other produce that thrive in the moderate climate of the Mediterranean region. Warm, dry summers and cool, rainy winters provide ideal growing conditions for a variety of fruits, many of which had their origins in the region.

ANCIENT WARRIORS. Soldiers and horsemen from Thrace, an ancient territory in present-day Bulgaria and Greece, wore masks as they rode into battle. Often serving as paid fighters in other armies, the Thracians were allies of Troy in Homer's *Iliad*.

1 2 3 4 5 6 7 8

SLOVAKIA

UKRAINE

CARPATHIAN

Dniester

AUSTRIA

HUNGARY

MOLDOVA

• Satu Mare
• Baia Mare

• Botoşani
• Suceava
Iaşi

Zalău •
TRANSYLVANIA

Piatra
Neamţ

Drava

Oradea •

• Bacău

Drava

Cluj-Napoca •

• Târgu-Mureş

SLOVENIA

Maribor •

ROMANIA

Sava

⊛ Zagreb

Subotica •

Arad •

MTS.

Ljubljana ⊛

Deva •

• Alba Iulia

CROATIA

DINARIC

Novi
Sad •

Timişoara •

Sibiu •

Braşov •

*Gulf of
Venice*

Rijeka •

Osijek •

Zrenjanin •

Reşiţa •

Tisza

Transylvanian Alps

Galaţi •
Brăila •

• Tulcea

Pula •

Prijedor •
Banja Luka •

Doboj •

Tuzla •

Sava

Šabac • Pančevo •

*Iron Gate
Dam*

Râmnicu
Vâlcea •

• Buzău

Ploieşti •

BOSNIA AND

DALMATIA

Zenica •

Belgrade ⊛

SERBIA

Smederevo •

Drobeta-
Turnu
Severin •

Piteşti •

⊛ Bucharest

Zadar •

HERZEGOVINA

Sarajevo ⊛

Čačak •

Kragujevac •

Danube

Craiova •

• Constanţa

Split •

Mostar •

ALPS

Kraljevo •

Kruševac •

Ruse •

Dobrich •

• Niš

Pleven •

Shumen •

Varna •

Leskovac •

BLACK
SEA

ADRIATIC

Dubrovnik •

MONTENEGRO

Priština ⊛

Teteven •

BULGARIA

Dryanovo •

Peja •

KOSOVO

Sofia ⊛

Tryavna •

Sliven •

Podgorica ⊛

Prizren •

Ferizaj •

BALKAN

MOUNTAINS

Burgas •

SEA

Shkodër •

Stara Zagora •

ITALY

Tetovo •

⊛ Skopje

RHODOPE MTS.

Plovdiv •

Bosporus

Durrës •

MACEDONIA

BLACK
SEA

Tirana ⊛

PENINSULA

Strait of Otranto

Elbasan •

• Bitola

Kavála •

BALKAN

Sea of
Marmara

ALBANIA

Thessaloníki •

• Vlorë

*Olympus
9,570 ft
2,917 m*

Halkidikí •

Límnos

TURKEY

Corfu

Lárissa •

AEGEAN

*Lesbos
(Mitilíni)*

IONIAN
SEA

Dardanelles

Vólos •

Chios

IONIAN
ISLANDS

GREECE

Map Key

⊛ Country capital

••• City or town

...... Boundary

0 ————— 100 miles
0 ————— 100 kilometers

Azimuthal Equidistant Projection

Pátra •

Píreas •

Corinth •

Athens ⊛
Kallithéa •

Sámos

SEA

⊹ Olympia •

Ikaría

Náxos

DODECANESE

PELOPONNESUS

Sparta •

CYCLADES

Gulf of Messinía

*Thíra
(Santoríni)*

Rhodes •
Rhodes •

MEDITERRANEAN

SEA OF CRETE

Irákli o •

Crete

SEA

See map page 85 for position

NORTHERN CYPRUS
(recognized only by Turkey)

CYPRUS

⊛ Nicosia

Lemesos •

Same Scale as Main Map

See map page 85 for position

REGION IN TURMOIL

AUSTRIA   HUNGARY

Former Yugoslavia
Border (1991)

SLOVENIA

ROMANIA

CROATIA

Adriatic Sea

BOSNIA
AND
HERZEGOVINA

SERBIA

BULGARIA

ITALY

KOSOVO

MONTENEGRO

ALBANIA

MACEDONIA

GREECE   TURKEY

**Political and social change brought an end to the
southern Slavic country of Yugoslavia. Seven new
countries emerged, but peace has been fragile.**

European Russia

THE BASICS

STATS*

Area
6,592,850 sq mi (17,075,400 sq km)

Population
143,165,000

Predominant languages
Russian, minority languages

Predominant religions
Christianity (Russian Orthodox), Islam

GDP per capita
$16,700

Life expectancy
66 years

Literacy rate
100%

*Note: These figures are for all of Russia.
For Asian Russia, see pages 108–109.

GEO WHIZ

St. Petersburg's many canals and hundreds of bridges have earned it the nickname Venice of the North.

The fertile Northern European Plain, which stretches west from the Urals, is home to most of Russia's population and industry, whereas most of its mineral resources lie east of the Urals in the Asian portion of the country.

Two of the world's most famous ballet companies are in Russia: the Kirov in St. Petersburg and the Bolshoi in Moscow.

Arkhangel'sk, founded in 1584, is Russia's oldest Arctic port. The rich timber resources that surround it and make up the bulk of its exports have been nicknamed "green gold."

The official residence of the President of Russia is inside a walled fortress known as the Kremlin in downtown Moscow. The site on which the Kremlin stands has been continuously occupied since 2000 B.C.

During the Soviet era (1920–1991), the city Nizhniy Novgorod was named Gorky after author Maxim Gorky. "Gorky" is a Russian word meaning "bitter."

Soviet dictator Josef Stalin used the GUM department store, located on Moscow's Red Square, to display propaganda posters and the body of his wife, who committed suicide in 1932.

◐ **CHECKMATE!** Bystanders watch intently as one player prepares to make his move in this chess game in a park in St. Petersburg. In Russia, chess is a national pastime, popular with people from all walks of life.

Home to four-fifths of Russia's 143 million people, European Russia contains most of the world's largest country's agriculture and industry. Here also is Moscow, its capital and Europe's largest city. Far to the north, Murmansk provides a year-round seaport—a gift of the warming currents of the North Atlantic Drift. This large, funnel-shaped portion of Russia, which spans 1,600 miles (2,575 km) from the icy Arctic to the imposing Caucasus Mountains, is home to the Volga, Europe's longest river, and Mount El'brus (18,510 ft/5,642 m), its highest peak. The Caucasus, together with the mineral-rich Urals, form a natural boundary between Europe and Asia. Although parts of Azerbaijan and Georgia in the south and Kazakhstan in the east span the continental boundary, only Russia is counted as part of Europe. To read about Asian Russia, see pages 108–109.

EUROPE'S GREAT RIVERS

River	Length
Volga	3,685 km (2,290 mi)
Danube	2,888 km (1,795 mi)
Dnieper	2,290 km (1,423 mi)
Rhine	1,320 km (820 mi)
Elbe	1,091 km (678 mi)
Vistula	1,047 km (651 mi)
Tagus	1,038 km (645 mi)
Loire	1,012 km (629 mi)
Rhône	800 km (497 mi)
Po	652 km (405 mi)

Europe's rivers, many linked by canals, form a transportation network that connects the continent's people and places to each other and the world beyond.

◑ **CATHEDRAL ON THE SQUARE.** The onion dome–topped towers of St. Basil's are a key landmark on Moscow's Red Square. Built between 1555 and 1561 to commemorate successful military campaigns by Ivan the Terrible, the building is rich in Christian symbolism.

◖ **RUSSIAN DELICACY.** Caviar, a distinctly Russian luxury food item, is the eggs (called roe) of sturgeon fish caught in the Caspian Sea. The eggs are aged in a salty brine before being packaged in cans (left) for shipment around the world.

THE CONTINENT:
EUROPE

ARCTIC OCEAN

NORWAY

NOVAYA
ZEMLYA

KARA
SEA

Yamal Peninsula

Gulf of Ob

BARENTS SEA

LAPLAND

Kolguyev I.

• Murmansk

• Vorkuta

ARCTIC CIRCLE

Kola
Peninsula

Kanin Peninsula

• Usinsk

SWEDEN

FINLAND

WHITE SEA

• Pechora

Pechora

See pages 108–109
for Asian part of Russia

Gulf of Bothnia

Northern Dvina

• Severodvinsk   • Arkhangel'sk

• Ukhta

• Sosnogorsk

URAL

• Zheleznodorozhnyy

• Petrozavodsk

• Syktyvkar

SIBERIA

Lake
Ladoga

Lake
Onega

• Kotlas

R

MOUNTAINS

Gulf of Finland

St. Petersburg

Sukhona

U

• Berezniki

BALTIC SEA

ESTONIA

Lake
Peipus

Cherepovets •
• Vologda

S

EUROPE-ASIA
BOUNDARY

• Velikiy
  Novgorod

Rybinsk Reservoir

• Kirov

Perm'

• Pskov

PLAIN

S

Kama

LATVIA

• Velikiye
  Luki

• Rybinsk
• Yaroslavl'
Volga

• Kostroma

• Izhevsk

KALININGRAD
(RUSSIA)

Tver' •

• Ivanovo

Nizhniy
Novgorod

Naberezhnyye
Chelny

Ufa

LITHUANIA

NORTHERN

Moscow ⊛

Vladimir

Kazan'

Ural

POLAND

• Smolensk

Oka

Cheboksary •

Volga

Magnitogorsk

BELARUS

EUROPEAN

• Kaluga
  • Tula

• Ryazan'

Ul'yanovsk

Sterlitamak •

Belaya

CENTRAL

Saransk •

Syzran'
Tol'yatti

• Bryansk

Oka

• Orel
  • Lipetsk

• Tambov

Penza •

Samara

Novotroitsk

RUSSIAN

• Kursk
  • Voronezh

Saratov •

• Balakovo

Orenburg •

Orsk

• Belgorod

UKRAINE

UPLAND

Dnieper

Don

• Kamyshin

KAZAKHSTAN

Donets

Ural

MOLDOVA

Dnieper

• Volgograd • Volzhskiy

CASPIAN DEPRESSION

• Shakhty

Don

Volga

SEA OF
AZOV

• Taganrog

• Rostov na Donu

CASPIAN

• Astrakhan'

• Krasnodar

• Stavropol'

Map Key

⊛ Country capital

• • City or town

······ Boundary

• Novorossiysk

• Maykop

El'brus
18,510 ft
5,642 m

• Pyatigorsk

CHECHNYA

CASPIAN SEA

BLACK SEA

• Sochi

CAUCASUS

Groznyy •

• Makhachkala

• Vladikavkaz

GEORGIA

MOUNTAINS

0 _____ 200 miles

0 _____ 300 kilometers

Azimuthal Equidistant Projection

TURKEY

ARMENIA

AZERBAIJAN

PHYSICAL			POLITICAL		
Land area 17,208,000 sq mi (44,570,000 sq km)	**Lowest point** **Dead Sea, Israel-Jordan** -1,385 ft (-422 m)	**Largest lake entirely in Asia** **Lake Baikal** 12,200 sq mi (31,500 sq km)	**Population** 4,191,414,100	**Largest country entirely in Asia** China 3,705,405 sq mi (9,596,960 sq km)	**Economy** **Farming:** rice, wheat **Industry:** petroleum, electronics **Services**
Highest point **Mount Everest, China-Nepal** 29,035 ft (8,850 m)	**Longest river** **Yangtze (Chang), China** 3,964 mi (6,380 km)		**Largest metropolitan area** **Tokyo, Japan** Pop. 36,500,000	**Most densely populated country** **Singapore** 19,679 people per sq mi (7,565 per sq km)	

Asia

Asia

A   B   C   D   E   F   G   H

9

8

7

6

5

4

3

2

1

PACIFIC OCEAN

ARCTIC OCEAN

ATLANTIC OCEAN

NORTH AMERICA

Greenland

Aleutian Islands

Commander Islands

Kamchatka Peninsula

Chukchi Peninsula

Bering Strait

BERING SEA

CHUKCHI SEA

Wrangel Island

EAST SIBERIAN SEA

New Siberian Islands

North Land

Franz Josef Land

LAPTEV SEA

KARA SEA

BARENTS SEA

Taymyr Peninsula

Gulf of Ob

Kolyma Range

Chersky Range

Aldan

Verkhoyansk Range

Lena

Stanovoy Range

Lena

Angara

Yenisey

Lake Baikal

CENTRAL SIBERIAN PLATEAU

SIBERIA

WEST SIBERIAN PLAIN

Ob

Irtysh

Ob

URAL MOUNTAINS

Ural

Volga

EUROPE

Europe–Asia Boundary

RUSSIA

SEA OF OKHOTSK

Sakhalin

Sikhote Alin Range

Amur

Amur

Kuril Islands

Hokkaido

JAPAN

Honshu

SEA OF JAPAN (EAST SEA)

Shikoku

Kyushu

Ryukyu Islands

Nampō Shotō

TROPIC OF CANCER

Mariana Islands

CAROLINE ISLANDS

PHILIPPINE SEA

NEW GUINEA

AUSTRALIA

ARAFURA SEA

TIMOR SEA

EAST TIMOR (TIMOR-LESTE)

Timor

LESSER SUNDA ISLANDS

BANDA SEA

Celebes

CELEBES SEA

MOLUCCAS

INDONESIA

Flores Sea

Java

GREATER SUNDA ISLANDS

JAVA SEA

Borneo

MALAYSIA

BRUNEI

SINGAPORE

Sumatra

Mindanao

SULU SEA

PHILIPPINES

PHILIPPINE ISLANDS

Luzon

SOUTH CHINA SEA

Hainan

Taiwan

EAST CHINA SEA

YELLOW SEA

SOUTH KOREA

NORTH KOREA

Yellow

North China Plain

Northeast China Plain

Greater Khingan Range

MONGOLIA

ALTAY MOUNTAINS

GOBI

CHINA

Yangtze

Yellow

Sichuan Basin

Yangtze

Three Gorges

Gongga Shan 24,790 ft 7,556 m

TIEN SHAN

TARIM BASIN

Taklimakan Desert

KUNLUN MOUNTAINS

PLATEAU OF TIBET

Qaidam Basin

Salween

Mekong

VIETNAM

LAOS

THAILAND

CAMBODIA

Mekong

Gulf of Thailand

MALAY PENINSULA

ANDAMAN SEA

Andaman Islands

Nicobar Islands

BAY OF BENGAL

MYANMAR (BURMA)

Salween

Brahmaputra

BHUTAN

BANGLADESH

NEPAL

HIMALAYA

Mt. Everest 29,035 ft 8,850 m World's highest point

Ganges

INDIA

DECCAN PLATEAU

Eastern Ghats

Western Ghats

SRI LANKA

LACCADIVE SEA

MALDIVES

INDIAN OCEAN

EQUATOR

Hindu Kush

KYRGYZSTAN

TAJIKISTAN

KAZAKHSTAN

Lake Balkhash

THE STEPPES

Syr Darya

Amu Darya

UZBEKISTAN

TURKMENISTAN

Aral Sea

AFGHANISTAN

PAKISTAN

Indus

Thar Desert

Great Indian Desert

Caspian Depression

Caspian Sea

IRAN

Elburz Mountains

Zagros Mountains

Gulf of Oman

Persian Gulf

UNITED ARAB EMIRATES

OMAN

QATAR

BAHRAIN

KUWAIT

Mesopotamia

Tigris

Euphrates

ARABIAN SEA

Rub al Khali

SAUDI ARABIA

ARABIAN PENINSULA

YEMEN

Gulf of Aden

RED SEA

AFRICA

EQUATOR

Caucasus Mts.

BLACK SEA

GEORGIA

ARMENIA

AZERBAIJAN

TURKEY

ANATOLIA

SYRIA

Syrian Desert

LEBANON

ISRAEL

JORDAN

Dead Sea −1,385 ft −422 m World's lowest point

Sinai

Suez Canal

Aegean Sea

Mediterranean Sea

Baltic Sea

Kolyma Range

Map Key

— Country boundary

1,000 miles

1,500 kilometers

0

0

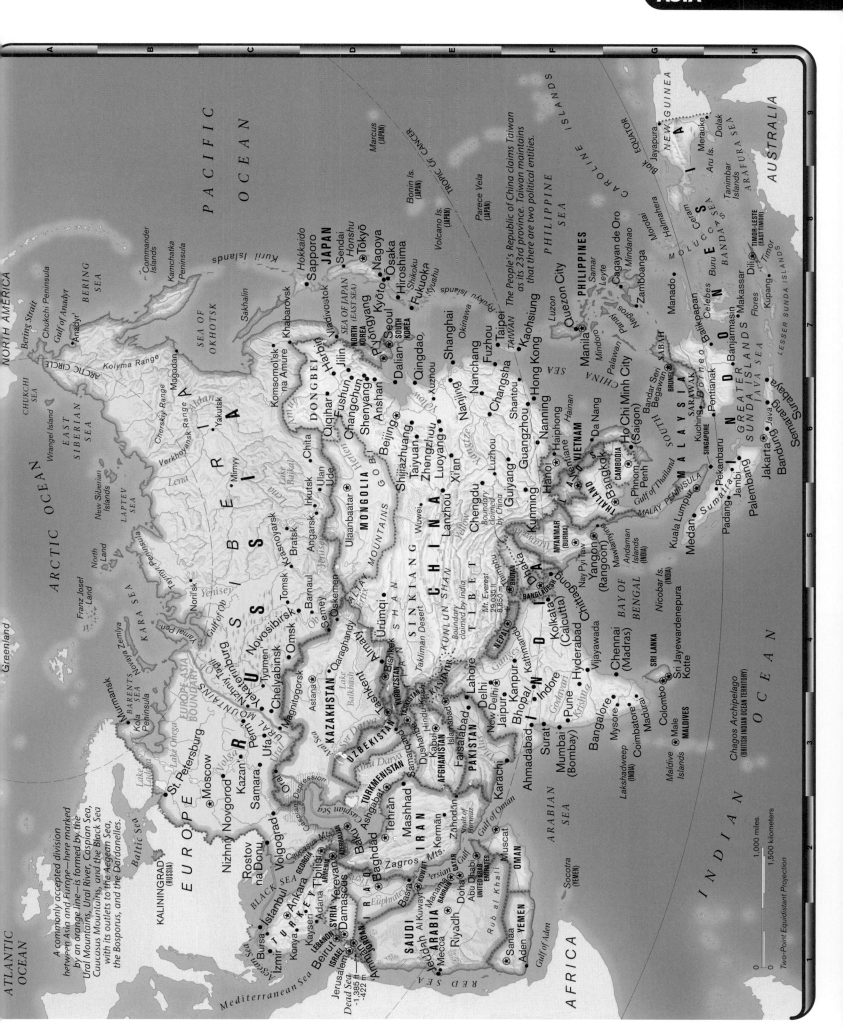

A B C D E F G H

9 8 7 6 5 4 3 2 1

ATLANTIC
OCEAN

Greenland

NORTH
AMERICA

PACIFIC
OCEAN

ARCTIC OCEAN

Commander
Islands

Kamchatka
Peninsula

Chukchi Peninsula

Gulf of Anadyr'

Anadyr'

BERING
SEA

Bering Strait

Chukchi
Peninsula

CHUKCHI
SEA

Wrangel Island

Kolyma Range

Magadan

Chersky Range

Verkhoyansk Range

Yakutsk

Aldan

SEA OF
OKHOTSK

Kuril Islands

Sakhalin

Komsomol'sk
na Amure

Khabarovsk

Amur

Hokkaido

Sapporo

JAPAN

Sendai

Honshu

Tōkyō

Nagoya

Osaka

Kyōto

Hiroshima

Fukuoka

Shikoku

Kyushu

Bonin Is.
(JAPAN)

Volcano Is.
(JAPAN)

Marcus
(JAPAN)

Parece Vela
(JAPAN)

TROPIC OF CANCER

The People's Republic of China claims Taiwan
as its 23rd province. Taiwan maintains
that there are two political entities.

CAROLINE ISLANDS

NEW GUINEA

Biak

Jayapura

EQUATOR

PHILIPPINE
SEA

PHILIPPINES

Manila

Quezon City

Luzon

Mindoro

Samar

Leyte

Panay

Negros

Cagayan de Oro

Mindanao

Zamboanga

Morotai

Halmahera

Manado

Celebes

MOLUCCAS

Buru

Ceram

BANDA SEA

Makassar

Kupang

Dili

TIMOR-LESTE
(EAST TIMOR)

Timor

Dolak

Merauke

Aru Is.

Tanimbar
Islands

ARAFURA
SEA

AUSTRALIA

LESSER SUNDA ISLANDS

Flores

BALI

Surabaya

Semarang

Bandung

Jakarta

Java

JAVA SEA

Palembang

Jambi

GREATER SUNDA ISLANDS

INDONESIA

Pontianak

Banjarmasin

Balikpapan

Borneo

SARAWAK

Kuching

SABAH

Bandar Seri
Begawan

BRUNEI

MALAYSIA

Kuala Lumpur

SINGAPORE

Pekanbaru

Medan

Sumatra

Padang

MALAY PENINSULA

SOUTH
CHINA
SEA

Gulf of
Thailand

Phnom
Penh

CAMBODIA

THAILAND

Bangkok

VIENTIANE

LAOS

VIETNAM

Ho Chi Minh City
(Saigon)

Da Nang

Haiphong

Hanoi

Hainan

MYANMAR
(BURMA)

Nay Pyi Taw

Yangon
(Rangoon)

Mawlamyine

Mandalay

Andaman
Islands
(INDIA)

ANDAMAN
SEA

Nicobar Is.
(INDIA)

BAY OF
BENGAL

Chennai
(Madras)

Vijayawada

Hyderabad

Bangalore

Mysore

Coimbatore

Madurai

SRI LANKA

Sri Jayewardenepura
Kotte

Colombo

MALDIVES

Male

Maldive
Islands

Lakshadweep
(INDIA)

Chagos Archipelago
(BRITISH INDIAN OCEAN TERRITORY)

INDIAN
OCEAN

ARABIAN
SEA

Socotra
(YEMEN)

Gulf of Aden

AFRICA

RED
SEA

Mediterranean Sea

Aden

Sanaa

YEMEN

Rub' al Khali

OMAN

Muscat

Gulf of Oman

Strait of
Hormuz

Persian
Gulf

UNITED ARAB
EMIRATES

Abu Dhabi

Doha

QATAR

Manama

BAHRAIN

Al Kuwayt

KUWAIT

Riyadh

Mecca

Jeddah

SAUDI
ARABIA

Basra

Baghdad

IRAQ

Zagros Mts.

Kermān

Zāhedān

Kabul

AFGHANISTAN

Karachi

PAKISTAN

Faisalabad

Islamabad

Lahore

KASHMIR

Boundary
claimed
by India

TIBET

Mt. Everest
29,035 ft
8,850 m

Kathmandu

NEPAL

BHUTAN
Thimphu

BANGLADESH

Dhaka

Chittagong

Kolkata
(Calcutta)

INDIA

Kanpur

Delhi

New Delhi

Jaipur

Indore

Bhopal

Ahmadabad

Surat

Mumbai
(Bombay)

Pune

Godavari

Krishna

Ganges

Kaveri

Indus

Mashhad

Tehrān

IRAN

Zāhedān

TURKMENISTAN

Ashgabat

Amu Darya

UZBEKISTAN

Dushanbe

TAJIKISTAN

Samarqand

Hindu Kush

Syr Darya

KYRGYZSTAN

Bishkek

Tashkent

Almaty

KAZAKHSTAN

Astana

Lake
Balkhash

Qaraghandy

Aral Sea

TIAN SHAN

Ürümqi

SINKIANG

Takliman Desert

KUNLUN SHAN

Yellow

CHINA

Lanzhou

Xian

Luoyang

Zhengzhou

Chengdu

Gulyang

Kunming

Nanning

Guangzhou

Hong Kong

Shantou

Changsha

Nanchang

Fuzhou

Taipei

TAIWAN

Kaohsiung

Okinawa

Ryukyu Islands

Shanghai

Nanjing

Qingdao

Yellow
Sea

Dalian

Beijing

Shijiazhuang

Taiyuan

Zhongzhou

Wuwe

Luzhou

ALTAI MOUNTAINS

GOBI

MONGOLIA

Ulaanbaatar

Helen River

DONGBEI

Harbin

Qiqihar

Jilin

Changchun

Shenyang

Fushun

Anshan

Vladivostok

SEA OF JAPAN
(EAST SEA)

NORTH
KOREA

Pyŏngyang

SOUTH
KOREA

Seoul

Chita

Ulan Ude

Irkutsk

Lake
Baikal

Angarsk

Bratsk

Krasnoyarsk

Tomsk

Novosibirsk

Barnaul

Semey

Öskemen

Omsk

Ob

Yenisey

Noril'sk

Yenisey

Yamal Pen.

KARA SEA

LAPTEV
SEA

EAST
SIBERIAN
SEA

New Siberian
Islands

North
Land

Taymyr Peninsula

Severnaya Zemlya

Franz Josef
Land

Novaya Zemlya

BARENTS
SEA

Kola
Peninsula

Murmansk

ARCTIC
OCEAN

ARCTIC CIRCLE

S I B E R I A

R U S S I A

Lena

Lena

Mirnyy

Vilyuy

Yekaterinburg

Chelyabinsk

Magnitogorsk

Nizhniy Tagil'

Perm'

Ufa

Samara

Kazan

Nizhniy Novgorod

Moscow

St. Petersburg

Lake Onega

Lake
Ladoga

Baltic
Sea

KALININGRAD
(RUSSIA)

EUROPE

URAL MOUNTAINS

EUROPE-ASIA
BOUNDARY

Volga

Ural

Oral

Tyumen'

Gulf of Ob

Qaraghandy

Rostov
na Donu

Volgograd

Astrakhan

Caspian
Depression

Caspian Sea

Baku

AZERBAIJAN

Yerevan

ARMENIA

Tbilisi

GEORGIA

Caucasus Mts.

BLACK SEA

Istanbul

Bursa

İzmir

Aegean Sea

Konya

Adana

Kayseri

Ankara

TURKEY

Damascus

SYRIA

Beirut

LEBANON

ISRAEL

Jerusalem
Dead Sea
-1,385 m
-422 m

Amman

JORDAN

Tigris

Euphrates

A commonly accepted division
between Asia and Europe—here marked
by an orange line—is formed by the
Ural Mountains, Ural River, Caspian Sea,
Caucasus Mountains, and the Black Sea
with its outlets to the Aegean Sea,
the Bosporus, and the Dardanelles.

0   1,000 miles
0   1,500 kilometers

Two-Point Equidistant Projection

Asia

WORLD CHAMPION

From Turkey to the eastern tip of Russia, Asia sprawls across nearly 180 degrees of longitude—almost half the globe! It boasts the highest (the Himalaya) and lowest (the Dead Sea) places on Earth's surface. Then there are Asia's people—more than four billion of them. That's more people than live on all the other continents put together. Asia has both the most farmers and the most million-plus cities. The world's first civilization arose in Sumer, in what is now southern Iraq. Rich cultures also emerged along rivers in present-day India and China, strongly influencing the world ever since.

⬤ **TASTY SNACK.** This black-and-white giant panda, native to China, munches on a stalk of bamboo, the mainstay of its diet.

◐ **NEW VS. OLD.** An Afghan woman, completely covered by a traditional burka, sits among young girls dressed in Western clothes in Kabul.

◗ **LUNAR NEW YEAR.**
Young men carry a writhing paper dragon on poles in this Chinese New Year's parade in Singapore.

◗ **NEON AVENUE.**
Bright lights and neon signs highlight bustling Nanjing Lu, Shanghai's main shopping street. With a population of more than 23 million, Shanghai is China's largest city.

◗ **WINGED HUNTER.**
A Kazakh falconer sits astride his pony as he releases his golden eagle to pursue prey on the dry Mongolian steppe.

more about
Asia

⬤ **EASTERN BELIEF.** From its origins in the foothills of the Himalaya, Buddhism has spread across much of eastern Asia. Statues of the Buddha, such as this one in Bangkok, Thailand, appear frequently in the landscape of the region.

⬤ **UP AND DOWN.** Traditional dress and a modern motorized walkway create a sharp contrast in a mall in Doha, Qatar.

⬤ **A FINAL TOUCH.** Silk kimonos and perfectly applied makeup are part of the tradition of a *maiko,* or apprentice geisha, in Kyoto, Japan.

STONE BARRIER. Construction on China's Great Wall began in 220 B.C. as a defense against invasion from the north and continued until the A.D. 1600s. Extending in sections for almost 4,000 miles (6,436 km), the wall attracts tourists from around the world.

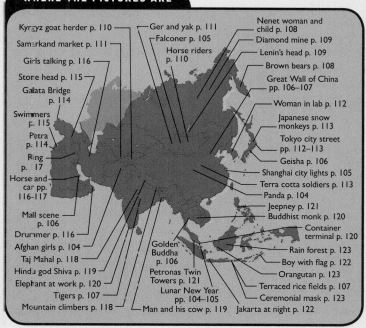

WHERE THE PICTURES ARE

Kyrgyz goat herder p. 110
Samarkand market p. 111
Girls talking p. 116
Stone head p. 115
Galata Bridge p. 114
Swimmers p. 115
Petra p. 114
Ring p. 117
Horse and cart pp. 116–117
Mall scene p. 106
Drummer p. 116
Afghan girls p. 104
Taj Mahal p. 118
Hindu god Shiva p. 119
Elephant at work p. 120
Tigers p. 107
Mountain climbers p. 118

Ger and yak p. 111
Falconer p. 105
Horse riders p. 110
Golden Buddha p. 106
Petronas Twin Towers p. 121
Lunar New Year pp. 104–105
Man and his cow p. 119

Nenet woman and child p. 108
Diamond mine p. 109
Lenin's head p. 109
Brown bears p. 108
Great Wall of China pp. 106–107
Woman in lab p. 112
Japanese snow monkeys p. 113
Tokyo city street pp. 112–113
Geisha p. 106
Shanghai city lights p. 105
Terra cotta soldiers p. 113
Panda p. 104
Jeepney p. 121
Buddhist monk p. 120
Container terminal p. 120
Rain forest p. 123
Boy with flag p. 122
Orangutan p. 123
Terraced rice fields p. 107
Ceremonial mask p. 123
Jakarta at night p. 122

MOUNTAIN STAIRWAY. Terraces cut into a steep mountainside create fields for rice on the island of Bali, in Indonesia. Rice is the staple grain crop in much of eastern Asia. In the foreground, a man nimbly climbs a palm tree to harvest coconuts.

MOTHER KNOWS BEST.
A Bengal tiger gently moves her cub to a safe hiding place before stalking her prey in India's Bandhavgarh National Park. Tigers are an endangered species.

Asian Russia

1   2   3

THE BASICS

STATS*

Area
6,592,850 sq mi (17,075,400 sq km)

Population
143,165,000

Predominant languages
Russian, minority languages

Predominant religions
Christianity (Russian Orthodox), Islam

GDP per capita
$16,700

Life expectancy
66 years

Literacy rate
100%

*These figures are for all of Russia.
For European Russia, see pages 98–99.

GEO WHIZ

The name Siberia comes from the Turkic language and means "Sleeping Land."

Trophy hunting, oil and gas exploration, and gold mining have reduced the brown bear population on the Kamchatka Peninsula from 20,000 during the Soviet era, when the peninsula was restricted to military use, to about 12,500.

A region of northern coniferous forest called taiga stretches across northern Russia as far west as Norway. It covers an area that is more than 11 times the size of Texas.

It takes at least six days to travel 6,000 miles (9,656 km) on the Trans-Siberian Railroad from Moscow to the Pacific port of Vladivostok. The trip crosses eight time zones.

Russia produces more natural gas than the next six countries combined. More than a quarter of the world's proven reserves are in Russia, mainly in Siberia, the Urals, and the region around the Volga River.

Lake Baikal, nicknamed Siberia's "blue eye," is home to 1,500 unique species of plants and animals, including the nerpa, the world's only freshwater seal.

The Chukchi, the largest group of native people in Siberia, take their name from a word that means "rich in reindeer." They share their name with their homeland, a peninsula that borders the Arctic and Pacific Oceans.

⬤ **NOMADIC HERDERS.** A Nenet woman and her grandson prepare to follow the family reindeer herd into northern Siberia for spring and summer grazing.

Forming more than half of gigantic Russia, this region stretches from the Ural Mountains east to the Pacific, and from the Arctic Ocean south to mountains and deserts along borders with Central Asia and China. Siberia, as this region is commonly known, has limited croplands but bountiful forests (the taiga) and rich mineral resources such as natural gas, oil, and gold. The Trans-Siberian Railroad, built between 1891 and 1905, opened up the region for settlement—but not too much. Only about one-sixth of Russia's population—fewer than 25 million people—lives in sprawling Siberia.

See page 99 for
European part of Russi

⬅ **FISHING FOR A MEAL.**
A brown bear and her cubs
hunt for fish in a river
below the snow-laced slopes
of a volcano on Russia's
Kamchatka Peninsula.
Part of the Pacific Ring of Fire,
this peninsula in far eastern Russia
has 29 active volcanoes.

◖ **REVOLUTIONARY LEADER.** Vladimir Ilyich Lenin, a founder of the Soviet Union, was honored with statues throughout the former Communist union and beyond. This one in Ulan Ude, in Siberia, is the largest still standing in Russia.

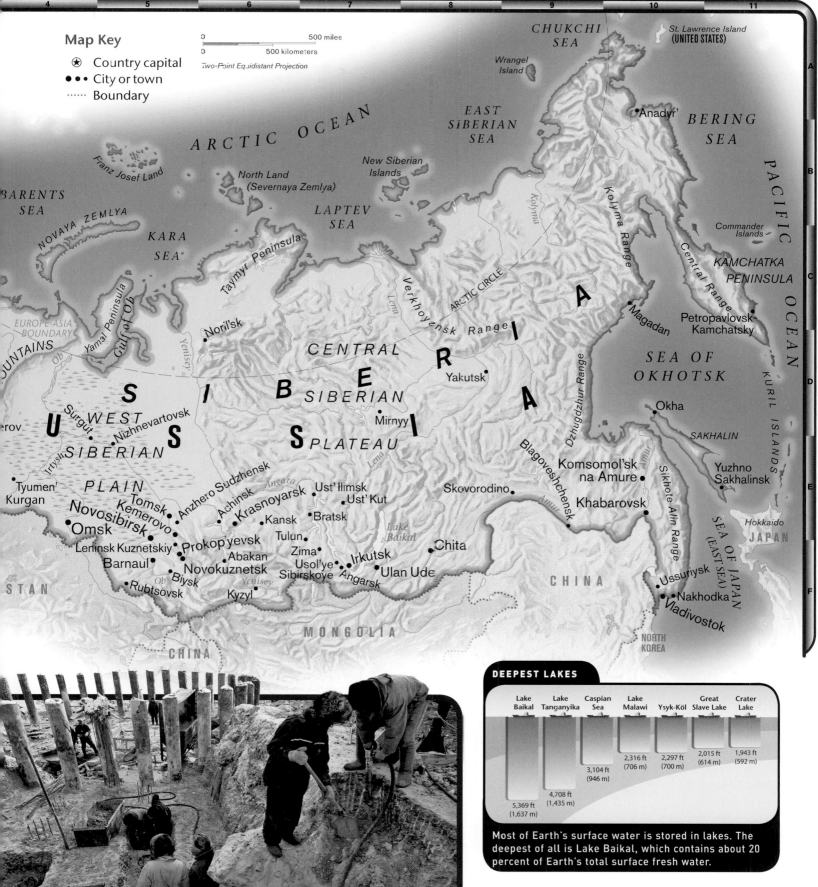

Map Key

⊛ Country capital
••• City or town
······ Boundary

0 ———— 500 miles
0 ———— 500 kilometers
Two-Point Equidistant Projection

ARCTIC OCEAN

CHUKCHI SEA

St. Lawrence Island
(UNITED STATES)

BERING SEA

PACIFIC OCEAN

EAST SIBERIAN SEA

Wrangel Island

•Anadyr'

Franz Josef Land

North Land
(Severnaya Zemlya)

New Siberian Islands

LAPTEV SEA

Commander Islands

BARENTS SEA

NOVAYA ZEMLYA

KARA SEA

Taymyr Peninsula

KAMCHATKA PENINSULA

Kolyma Range

Central Range

Yamal Peninsula

Gulf of Ob

Lena

Verkhoyansk Range

ARCTIC CIRCLE

•Magadan

Petropavlovsk-Kamchatsky

EUROPE-ASIA BOUNDARY

•Noril'sk

CENTRAL SIBERIAN

•Yakutsk

SEA OF OKHOTSK

KURIL ISLANDS

OUNTAINS

Ob

Yenisey

SIBERIA

•Okha

•erov

Surgut

WEST

•Nizhnevartovsk

Mirnyy

PLATEAU

SAKHALIN

•Tyumen'

SIBERIAN

Irtysh

Anzhero Sudzhensk

Lena

Dzhugdzhur Range

Blagoveshchensk

Komsomol'sk na Amure

Yuzhno Sakhalinsk

•Kurgan

PLAIN

•Tomsk

Achinsk

Angara

Ust' Ilimsk

•Skovorodino

Amur

Khabarovsk

Hokkaido

Kemerovo

Krasnoyarsk

Ust' Kut

Sikhote Alin Range

JAPAN

•Omsk

Novosibirsk

Kansk

•Bratsk

Lake Baikal

SEA OF JAPAN
(EAST SEA)

Leninsk Kuznetskiy

Prokop'yevsk

Tulun

•Chita

Barnaul

Abakan

Zima

Irkutsk

•Ussuriysk

Novokuznetsk

Usol'ye Sibirskoye

Angarsk

Ulan Ude

•Nakhodka

•Biysk

Ob

CHINA

Vladivostok

•Rubtsovsk

Yenisey

Kyzyl

NORTH KOREA

STAN

MONGOLIA

CHINA

DEEPEST LAKES

Lake Baikal	Lake Tanganyika	Caspian Sea	Lake Malawi	Ysyk-Köl	Great Slave Lake	Crater Lake
5,369 ft (1,637 m)	4,708 ft (1,435 m)	3,104 ft (946 m)	2,316 ft (706 m)	2,297 ft (700 m)	2,015 ft (614 m)	1,943 ft (592 m)

Most of Earth's surface water is stored in lakes. The deepest of all is Lake Baikal, which contains about 20 percent of Earth's total surface fresh water.

◖ **GEMS IN THE ROUGH.** Miners bundled in warm clothing cut through permafrost in the Mir diamond mine in northern Siberia. Although mined out and closed in 2004, it once produced two million carats a year.

THE BASICS

STATS

Largest country
Kazakhstan 1,049,155 sq mi
(2,717,300 sq km)

Smallest country
Tajikistan 55,251 sq mi (143,100 sq km)

Most populous country
Uzbekistan 29,780,000

Least populous country
Mongolia 2,873,000

Predominant languages
Russian, Kazakh, Uzbek, Kyrgyz, Tajik, Mongol, Turkmen

Predominant religions
Islam, Christianity (Orthodox), Buddhism

Highest GDP per capita
Kazakhstan $13,000

Lowest GDP per capita
Tajikistan $2,100

Highest life expectancy
Uzbekistan 73 years

Highest literacy rate
Kazakhstan, Tajikistan
100%

GEO WHIZ

The main musical instrument of the steppes in Kazakhstan is the *dombra*, a long-necked lute with two strings.

Uzbekistan is among the world's top ten gold-producing countries, and the world's largest open-pit gold mine is at Muruntau in the Qizilqum Desert some 250 miles (400 km) from Tashkent.

The world's only surviving breed of wild horse, the *takh*, or Prezewalski, was "discovered" in southwestern Mongolia in the 1880s by Count Prezewalski. The largest number—some 300—now live in zoos around the world, but a select few that have been reintroduced into the wild graze on the steppe in Mongolia's Hustai National Park.

Kazakhstan's Baikonur Cosmodrome, site of most of the space flights launched by the Soviet Union from the late 1950s to the 1980s, is the world's oldest space-launch facility. It is still managed by the Russian Federal Space Agency.

The Pamir and the Tian Shan are among the mountain ranges that cover more than 90 percent of Tajikistan.

Central Asia

Mongolia and five *stans*—"homelands"—make up Central Asia. Kazakhs, Turkmen, Uzbeks, Tajiks, and Kyrgyz form the majority of the population in these largely Muslim countries. Russians are still present in each, a result of decades of Soviet efforts to control these lands. Sparsely settled, largely Buddhist Mongolia consists of valley grasslands and dry basins beneath towering peaks. Kazakhstan's short-grass steppes give way to deserts, arid plateaus, and rugged mountains to the south. Irrigation provides water for wheat, cotton, and fruit crops. Though far from any ocean, this region possesses several inland seas, including the salty Caspian. Beneath its floor lie huge oil deposits, both tapped and undeveloped, which will add to the region's future importance.

BEST FRIENDS. A boy carries his goat in mountainous Kyrgyzstan, where almost half the land is used for pasture and hay to support herds of goats and sheep.

SKILLED RIDERS.
Young people ride their horses across the steppe in the Darhad Valley, a region of nomadic herders in northern Mongolia. From the time of Genghis Khan's 13th-century armies, Mongolians have been known for their skill on horseback.

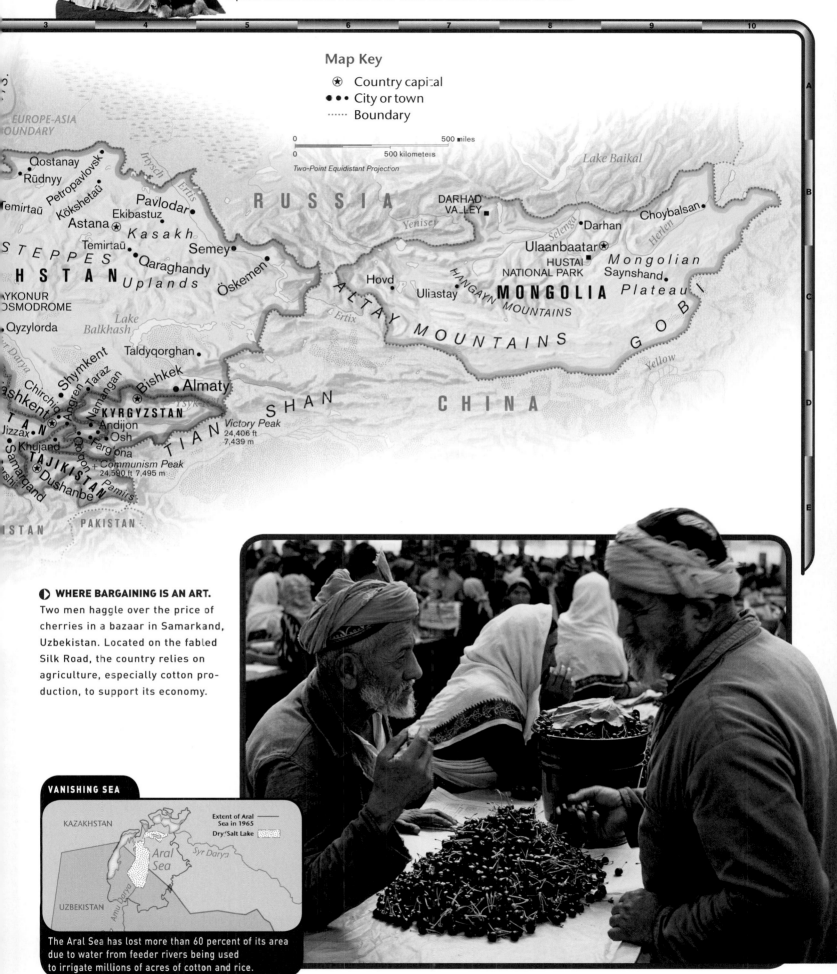

◐ **HOME ON THE STEPPE.** A *ger*, made of a wooden frame overlaid with felt, is the traditional Mongolian dwelling. The cowlike yak works as a pack animal and is a source of milk. Its waste is burned as fuel.

Map Key

⊛ Country capital
●●● City or town
········ Boundary

0 _____ 500 miles
0 _____ 500 kilometers
Two-Point Equidistant Projection

Lake Baikal

EUROPE-ASIA
BOUNDARY

Qostanay
Rūdnyy
Petropavlovsk
Temirtaū
Kökshetaū
Pavlodar
Astana ⊛
Ekibastuz
Temirtaū
Semey
Qaraghandy
Öskemen
Qyzylorda
Lake Balkhash
Taldyqorghan

STEPPES
KASAKH
HSTAN
Uplands
AYKONUR
OSMODROME

RUSSIA

DARHAD
VALLEY
Yenisey
Selenga
Darhan
Choybalsan
Herlen

Hovd
Ulaanbaatar ⊛
HUSTAI
NATIONAL PARK
Uliastay
MONGOLIA
Saynshand
Mongolian
Plateau

HANGAYN
MOUNTAINS

ALTAY MOUNTAINS

Ertix

GOBI

Yellow

Shymkent
Chirchiq
Angren
Taraz
Namangan
Bishkek
Almaty
ashkent
Jizzax
Andijon
Osh
Farg'ona
KYRGYZSTAN
Ysyk
Victory Peak
24,406 ft
7,439 m

TIAN SHAN

CHINA

Khujand
Samarqand
Dushanbe
TAJIKISTAN
Communism Peak
24,590 ft 7,495 m
Pamirs

PAKISTAN
ISTAN

◐ **WHERE BARGAINING IS AN ART.** Two men haggle over the price of cherries in a bazaar in Samarkand, Uzbekistan. Located on the fabled Silk Road, the country relies on agriculture, especially cotton production, to support its economy.

VANISHING SEA

KAZAKHSTAN
Extent of Aral
Sea in 1965 ——
Dry Salt Lake
Aral Sea
Syr Darya
Amu Darya
UZBEKISTAN

The Aral Sea has lost more than 60 percent of its area due to water from feeder rivers being used to irrigate millions of acres of cotton and rice.

East Asia

China takes up most of this region, with the Koreas and Japan lining the Pacific edge. With more than 1.3 billion people, China's population is unrivaled in size. Rich river valleys have nourished Chinese civilization for more than four millennia. The Tibetan Plateau, dry basins, and the hulking Himalaya border China's western regions. Rugged uplands limit living space in Japan and the Koreas. Japan's economic success—especially in technology and manufacturing—has made it a global powerhouse. South Korea has followed a similar economic path, whereas North Korea's dictator prefers to isolate his country. A gradual move to capitalism has led communist China near the top of the global marketplace.

THE BASICS

STATS

Largest country
China 3,705,405 sq mi (9,596,960 sq km)

Smallest country
South Korea 38,321 sq mi (99,250 sq km)

Most populous country
China 1,350,378,000

Least populous country
North Korea 24,589,000

Predominant languages
Standard Chinese or Mandarin, Japanese, Korean, local dialects

Predominant religions
Daoism, Buddhism, Shintoism, Christianity, Confucianism

Highest GDP per capita
Japan $34,700

Lowest GDP per capita
North Korea $1,800

Highest life expectancy
Japan 83 years

Highest literacy rate
Japan, North Korea 99%

GEO WHIZ

The Seikan Tunnel, the world's longest railroad tunnel, links Japan's two largest islands: Honshu and Hokkaido.

Roughly 900 square miles (2,300 sq km) of farmland in northern China are blown away by the wind each year. Huge dust plumes travel hundreds of miles to Beijing and other cities. The clouds are often so thick that they hide the sun, slow traffic, and close airports.

Each year on October 9, people in South Korea celebrate their alphabet, which was created in 1446 to increase literacy.

Construction of the Three Gorges Dam across the Yangtze River created a reservoir that forced more than a million people to find new homes.

Kim Il-sung, who ruled North Korea from its founding in 1948 to his death in 1994, is referred to in the country's constitution as the Eternal President. Both his birthday and the anniversary of his death are public holidays.

Only about 18 percent of Japan's land is suitable for people to live on. Most people choose to live in cities along the narrow coastal plain.

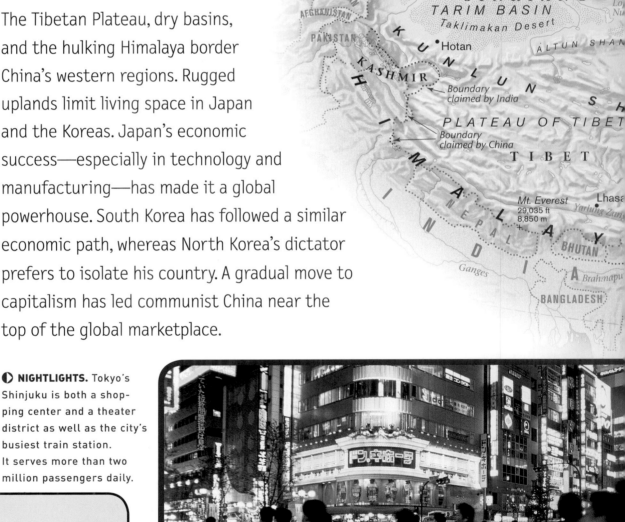

HIGH TECH. This young South Korean woman works in a laboratory that makes microcircuits in a semiconductor plant in Seoul.

RUSSIA

ALTAY

KAZAKHSTAN

Yining Changji Karamay Altay

Ürümq

KYRGYZSTAN T I A N S H A N

Turpan Depression
-505 m
-154 m

Aksu Tarim Korla

TAJIKISTAN

Kashi S I N K I A N G

AFGHANISTAN TARIM BASIN

Taklimakan Desert

PAKISTAN Hotan ALTUN SHAN

KASHMIR K U N L U N Sh

Boundary claimed by India

PLATEAU OF TIBET

Boundary claimed by China

T I B E T

H I M A L A Y Mt. Everest Lhasa
29,035 ft
8,850 m Yarlung Zang

NEPAL BHUTAN

I N D I A Brahmapu

Ganges BANGLADESH

NIGHTLIGHTS. Tokyo's Shinjuku is both a shopping center and a theater district as well as the city's busiest train station. It serves more than two million passengers daily.

AUTO GIANTS

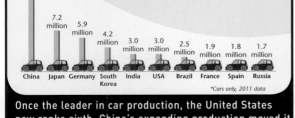

14.5 million*	7.2 million	5.9 million	4.2 million	3.0 million	3.0 million	2.5 million	1.9 million	1.8 million	1.7 million
China	Japan	Germany	South Korea	India	USA	Brazil	France	Spain	Russia

*Cars only, 2011 data

Once the leader in car production, the United States now ranks sixth. China's expanding production moved it from number two a few years ago to the top spot.

STANDING GUARD. Lifelike terra cotta statues formed part of the "army" buried in 141 B.C. with Han Dynasty emperor Jing Di. The emperor believed the army, arranged in battle formation and facing enemy territory, would protect him after death.

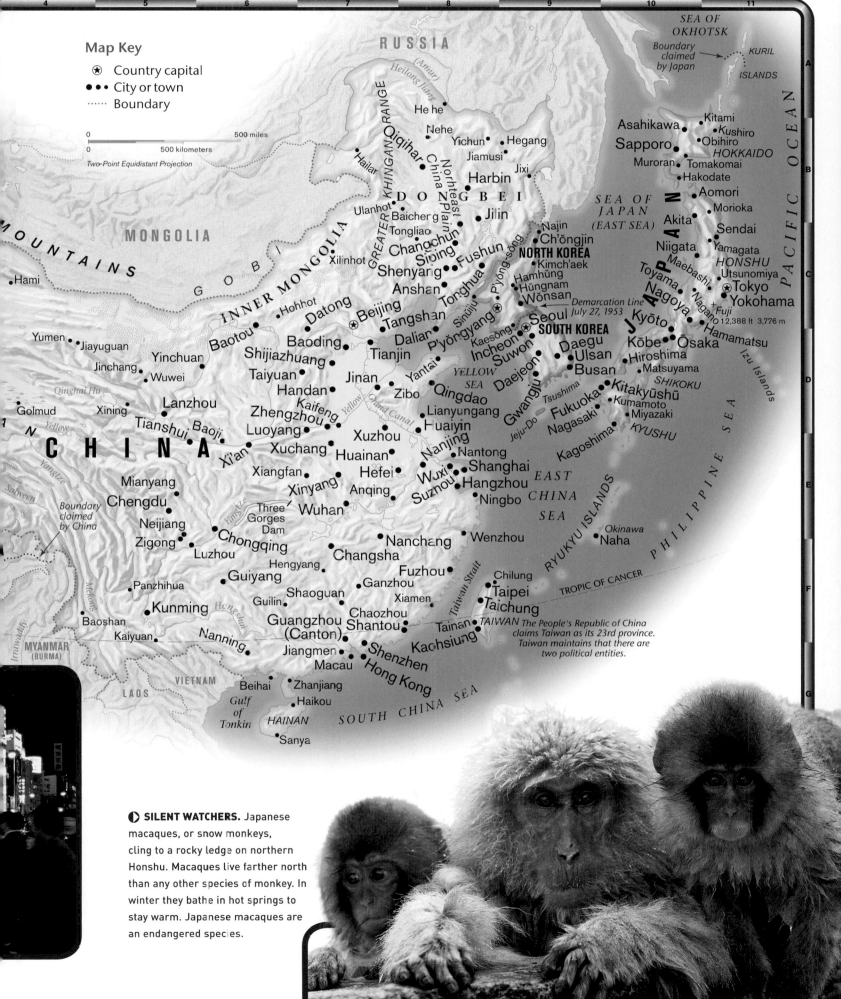

Map Key

⊛ Country capital

••• City or town

⋯⋯ Boundary

0 ——— 500 miles

0 ——— 500 kilometers

Two-Point Equidistant Projection

SEA OF OKHOTSK

Boundary claimed by Japan → KURIL ISLANDS

RUSSIA

MONGOLIA

Heilong Jiang (Amur)

He he
Nehe
Yichun • Hegang
Jiamusi
Jixi
Harbin

GREATER KHINGAN RANGE
Qiqihar
Hailar
Ulanhot
Baicheng
Tongliao
Xilinhot
Changchun
Siping
Shenyang
Anshan
Jilin
Fushun
Tonghua

Northeast China Plain

DONGBEI

Najin
Ch'ŏngjin
NORTH KOREA
Kimch'aek
Hamhŭng
Hŭngnam
Wŏnsan
Sinŭiju
Pyongyang
Pyong-song

Kitami • Kushiro
Asahikawa
Sapporo • Obihiro
HOKKAIDO
Muroran • Tomakomai
Hakodate
Aomori
Morioka
Akita
Sendai
Yamagata
Niigata
Maebashi
Utsunomiya
HONSHU
Toyama
Nagano
Tokyo
Nagoya
Yokohama
Fuji 12,388 ft 3,776 m

SEA OF JAPAN (EAST SEA)

PACIFIC OCEAN

INNER MONGOLIA

GOBI

Hami

MOUNTAINS

Hohhot
Datong
Baotou
Baoding
Beijing ⊛
Tangshan
Dalian
Tianjin
Yantai
YELLOW SEA

Hami

Yumen • Jiayuguan
Jinchang
Yinchuan
Wuwei
Shijiazhuang
Taiyuan
Handan
Jinan
Zibo
Qingdao

Qinghai Hu

Golmud • Xining
Lanzhou
Zhengzhou
Kaifeng
Luoyang
Lianyungang
Huaiyin

Yellow

Tianshui
Baoji
Xuzhou
Huainan

CHINA

Xi'an
Xuchang
Huainan
Nanjing
Nantong
Shanghai
Wuxi
Suzhou
Hangzhou
Ningbo

Seoul ⊛
SOUTH KOREA
Incheon
Kaesŏng
Suwon
Daejeon
Gwangju
Daegu
Ulsan
Busan

Demarcation Line July 27, 1953

Tsushima
Jeju-Do

Fukuoka
Kitakyūshū
Kumamoto
Nagasaki
Miyazaki
Kagoshima
KYUSHU

Hiroshima
Matsuyama
SHIKOKU

Kōbe
Ōsaka
Kyōto
Hamamatsu

JAPAN

Xiangfan
Mianyang
Chengdu
Neijiang
Zigong
Luzhou

Boundary claimed by China

Three Gorges Dam
Yangtze
Wuhan
Xinyang
Anqing
Hefei

Chongqing
Changsha
Hengyang
Nanchang
Wenzhou

EAST CHINA SEA

RYUKYU ISLANDS
Okinawa
Naha

PHILIPPINE SEA

IZU Islands

Salween

Mekong

Panzhihua

Guiyang
Guilin
Shaoguan
Fuzhou
Ganzhou
Xiamen
Chaozhou

Kunming
Baoshan
Kaiyuan

Hongshui

Guangzhou (Canton)
Shantou
Jiangmen
Macau
Shenzhen
Hong Kong

Chilung
Taipei
Taichung
Tainan
Kaohsiung

TAIWAN *The People's Republic of China claims Taiwan as its 23rd province. Taiwan maintains that there are two political entities.*

Taiwan Strait

TROPIC OF CANCER

MYANMAR (BURMA)
Irrawaddy

VIETNAM
LAOS

Nanning
Beihai
Zhanjiang
Haikou
Gulf of Tonkin
HAINAN
Sanya

SOUTH CHINA SEA

SILENT WATCHERS. Japanese macaques, or snow monkeys, cling to a rocky ledge on northern Honshu. Macaques live farther north than any other species of monkey. In winter they bathe in hot springs to stay warm. Japanese macaques are an endangered species.

Eastern Mediterranean

ANCIENT MYSTERY. A camel walks before El-Khazneh in Petra, a World Heritage site in Jordan. Carved out of the mountainside more than 2,500 years ago, Petra was the capital of the Nabateans.

This region forms a bridge between Europe and Asia, from the Caucasus Mountains to the desert lands of Jordan. Turkey, framed by the Black, Aegean, and Mediterranean Seas, leads the region in population and area. The historic and life-giving Tigris and Euphrates Rivers begin in Turkey and flow southeast through arid Syria and Iraq. Israel, Lebanon, and Syria share the Mediterranean shore. While Islam claims the majority of followers across these lands, Jewish, Christian, and other faiths are present. Indeed, the holiest places to Christians and Jews occupy Israeli soil in Jerusalem, adjacent to the third holiest site for Muslims, a situation that continues to cause tension and conflict.

THE BASICS

STATS

Largest country
Turkey 300,948 sq mi (779,452 sq km)

Smallest country
Lebanon 4,036 sq mi (10,452 sq km)

Most populous country
Turkey 74,885,000

Least populous country
Armenia 3,282,000

Predominant languages
Turkish, Arabic, Azeri, Hebrew, Armenian, Azerbaijani, Georgian, English, Kurdish

Predominant religions
Islam, Judaism, Christianity

Highest GDP per capita
Israel $31,500

Lowest GDP per capita
Syria $5,100

Highest life expectancy
Israel 81 years

Highest literacy rate
Armenia, Georgia, Azerbaijan 100%

GEO WHIZ

A 1.75-million-year-old skull recently discovered in the Republic of Georgia is forcing scientists to rethink humankind's first great migration.

Nagorno-Karabakh is an Armenian Christian enclave surrounded by Muslim Azerbaijan that has been the focus of bitter conflict between Armenians and Azeris for decades.

Mount Ararat, near Turkey's border with Iran and Armenia, is believed by some to be the resting place for the ark that—according to the Bible—Noah built to survive the great flood.

To capture Tyre, capital of ancient Phoenicia and now a port in Lebanon, Alexander the Great destroyed the mainland portion of the city, then used the rubble to build a causeway to the island fortress.

Israelis capture runoff from seasonal rains to support crops in the Negev, a desert region that extends across more than half their country.

WEST BANK & GAZA STRIP
Captured by Israel in the 1967 Six Day War, areas of the West Bank and Gaza have limited Palestinian self-rule under a 1993 peace agreement. The future for these areas and four million Palestinians is subject to Israeli-Palestinian negotiations.

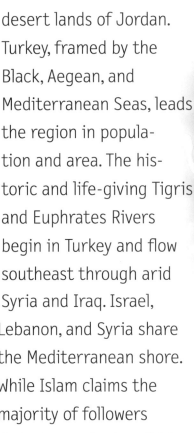

BELOW SEA LEVEL

sea level

Empire State Building

-1,385 ft (-422 m)   -1,250 ft (-381 m)

Dead Sea

Not every place with an elevation below sea level is under the ocean. The Dead Sea, in western Asia, plunges to -1,385 feet (-422 m) below sea level.

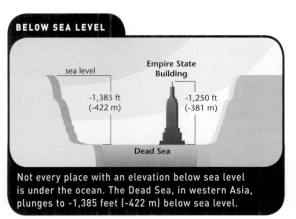

◑ WATCHERS FROM THE PAST. Giant stone heads, representing Greek gods, guard the first-century B.C. burial site of King Antiochus I in remote southeastern Turkey. Many of the heads have been toppled in this earthquake-prone region.

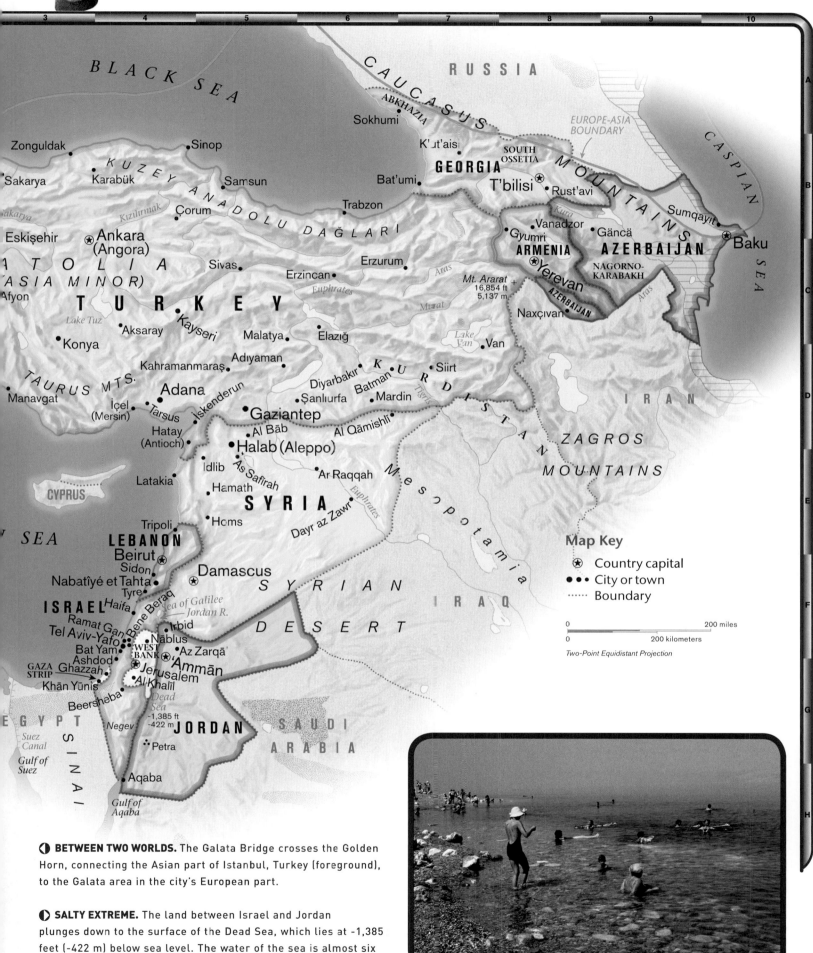

◑ BETWEEN TWO WORLDS. The Galata Bridge crosses the Golden Horn, connecting the Asian part of Istanbul, Turkey (foreground), to the Galata area in the city's European part.

◑ SALTY EXTREME. The land between Israel and Jordan plunges down to the surface of the Dead Sea, which lies at -1,385 feet (-422 m) below sea level. The water of the sea is almost six times saltier than the ocean.

Map Key
⊛ Country capital
••• City or town
····· Boundary

0   200 miles
0   200 kilometers
Two-Point Equidistant Projection

Southwest Asia

This region, made up largely of deserts and mountains, includes the countries of the Arabian Peninsula and those that border the Persian Gulf. Islam is the dominant religion in each, and the two holiest places for Muslims—Mecca and Medina—are here. Arabic is the principal language everywhere but Iran, where most people speak Farsi. While water has been the most important natural resource here for millennia, global attention has focused in recent decades on the region's oil wealth. With the majority of the world's reserves found here, oil has brought outside influences and military conflict. Long a cradle of civilization, Southwest Asia continues to hold the world's attention.

🌐 **GIRL TALK.** Young Iranian girls get together at a film festival in Tehran. The scarves they are wearing are part of the Islamic dress code, hijab, which says that women and girls must cover their heads and dress modestly.

🌐 **HE'S GOT THE BEAT.** This Omani drummer plays at a dance in the Arabian Sea port of Qurayyat. Though modernizing in many ways, Oman works hard to preserve its traditional culture.

◖ **DIFFERENT WORLDS.** This roadside meeting in Qatar displays a contrast between horse and horsepower and that of traditional Arab and Western clothing styles. This Persian Gulf country preserves a rich history of Arabian horse breeding and continues to produce champions.

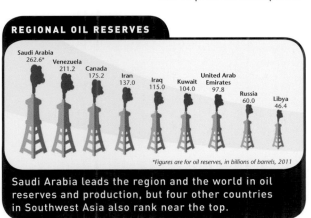

REGIONAL OIL RESERVES

Saudi Arabia
262.6*

Venezuela
211.2

Canada
175.2

Iran
137.0

Iraq
115.0

Kuwait
104.0

United Arab
Emirates
97.8

Russia
60.0

Libya
46.4

*Figures are for oil reserves, in billions of barrels, 2011

Saudi Arabia leads the region and the world in oil reserves and production, but four other countries in Southwest Asia also rank near the top.

LOST AND FOUND. Thousands of treasures dating from ancient Mesopotamia were destroyed, lost, or stolen during the invasion of Iraq in April 2003. This ring is among the few items recovered.

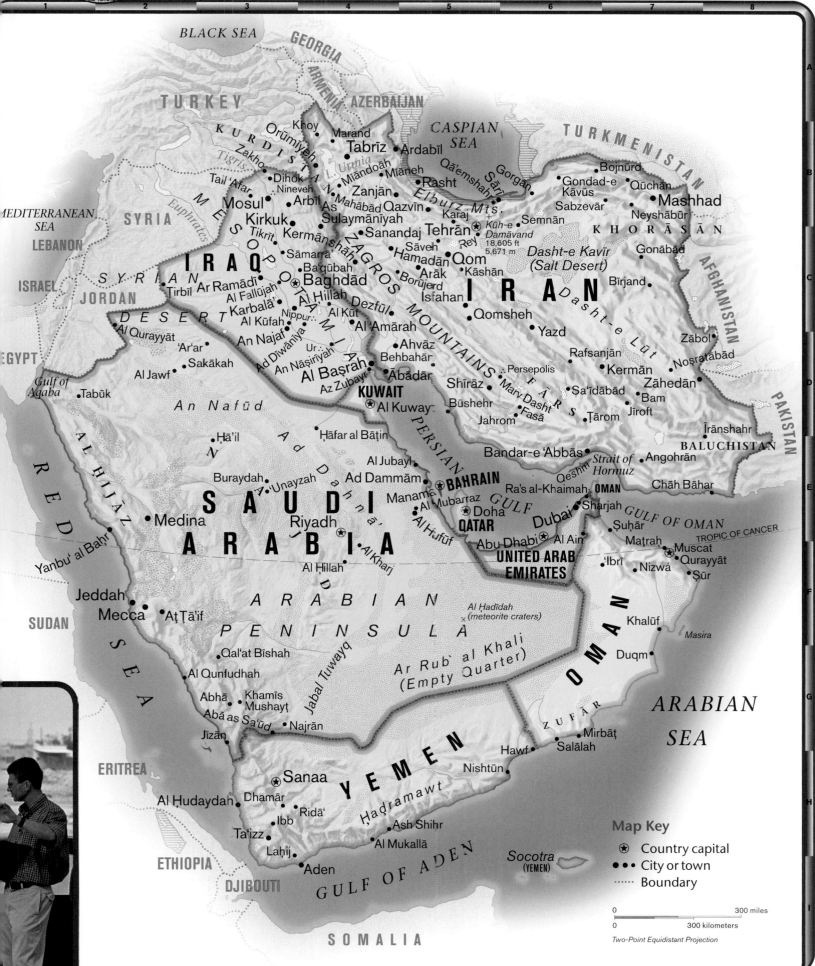

BLACK SEA

GEORGIA

ARMENIA

AZERBAIJAN

TURKEY

TURKMENISTAN

CASPIAN SEA

Khoy
Orūmīyeh
Marand
Tabrīz
Ardabīl
Qā'emshahr
Gorgān
Sārī
Bojnūrd
Qūchān
Mashhad

KURDISTĀN

Zakho
Dihōk
Nineveh
Miāndoāb
Miāneh
Rasht
Gondad-e Kāvūs
Sabzevār
Neyshābūr

Tail 'Afar
Zanjān
Elburz Mts.
Karaj
Semnān
KHORĀSĀN

Mosul
Arbīl
As Sulaymānīyah
Qazvīn
Tehrān
Kūh-e Damāvand 18,605 ft 5,671 m
Gonābād

Kirkuk
Kermānshāh
Sanandaj
Rey
Dasht-e Kavīr (Salt Desert)

Tikrīt
Sāmarrā'
Hamadān
Qom
Kāshān
Bīrjand

IRAQ
MESOPOTAMIA
Ba'qūbah
Baghdad
Sāveh
Arāk
Qomsheh

SYRIA

MEDITERRANEAN SEA

LEBANON

ISRAEL

JORDAN

EGYPT

Tirbīl
Ar Ramādī
Al Fallūjah
Al Hillah
Dezfūl
Isfahan
Zābol
Noṣratābād

Karbalā'
Nippur
Al Kūfah
Al Kūt
Al 'Amārah
Yazd

DESERT
Al Qurayyāt
An Najaf
Ad Dīwānīya
Ur
Ahvāz
Behbahār
Rafsanjān
Kermān
Zāhedān

'Ar'ar
Sakākah
An Nāṣirīyah
Al Başrah
Ābādar
Shīrāz
Persepolis
Marv Dasht
Sa'īdābād
Bam
Jīroft

Al Jawf
Az Zubayr
KUWAIT
Būshehr
Jahrom
Fasā
Ṭārom

An Nafūd
Al Kuway
Bandar-e 'Abbās
Īrānshahr

Tabūk
Ḥā'il
Ḥafar al Bāṭin
Angohrān
BALUCHISTAN

Gulf of Aqaba

Buraydah
'Unayzah
Al Jubayl
Ad Dammām
Ra's al-Khaimah
OMAN
Chāh Bāhar

Medina
Riyadh
Manama
Al Mubarraz
Doha
Dubai
Sharjah
GULF OF OMAN

SAUDI ARABIA
Al Hufūf
QATAR
Abu Dhabi
Al Ain
Ṣuḥār
Maṭrah
TROPIC OF CANCER
Muscat

Al Hillah
Al Kharj
UNITED ARAB EMIRATES
'Ibrī
Nizwá
Qurayyāt
Ṣūr

PERSIAN GULF
BAHRAIN

Jeddah
Mecca
Aṭ Ṭā'if
ARABIAN PENINSULA
Al Ḥadīdah x (meteorite craters)
Khalūf
Masira

AL ḤIJĀZ
RED SEA

Qal'at Bīshah
Jabal Tuwayq
Ar Rub' al Khali (Empty Quarter)
OMAN
Duqm

Al Qunfudhah

SUDAN

Abhā
Khamīs Mushayṭ
Abā as Sa'ūd
Najrān
ZUFĀR

Jīzan
YEMEN
Mirbāṭ
Salālah
Hawf
ARABIAN SEA

ERITREA
Sanaa
Nishtūn

Dhamār
Ḥaḍramawt

Al Hudaydah
Ridā'
Ash Shihr

Ibb
Al Mukallā

Ta'izz
Lahij

ETHIOPIA
Aden
Socotra (YEMEN)
GULF OF ADEN

DJIBOUTI

SOMALIA

Map Key
⊛ Country capital
••• City or town
······ Boundary

0 ———— 300 miles
0 ———— 300 kilometers

Two-Point Equidistant Projection

THE CONTINENT:
ASIA

STATS

Largest country
India 1,269,221 sq mi (3,287,270 sq km)

Smallest country
Maldives 115 sq mi (298 sq km)

Most populous country
India 1,259,721,000

Least populous country
Maldives 331,000

Predominant languages
Hindi, English, Punjabi, Bangla, Dari, Burmese, Pashtu, Urdu, Sinhala, Nepali, Dzongkha

Predominant religions
Hindu, Islam, Buddhism

Highest GDP per capita
Maldives $8,600

Lowest GDP per capita
Afghanistan $1,000

Highest life expectancy
Sri Lanka 76 years

Highest literacy rate
Maldives
94%

GEO WHIZ

India's rail system transports four billion passengers each year across nearly 38,000 miles (61,155 km) of track.

Bhutan, a Himalayan country known as Land of the Thunder Dragon, is the world's only Buddhist kingdom.

Nepal has the only national flag that is not a rectangle or a square. Its shape evokes the high Himalayan peaks that dominate its landscape (see page 172).

The mountains of the Hindu Kush in northeastern Afghanistan have been a source of rubies, silver, and other mineral wealth for thousands of years. The lapis lazuli that adorns the golden funeral mask of Egypt's King Tutankhamun was mined in this region.

Beaches along the southern and western coasts of Sri Lanka are nesting sites for five species of endangered sea turtle. The December 2004 tsunami wiped out several hatcheries, but the devastation has not kept the turtles from returning to their nesting areas.

South Asia

This region is home to the world's highest peaks, and three of the world's storied rivers—the Indus, Ganges, and Brahmaputra—support the hundreds of millions of people

who live here. India is at the center, with greater area than the other countries combined and three times their population. Born in India, Hinduism and Buddhism were spread to other places by traders, teachers, and priests. Muslims form the majority in Afghanistan, Pakistan, and Bangladesh, whereas there are large numbers of Buddhists in Bhutan, Nepal, Sri Lanka, and Myanmar. Poverty and prosperity live side by side across the region, with streams of migrants flowing from rural areas to mushrooming cities.

⬣ **TAJ MAHAL.** In 1631 in Agra, India, the Mughal emperor Shah Jehan began construction of this magnificent marble memorial to his deceased wife.

◗ **TOP OF THE WORLD.** Climbers make their way through Nepal's treacherous Khumbu Icefall on their approach to Mount Everest.

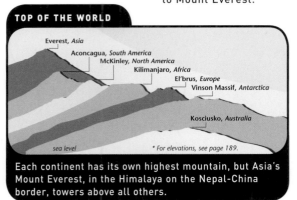

TOP OF THE WORLD

Everest, *Asia*
Aconcagua, *South America*
McKinley, *North America*
Kilimanjaro, *Africa*
El'brus, *Europe*
Vinson Massif, *Antarctica*
Kosciusko, *Australia*
sea level   * For elevations, see page 189.

Each continent has its own highest mountain, but Asia's Mount Everest, in the Himalaya on the Nepal-China border, towers above all others.

◐ EASTERN BELIEF. The god Shiva is part of the Hindu trinity, which also includes the gods Brahma and Vishnu. With more than 900 million followers, Hinduism is the world's third largest religion, after Christianity and Islam.

2 3 4 5 6 7 8 9

Map Key
- ⊛ Country capital
- ••• City or town
- ······ Boundary

0 — 300 miles
0 — 300 kilometers
Two-Point Projection

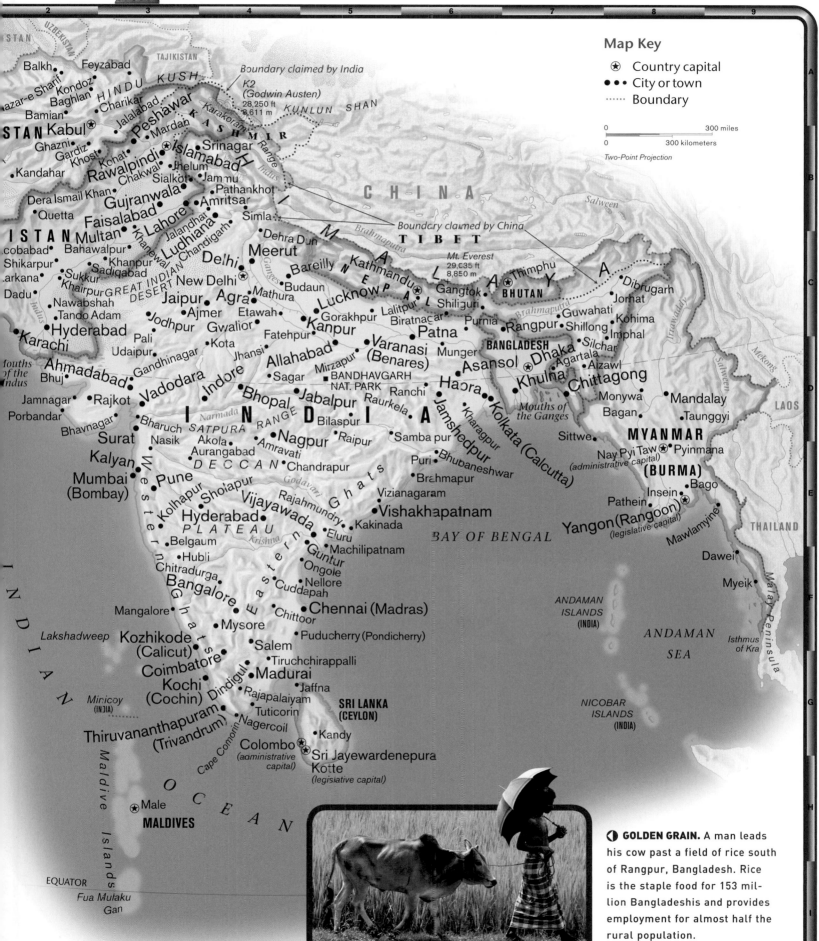

UZBEKISTAN
TAJIKISTAN

Balkh
Feyzabad
Mazar-e Sharif
Kondoz
Baghlan
Charikar
Bamian
Jalalabad
HINDU KUSH
Peshawar
Mardan
STAN Kabul ⊛
Ghazni
Gardiz
Khost
Kohat
Chakwal
Rawalpindi
Islamabad ⊛
Srinagar
Kandahar
KASHMIR
Jammu
Pathankot
Sialkot
Jhelum

Boundary claimed by India
K2
(Godwin Austen)
28,250 ft
8,611 m
KARAKORAM Range
KUNLUN SHAN
Indus
Salween

CHINA

Dera Ismail Khan
Gujranwala
Amritsar
Quetta
Faisalabad
Lahore
Jalandhar
Simla
ISTAN Multan
Khanewal
Ludhiana
Chandigarh
Dehra Dun
cobabad
Bahawalpur
Khanpur
Sadiqabad
Meerut
Shikarpur
Sukkur
GREAT INDIAN New Delhi ⊛
arkana
Khairpur **DESERT**
Delhi
Dadu
Nawabshah
Jaipur
Agra
Tando Adam
Ajmer
Etawah
Hyderabad
Jodhpur
Gwalior
Pali
Kota
Fatehpur
Karachi
Udaipur
Gandhinagar
Jhansi
Kanpur
Mathura
Budaun
Lucknow
NEPAL
Kathmandu ⊛
Gangtok
Boundary claimed by China
TIBET
Mt. Everest
29,035 ft
8,850 m
Thimphu ⊛
BHUTAN
Dibrugarh
Jorhat
Shiliguri
Biratnagar
Gorakhpur
Lalitpur
Purnia
Guwahati
Kohima
Shillong
Imphal
Brahmaputra

Mouths
of the
Indus
Ahmadabad
Bhuj
Allahabad
Varanasi
(Benares)
Patna
Munger
Rangpur
Silchar
Aizawl
Mirzapur
BANGLADESH
Dhaka ⊛
Agartala
Jamnagar
Rajkot
INDIA
Sagar
BANDHAVGARH NAT. PARK
Asansol
Haora
Khulna
Chittagong
Porbandar
Vadodara
Indore
Bhopal
Jabalpur
Raurkela
Ranchi
Kolkata (Calcutta)
Monywa
Mandalay
Bhavnagar
Bharuch
Bilaspur
Jamshedpur
Kharagpur
Mouths of the Ganges
Bagan
Taunggyi
LAOS
Narmada
SATPURA RANGE
Nagpur
Raipur
Samba pur
Surat
Nasik
Akola
Amravati
Chandrapur
Puri
Bhubaneshwar
Sittwe
MYANMAR
Kalyan
Aurangabad
DECCAN
Brahmapur
(BURMA)
Mumbai (Bombay)
Pune
Vijayawada
Rajahmundry
Vizianagaram
Nay Pyi Taw ⊛ Pyinmana
(administrative capital)
Kolhapur
Sholapur
PLATEAU
Eluru
Vishakhapatnam
Insein
Bago
Hyderabad
Belgaum
Krishna
Kakinada
Yangon (Rangoon)
(legislative capital)
Pathein
Hubli
Guntur
Machilipatnam
BAY OF BENGAL
Mawlamyine
THAILAND
Chitradurga
Ongole
Bangalore
Cuddapah
Nellore
Dawei
Mangalore
Chennai (Madras)
Chittoor
Mysore
ANDAMAN ISLANDS (INDIA)
Myeik
Malay Peninsula
Kozhikode
(Calicut)
Salem
Puducherry (Pondicherry)
ANDAMAN SEA
Isthmus of Kra
Coimbatore
Tiruchchirappalli
Kochi
(Cochin)
Dindigul
Madurai
Lakshadweep (INDIA)
Rajapalaiyam
Jaffna
NICOBAR ISLANDS (INDIA)
Thiruvananthapuram
(Trivandrum)
Tuticorin
SRI LANKA (CEYLON)
Miricoy (INDIA)
Nagercoil
Kandy
INDIAN
Cape Comorin
Colombo
(administrative capital)
Sri Jayewardenepura Kotte
(legislative capital)

⊛ Male
MALDIVES
OCEAN
Maldive Islands

EQUATOR
Fua Mulaku
Gan

◐ GOLDEN GRAIN. A man leads his cow past a field of rice south of Rangpur, Bangladesh. Rice is the staple food for 153 million Bangladeshis and provides employment for almost half the rural population.

Largest country
Thailand 198,115 sq mi (513,115 sq km)

Smallest country
Singapore 255 sq mi (660 sq km)

Most populous country
Philippines 96,218,000

Least populous country
Brunei 413,000

Predominant languages
Filipino (based on Tagalog),
English, Vietnamese, Thai,
Khmer, Lao, French, Malay,
Bahasa Melayu, Mandarin

Predominant religions
Christianity, Buddhism, Islam

Highest GDP per capita
Singapore $59,700

Lowest GDP per capita
Cambodia $2,200

Highest life expectancy
Singapore 84 years

Highest literacy rate
Vietnam
94%

GEO WHIZ

Cambodia's Mekong Fish Conservation Project pays fishermen more than the market price to release any giant fish they catch. This includes catfish as long as 10 feet (3 m) weighing up to 600 pounds (270 kg).

The Philippines has one of the highest rates of deforestation in the world. Based on the current rate of removal, studies estimate that the country's virgin forests are in danger of disappearing as soon as 2025.

The Cathedral of Notre Dame in Ho Chi Minh City, capital of predominantly Buddhist Vietnam, was built in the late 1800s during French colonial times, when the city was named Saigon.

The Plain of Jars, in northern Laos, takes its name from hundreds of huge stone urns spread across the ground. Archaeologists believe the jars were made by Bronze Age people who used them to hold the cremated remains of their dead.

Thailand means "Land of the Free." It is the only country in Southeast Asia that has never been ruled by a colonial power.

Singapore is a melting pot of cultures. Its name comes from the Sanskrit *Singha Pura* (Lion City), its national anthem is sung in Malay, and English is the lingua franca.

Southeast Asia

The countries of Southeast Asia have long been influenced by neighboring giants India and China. The result is a dazzling mix of cultures, rich histories, terrible conflicts, and future promise. Cambodia's spectacular 12th-century Angkor Wat provides a glimpse of former greatness. Colonial rule brought division and change, and struggles for independence took a heavy toll, as in Vietnam. Mainland countries are largely Buddhist, whereas peninsular Malaysia is mostly Muslim, and Christians dominate the Philippines. All but Laos have ocean access, with fisheries providing jobs and food for millions. Rivers like the Chao Phraya and the mighty Mekong provide transport and water-rich croplands dominated by rice growing. Tiny Singapore has gained global importance with its bustling port operations and high-tech focus.

⬤ **SMILING BUDDHA.** A Buddhist monk admires a sculpture on a temple wall near Siem Reap, Cambodia. Built between A.D. 800 and 1200 by the Khmer, Angkor Wat includes Buddhist and Hindu temples.

⬤ **WILLING WORKER.** Smaller and more easily tamed than the African variety, Asian elephants have been a part of the workforce for centuries. They are found from India to Indonesia.

◗ **SHIPPING HUB.** Huge container terminals, such as this one at Tanjong Pagar, make Singapore the world's busiest trans-shipment center, moving about one-seventh of the world's containers.

◀ **FLASHY RIDE.** Colorful Philippine taxis, called jeepneys, are a common sight on the streets of Manila. Originally rebuilt WWII jeeps, these wildly decorated vehicles offer inexpensive, but crowded, transportation.

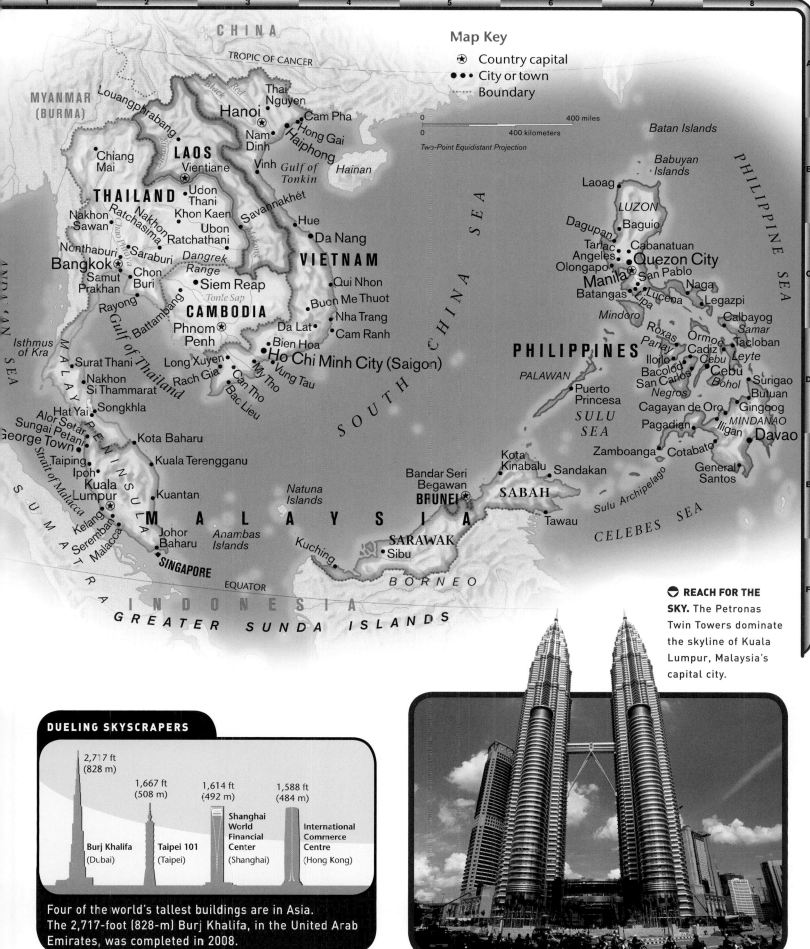

CHINA

TROPIC OF CANCER

Map Key
★ Country capital
●●● City or town
---- Boundary

0   400 miles
0   400 kilometers
Two-Point Equidistant Projection

MYANMAR (BURMA)

Louangphrabang

Black   Red

Thai Nguyen
Hanoi ★
Cam Pha
Nam Dinh
Hong Gai
Haiphong
Vinh   Gulf of Tonkin
Hainan
Batan Islands

LAOS
Vientiane ★

Chiang Mai

THAILAND
Udon Thani
Khon Kaen
Savannakhet

Nakhon Sawan
Ratchasima
Nakhon Ratchasima
Ubon Ratchathani
Hue
Da Nang

Nonthaburi
Chao Phraya
Saraburi
Dangrek Range
Mekong
VIETNAM

Bangkok ★
Samut Prakhan
Chon Buri
Siem Reap
Tonle Sap
Qui Nhon
Buon Me Thuot

Rayong
CAMBODIA
Battambang
Nha Trang
Da Lat
Cam Ranh
Phnom Penh ★
Bien Hoa

Isthmus of Kra
Surat Thani
Long Xuyen
Ho Chi Minh City (Saigon)
My Tho
Vung Tau

Nakhon Si Thammarat
Rach Gia
Can Tho
Bac Lieu

Hat Yai
Songkhla
Kota Baharu

Alor Setar
Sungai Petani
George Town
Kuala Terengganu

Taiping
Ipoh
Kuantan

Kuala Lumpur
MALAYSIA

Kelang
Seremban
Malacca
Johor Baharu
Anambas Islands
Kuching
Sibu
SARAWAK

SINGAPORE

EQUATOR

SUMATRA
INDONESIA
GREATER SUNDA ISLANDS

Natuna Islands

BORNEO

Bandar Seri Begawan ★
BRUNEI
SABAH
Tawau
Kota Kinabalu
Sandakan

SOUTH CHINA SEA

PHILIPPINE SEA

Babuyan Islands
Laoag
LUZON
Dagupan
Baguio
Tarlac
Cabanatuan
Angeles
Quezon City
Olongapo
San Pablo
Manila ★
Naga
Batangas
Lucena
Lipa
Legazpi

Mindoro
Calbayog
Samar
Roxas
Panay
Ormoc
Tacloban
Iloilo
Cadiz
Cebu
Leyte
Bacolod
San Carlos
Cebu
Negros
Bohol
Surigao
Butuan
PALAWAN
Cagayan de Oro
Gingoog
Puerto Princesa
MINDANAO
Iligan
Pagadian
Davao

PHILIPPINES

SULU SEA
Zamboanga
Cotabato
General Santos

Sulu Archipelago

CELEBES SEA

MALAY PENINSULA
Gulf of Thailand
ANDAMAN SEA
Strait of Malacca

◆ **REACH FOR THE SKY.** The Petronas Twin Towers dominate the skyline of Kuala Lumpur, Malaysia's capital city.

DUELING SKYSCRAPERS

2,717 ft (828 m) — Burj Khalifa (Dubai)
1,667 ft (508 m) — Taipei 101 (Taipei)
1,614 ft (492 m) — Shanghai World Financial Center (Shanghai)
1,588 ft (484 m) — International Commerce Centre (Hong Kong)

Four of the world's tallest buildings are in Asia. The 2,717-foot (828-m) Burj Khalifa, in the United Arab Emirates, was completed in 2008.

THE BASICS

STATS

Largest country
Indonesia 742,308 sq mi (1,922,570 sq km)

Smallest country
Timor-Leste 5,640 sq mi (14,609 sq km)

Most populous country
Indonesia 240,990,000

Least populous country
Timor-Leste 1,126,000

Predominant languages
Indonesian, English, Dutch, Javanese, Tetum, Portuguese

Predominant religions
Islam, Christianity

Highest GDP per capita
Timor-Leste $8,700

Lowest GDP per capita
Indonesia $4,700

Highest life expectancy
Indonesia 72 years

Highest literacy rate
Indonesia
90%

GEO WHIZ

Two species of sharks that use their fins to "walk" on coral reefs were discovered off the northwestern coast of Indonesia's Papua province in 2006. Scientists believe they might be similar to the first vertebrates that moved from sea to land.

In an effort to reduce crowding on Java, the government adopted a program of relocating landless people to more remote islands, a policy that has created tensions and that led to Timor-Leste's independence in 2002.

With a length of 10 feet (3 m) and a weight of more than 300 pounds (135 kg), the Komodo dragon is Earth's heaviest lizard. This meat eater lives only on Indonesia's Lesser Sunda Islands, where it eats all types of prey—including people sometimes!

When seen from the air, Timor Island resembles a crocodile. According to local legend, a crocodile turned itself into the island as a way of saying thank you to a boy who saved its life.

In December 2004 an earthquake off the coast of Sumatra, measuring 9.1 on the Richter scale, triggered a massive tsunami that killed hundreds of thousands of people and left millions homeless in countries around the Indian Ocean, from Indonesia to Africa's east coast.

Indonesia & Timor-Leste

Stretching more than 2,200 miles (3,520 km) from Sumatra to New Guinea, Indonesia is the world's largest island nation and the fourth most populous country. Most of its 241 million people live on the volcanically active island of Java. Indonesia shares rainforested Borneo with Malaysia and Brunei. Most Indonesians are of Malay ethnicity, though there are large numbers of Melanesians, Chinese, and East Indians. Arab traders brought Islam to the islands in the 13th century, and today six of seven Indonesians are Muslim. Timor-Leste gained independence from Indonesia in 2002. It and the Philippines are Asia's only predominantly Catholic countries.

◆ NEWLY INDEPENDENT.
A young boy smiles broadly as he waves Timor-Leste's flag in Dili, the capital city. The country is also known as East Timor.

◑ CITY ON THE MOVE.
Skyscrapers and a busy freeway are just one face of Jakarta, Indonesia. In this city of almost 10 million people—national capital and center of trade and industry—the modern and traditional, the rich and poor, live side by side. Just like Indonesia as a whole, the city has a very diverse population.

◗ **SPIRIT WORLD.** Hand-carved masks, such as this one from Bali, Indonesia, were probably first created for traditional dance and storytelling rituals. Later, they incorporated Hindu and Islamic beliefs as well.

◗ **GIANT APE.** An adult male Borneo orangutan peers through the forest foliage. An endangered species, orangutans are found only on Sumatra and Borneo. They are the largest tree-living mammals in the world.

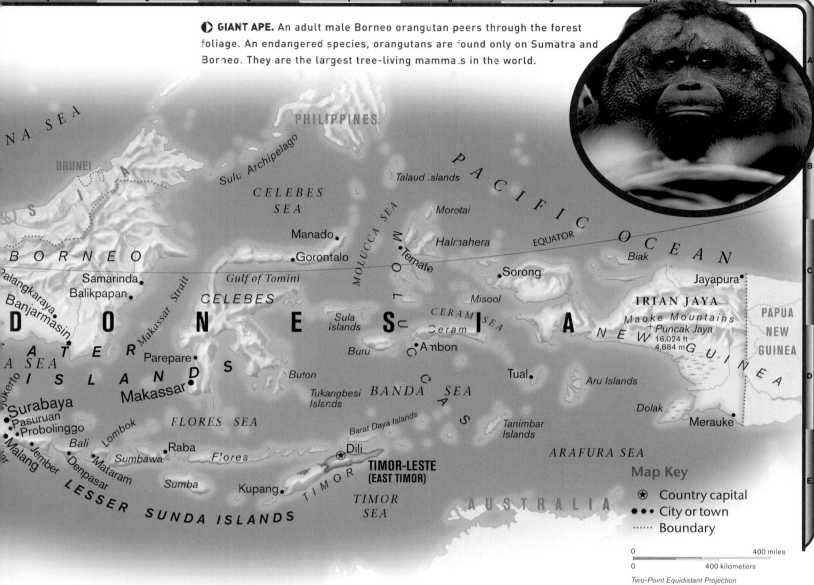

Map Key

⊛ Country capital
••• City or town
······ Boundary

0 ——————— 400 miles
0 ——————— 400 kilometers

Two-Point Equidistant Projection

FOLLOWERS OF ISLAM

Country	Followers (millions)
Indonesia	204.8*
Pakistan	178.1
India	177.3
Bangladesh	148.6
Egypt	80.0
Nigeria	75.7
Iran	74.8
Turkey	74.7
Algeria	34.8
Morocco	32.4

*Figures are in millions, 2010 data

Islam's origins trace to southwestern Asia, but the religion has spread around the world. The country with the largest Muslim population is Indonesia.

◗ **GENETIC STOREHOUSE.** About 75 percent of Indonesia's Kalimantan Province in eastern Borneo remains covered in rain forest that is home to 221 different types of mammals and 450 different species of birds. The forest and its inhabitants are at risk due to widespread logging and mining.

THE CONTINENT:
AFRICA

PHYSICAL

Land area	Lowest point	Largest lake
11,608,000 sq mi	Lake Assal, Djibouti	Victoria
(30,065,000 sq km)	-512 ft (-156 m)	26,800 sq mi (69,500 sq km)
Highest point	Longest river	
Kilimanjaro, Tanzania	Nile	
19,340 ft (5,895 m)	4,241 mi (6,825 km)	

POLITICAL

Population	Largest metropolitan area	Economy
1,061,224,000	Cairo, Egypt	Farming: fruit, grains
Largest country	Pop. 10,902,000	Industry: chemicals,
Algeria	Most densely populated country	mining, cement
919,595 sq mi	Mauritius	Services
(2,381,741 sq km)	1,638 people per sq mi (630 per sq km)	

Africa

Africa

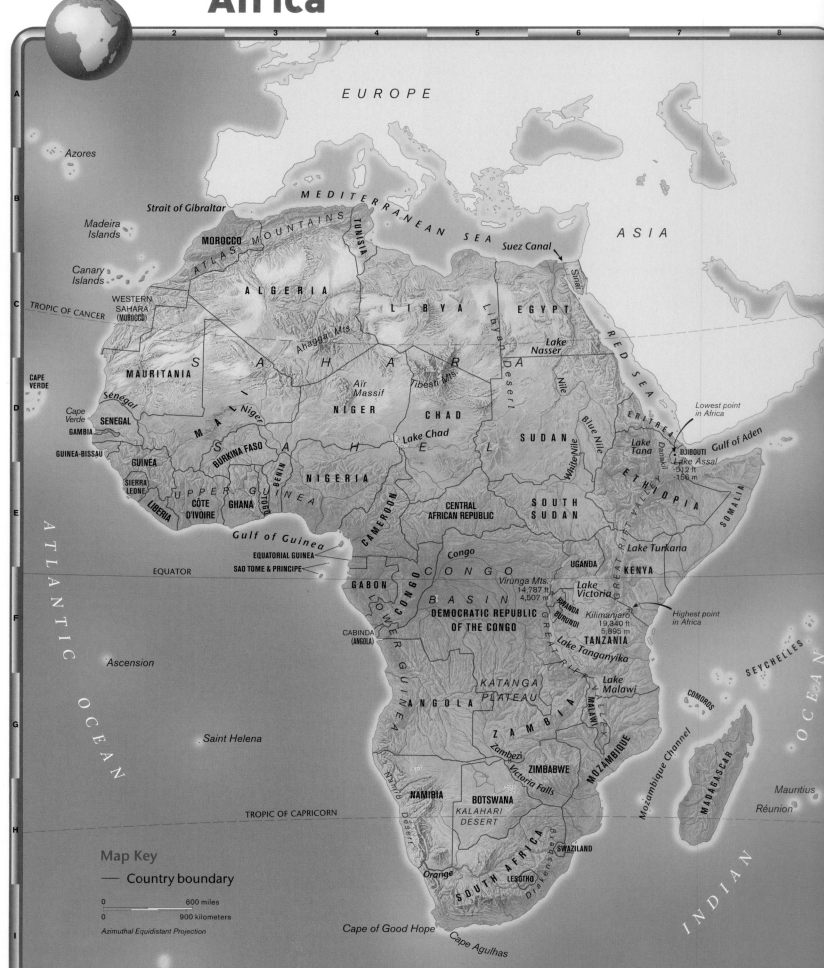

EUROPE

MEDITERRANEAN SEA

ASIA

Azores

Madeira Islands

Strait of Gibraltar

MOROCCO

ATLAS MOUNTAINS

TUNISIA

Suez Canal

Canary Islands

WESTERN SAHARA (MOROCCO)

ALGERIA

LIBYA

EGYPT

Sinai

RED SEA

TROPIC OF CANCER

CAPE VERDE

MAURITANIA

S   A   H   A   R   A

Ahaggar Mts.

Libyan Desert

Lake Nasser

Lowest point in Africa

Cape Verde

Senegal

M
A
L
I

Niger

Aïr Massif

Tibesti Mts.

NIGER

CHAD

Nile

Blue Nile

ERITREA

Gulf of Aden

SENEGAL

GAMBIA

GUINEA-BISSAU

GUINEA

BURKINA FASO

S
A
H
E
L

Lake Chad

SUDAN

White Nile

Lake Tana

DJIBOUTI
Lake Assal
-512 ft
-156 m

Danakil

SIERRA LEONE

LIBERIA

UPPER GUINEA

CÔTE D'IVOIRE

GHANA

BENIN

TOGO

NIGERIA

CAMEROON

CENTRAL AFRICAN REPUBLIC

SOUTH SUDAN

ETHIOPIA

SOMALIA

Gulf of Guinea

EQUATORIAL GUINEA

SAO TOME & PRINCIPE

EQUATOR

GABON

Congo

CONGO

Virunga Mts.
14,787 ft
4,507 m

UGANDA

Lake Turkana

KENYA

Lake Victoria

RWANDA

BURUNDI

ATLANTIC OCEAN

Ascension

LOWER GUINEA

DEMOCRATIC REPUBLIC OF THE CONGO

B A S I N

CONGO

Kilimanjaro
19,340 ft
5,895 m

Highest point in Africa

CABINDA (ANGOLA)

GREAT RIFT VALLEY

TANZANIA

Lake Tanganyika

SEYCHELLES

Saint Helena

KATANGA PLATEAU

Lake Malawi

COMOROS

ANGOLA

ZAMBIA

MALAWI

MOZAMBIQUE

Mozambique Channel

MADAGASCAR

INDIAN OCEAN

Zambezi

Victoria Falls

ZIMBABWE

Mauritius

Réunion

TROPIC OF CAPRICORN

NAMIBIA

Namib Desert

BOTSWANA

KALAHARI DESERT

SWAZILAND

Map Key

— Country boundary

0   600 miles
0   900 kilometers

Azimuthal Equidistant Projection

Orange

SOUTH AFRICA

LESOTHO

Drakensberg

Cape of Good Hope

Cape Agulhas

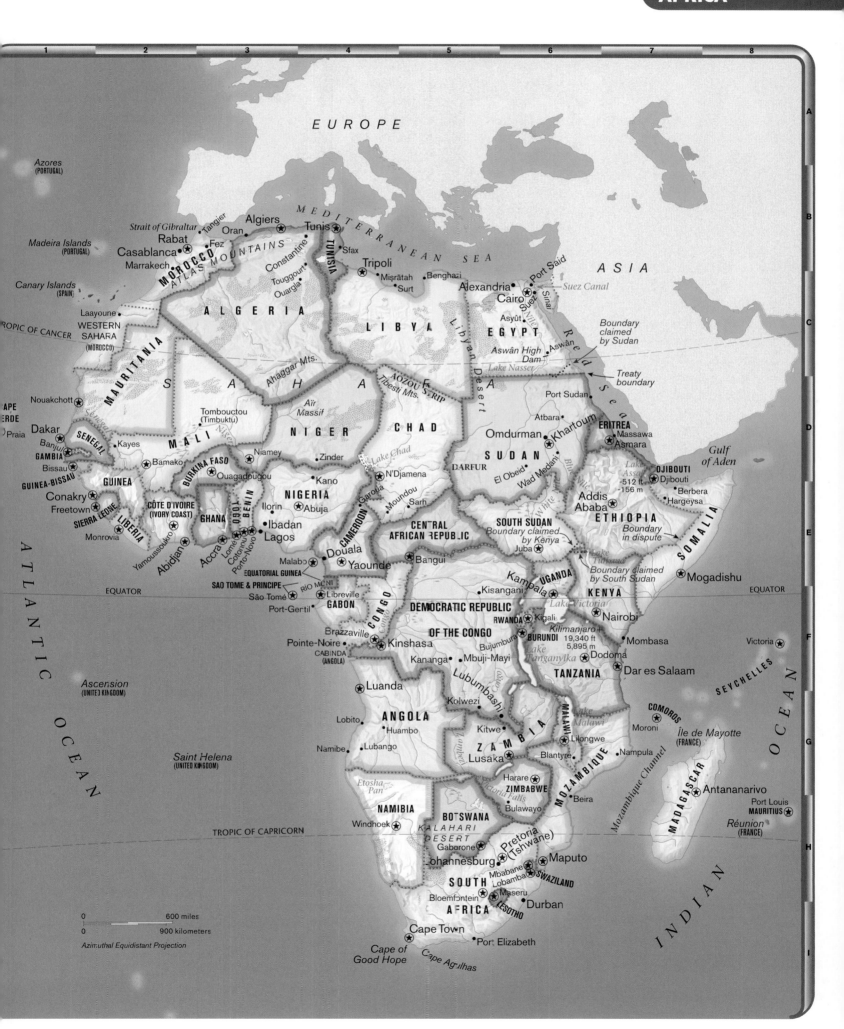

EUROPE

Azores
(PORTUGAL)

Madeira Islands
(PORTUGAL)

Canary Islands
(SPAIN)

ROPIC OF CANCER

CAPE
VERDE
• Praia

MEDITERRANEAN SEA

Strait of Gibraltar
• Tangier
Oran
Algiers ⭐
Tunis ⭐
Rabat ⭐ • Fez
Casablanca •
Marrakech •
MOROCCO
ATLAS MOUNTAINS
Constantine •
TUNISIA
• Sfax
Tripoli ⭐
• Mişrātah
• Surt
Benghazi •

ASIA

Port Said •
Alexandria •
Cairo ⭐ • Suez
Suez Canal
Asyût •
Sinai

Laayoune •
WESTERN
SAHARA
(MOROCCO)

ALGERIA

LIBYA

EGYPT

Aswân High
Dam • • Aswân
Lake Nasser

Boundary
claimed
by Sudan

Treaty
boundary

MAURITANIA
Nouakchott •

S   A   H   A
Ahaggar Mts.
Tibesti Mts.
AOZOU STRIP

R   A

Libyan Desert

Port Sudan •
Atbara •

Red Sea

ERITREA
• Massawa
Asmara ⭐

Gulf
of Aden

Dakar ⭐
Banjul ⭐
GAMBIA
Bissau ⭐
GUINEA-BISSAU

SENEGAL
Kayes •

MALI
Bamako •

Aïr
Massif
Tombouctou •
(Timbuktu)
Niamey ⭐
NIGER
• Zinder

N'Djamena ⭐
Lake Chad

CHAD

DARFUR

Omdurman •
El Obeid •

SUDAN
• Khartoum
Wad Medani •

Lake
Assal
-512 ft
-156 m
DJIBOUTI
Djibouti ⭐
• Berbera
Hargeysa •

Conakry ⭐
Freetown •
GUINEA
SIERRA LEONE
Monrovia •
LIBERIA

BURKINA FASO
Ouagadougou ⭐
• Kano
Garoua •
CÔTE D'IVOIRE
(IVORY COAST)
GHANA
Yamoussoukro ⭐
Abidjan •
Accra
TOGO BENIN
Lomé
Cotonou
Porto-Novo
Malabo •

Ilorin •
NIGERIA
Abuja ⭐
• Ibadan
Lagos •
CAMEROON
Douala •
Yaounde ⭐

Moundou •
Sarh •

CENTRAL
AFRICAN REPUBLIC
Bangui ⭐

White Nile
Blue Nile

Addis
Ababa ⭐

ETHIOPIA

SOMALIA

Boundary
in dispute

⭐ Mogadishu

EQUATORIAL GUINEA
SAO TOME & PRINCIPE
São Tomé ⭐
Port-Gentil •
RIO MUNI
• Libreville ⭐
GABON

SOUTH SUDAN
Boundary claimed
by Kenya
Juba ⭐

Kampala ⭐
Kisangani •
UGANDA
Lake Victoria

Boundary claimed
by South Sudan
Lake
Turkana

EQUATOR

KENYA
Nairobi ⭐

Mogadishu

EQUATOR

CONGO
Brazzaville ⭐
Pointe-Noire •
CABINDA
(ANGOLA)

Congo

DEMOCRATIC REPUBLIC
OF THE CONGO
RWANDA Kigali ⭐
BURUNDI ⭐
Bujumbura
Kananga •
Mbuji-Mayi •
Kinshasa ⭐

Kilimanjaro +
19,340 ft
5,895 m
• Mombasa

Dodoma ⭐
TANZANIA
Dar es Salaam •

Victoria ⭐
SEYCHELLES

ATLANTIC OCEAN

Ascension
(UNITED KINGDOM)

Saint Helena
(UNITED KINGDOM)

Luanda ⭐
Kolwezi •
Lobito •
ANGOLA
Huambo •
Namibe • Lubango •

Lubumbashi •
Kitwe •
Z A M B I A
Lusaka ⭐
Harare ⭐

Lake
Tanganyika

MALAWI
Lilongwe ⭐
Lake
Malawi
Blantyre •
Zambezi
MOZAMBIQUE

COMOROS
Moroni •

Île de Mayotte
(FRANCE)

INDIAN OCEAN

Nampula •

TROPIC OF CAPRICORN

ZIMBABWE
Victoria Falls
Bulawayo •
Beira •

Mozambique Channel

MADAGASCAR
Antananarivo ⭐
Port Louis
MAURITIUS ⭐
Réunion
(FRANCE)

NAMIBIA
Windhoek ⭐

Etosha
Pan

BOTSWANA
KALAHARI
DESERT
Gaborone ⭐

Pretoria ⭐
(Tshwane)
Johannesburg •
Mbabane ⭐
SWAZILAND
Lobamba
Maputo ⭐

SOUTH
AFRICA
Bloemfontein ⭐
Maseru ⭐
LESOTHO
• Durban

Cape Town ⭐
• Port Elizabeth
Cape of
Good Hope
Cape Agulhas

0   600 miles
0   900 kilometers
Azimuthal Equidistant Projection

Africa

A COMPLEX GIANT

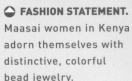

Africa spans nearly as far west to east as it does north to south. The Sahara—the world's largest desert—covers Africa's northern third, while to the south lie bands of grassland, tropical rain forest, and more desert. The East African Rift system marks where shifting plates are splitting off the continent's edge. Africa has a wealth of cultures, speaking some 1,600 languages—more than on any other continent. Though the continent is still largely rural, Africans increasingly migrate to booming cities like Cairo, Lagos, and Johannesburg. While rich in natural resources, from oil and coal to gemstones and precious metals, Africa is the poorest continent, long plagued by outside interference, corruption, and disease.

⬤ **FASHION STATEMENT.** Maasai women in Kenya adorn themselves with distinctive, colorful bead jewelry.

⬤ **CHARGE!** Sensing danger, an African elephant charges. The world's largest land mammal, African elephants are at risk due to poaching and loss of habitat.

⬤ **COLORFUL NEIGHBORHOOD.** With houses dating to the 18th century, Bo-Kaap was once known as the Malay Quarter because of its early settlers. This multicultural suburb overlooks Cape Town's city center.

⬡ **AFRICAN SAVANNA.** Zebras graze on the tall grasses of the Serengeti Plain, in East Africa. Each year more than 200,000 zebras migrate through Serengeti, following the seasonal rains.

⬡ **CRYSTAL WATERS.** A snorkeler swims in the clear blue waters off the Seychelles, one of Africa's island countries. Made up of 116 granite and coral islands, it lies about 1,000 miles (1,600 km) east of Kenya.

◗ **FREE RIDE.** A woman in Kumasi, Ghana, goes about her daily chores, with her infant wrapped snugly on her back in a colorful cloth.

THE CONTINENT:
AFRICA

more about
Africa

◗ **WORSHIPPERS IN THE DESERT.** Muslim faithful gather before the Great Mosque in Mopti, Mali. An earthen structure typical of Muslim architecture in Africa's Sahel, the mosque was built between 1936 and 1943.

◗ **WINDOW ON THE PAST.** Traditional Egyptian sailing vessels called feluccas skim along the Nile River below the ruins at Qubbat al-Hawa. Tombs from ancient Egypt's 6th dynasty are carved into the hillside.

◗ **MODERN SKYLINE.** Established in 1899 as a railway supply depot, Nairobi, Kenya, is now one of Africa's most modern cities. In Maasai, the name means "place of cold water."

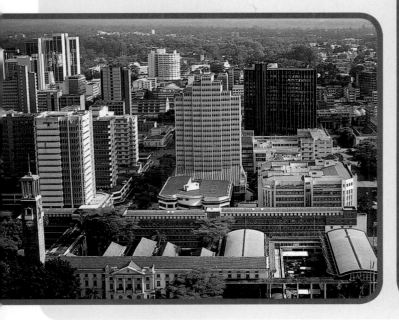

◐ **TALL LOAD.** A woman carries a stack of brightly dyed cotton cloth, called wax prints, through a market in Lomé, Togo.

WHERE THE PICTURES ARE

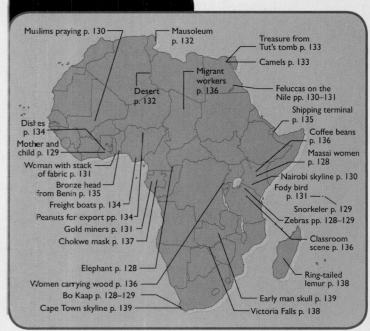

Muslims praying p. 130
Mausoleum p. 132
Treasure from Tut's tomb p. 133
Camels p. 133
Migrant workers p. 136
Desert p. 132
Feluccas on the Nile pp. 130–131
Shipping terminal p. 135
Dishes p. 134
Coffee beans p. 136
Mother and child p. 129
Maasai women p. 128
Woman with stack of fabric p. 131
Nairobi skyline p. 130
Bronze head from Benin p. 135
Fody bird p. 131
Freight boats p. 134
Snorkeler p. 129
Peanuts for export pp. 134
Zebras pp. 128–129
Gold miners p. 131
Chokwe mask p. 137
Classroom scene p. 136
Elephant p. 128
Women carrying wood p. 136
Ring-tailed lemur p. 138
Bo Kaap p. 128–129
Early man skull p. 139
Cape Town skyline p. 139
Victoria Falls p. 138

◗ **DIGGING FOR GOLD.** Miners dig a pit mine near the edge of the rain forest in Gabon. Oil and mineral extraction is an important part of Gabon's economy. While searching for traces of gold, however, they expose the fragile soil to erosion.

◯ **TROPICAL JEWEL.**
A ruby red fody bird perches on a forest branch on Mahé Island in the Seychelles. Native to neighboring Madagascar, the fody eats seeds and insects.

North Africa

This region, which is made up of five countries, stretches from the Atlantic Ocean in the west to the Red Sea in the east. To the north the region is bounded by the Mediterranean Sea, while to the south lies the vast dry expanse of the Sahara. The world's longest river—the Nile—winds northward through Egypt, but most of the region is arid—meaning there is too little moisture to support trees or extensive vegetation. Most of the region's population lives in coastal areas or in the fertile valley of the Nile River. In recent years, the region has experienced widespread instability as a result of tensions between conservative Islamic groups and more liberal groups seeking modernization and democratic rule.

THE BASICS

STATS

Largest country
Algeria 919,595 sq mi (2,381,741 sq km)

Smallest country
Tunisia 63,170 sq mi (163,610 sq km)

Most populous country
Egypt 82,283,000

Least populous country
Libya 6,469,000

Predominant languages
Arabic, French, various indigenous languages

Predominant religions
Islam, indigenous beliefs

Highest GDP per capita
Libya $14,500

Lowest GDP capita
Morocco $3,100

Highest life expectancy
Libya 78 years

Highest literacy rate
Libya 89%

GEO WHIZ

Ibn Battuta, who was born in Tangier, Morocco, in 1304, set off on a pilgrimage to Mecca that turned into a 29-year, 75,000-mile (120,675-km) journey that took him from the Middle East to India, China, the East Indies, and back home.

Lake Nasser in southern Egypt, formed by the Aswan High Dam, is the world's third largest reservoir. Built to provide water for farms along the Nile in years of drought, it also produces more than 10 billion kilowatt hours of electricity every year.

The city of Kairouan in eastern Tunisia is considered by many to be the fourth holiest Islamic city after Mecca, Medina, and Jerusalem. A UNESCO World Heritage site, the city was founded in A.D. 670 and became a center for Islamic learning.

◗ **SEA OF SAND.** Towering dunes, as well as barren, rocky expanses define Earth's largest desert—the Sahara, which separates North Africa from the rest of the continent.

◖ **LEADER REMEMBERED.** Arab influence in North Africa is reflected in the dramatic mausoleum of Tunisia's first president, Habib Bourguiba, in the coastal town of Al Munastîr. Bourguiba led Tunisia's fight for independence from colonial rule by France.

◀ **SPIRIT OF THE PAST.** A gold hawk pendant adorned with semiprecious stones and colored glass may represent the god Horus, one of the oldest Egyptian gods. This treasure was found in the tomb of King Tut.

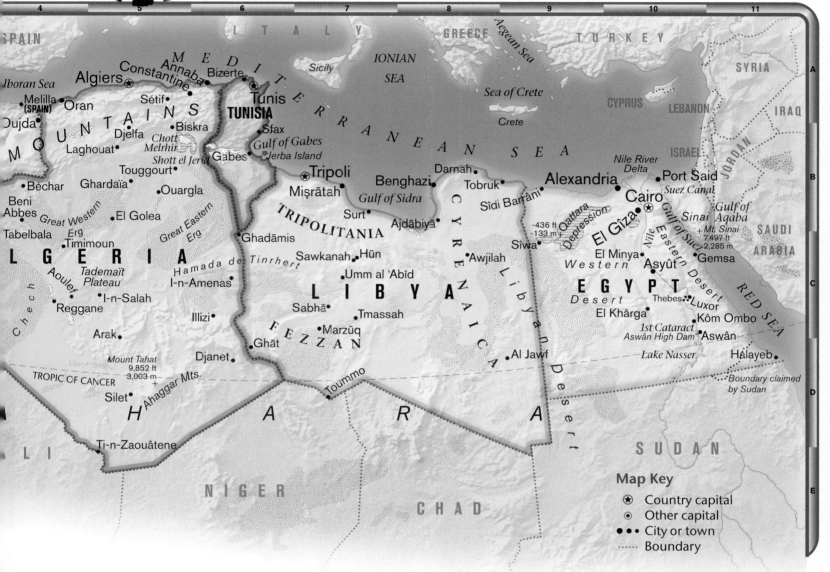

Map Key
★ Country capital
⊙ Other capital
••• City or town
····· Boundary

🜨 **BLACK GOLD.** Silhouetted against the setting sun, oil wells draw this valuable resource from beneath desert sands. Libya holds the largest proven oil reserves in Africa.

⬢ **SYMBOLS OF ANCIENT EGYPT.** Camels plod through the desert as the sun sets behind the ancient pyramids of Giza. Built 4,500 years ago, the pyramids were monumental tombs of pharaohs.

CHANGING THE LAND

☐ true desert
☐ severe risk of desertification
☐ moderate to great risk

Source: UN Food and Agricultural Organization

Overgrazing, removal of vegetation by farmers, and unreliable rainfall are turning some land in Africa into desert—a process called desertification.

West Africa

Stretching from Mauritania in the northwest to Gabon astride the equator in the southeast, 20 countries make up the region of West Africa. Three countries—Burkino Faso, Mali, and Niger—are landlocked. The remaining seventeen have coastlines along the Atlantic Ocean or the Gulf of Guinea. Early kingdoms thrived in Mali, Ghana, and Benin, but European conquest disrupted traditional societies and took away vast wealth, leaving a colonial legacy of disorder and conflict. Widespread use of French and English also reflect the colonial past. Palm oil, rubber, and cacao are produced in tropical areas. Drier lands grow peanuts and cotton. Nigeria, Equatorial Guinea, and Gabon are also major oil producers.

RIVER TRANSPORT. Traditional river boats are an important link in the movement of cargo and people along the Niger River.

THE BASICS

STATS

Largest country
Niger 489,191 sq miles (1,267,000 sq km)

Smallest country
São Tomé and Principe 372 sq miles (964 sq km)

Most populous
Nigeria 170,124,000

Least populous
São Tomé and Principe 183,000

Predominant languages French, English, Portuguese, Arabic, Spanish, various indigenous languages and dialects

Predominant religions
Islam, Christianity, indigenous beliefs

Highest GDP per capita
Equatorial Guinea $15,500

Lowest GDP per capita
Niger $434

Highest life expectancy
Cape Verde 71 years

Highest literacy rate
Equatorial Guinea 93.9%

GEO WHIZ

Nigeria is Africa's largest producer and exporter of oil. Port Harcourt, in the Niger River delta, is the center of the country's oil industry.

For more than 300 years, the Slave House on Senegal's Gorée Island served as a holding pen for slaves before they were sent to the Americas and elsewhere. Today, it is a museum and a memorial to those slaves.

Measuring a foot (32 cm) long and weighing seven pounds (3 kg), the goliath frog has a hind foot bigger than a man's palm. The world's largest frog lives only in the rain forests of Cameroon and Equatorial Guinea.

Income from oil production gives Equatorial Guinea the highest GDP per capita in the region, but wealth is unevenly distributed. Most people still practice subsistence farming and enjoy few benefits from oil revenues.

WAITING FOR SHIPMENT. Sacks of peanuts create an artificial mountain in Kano, Nigeria, where they wait for transport to Lagos and then export to world markets. The Kano region produces about half of Nigeria's peanut crop.

FULL OF COLOR. Artistic ceramic plates brighten an outdoor marketplace in Kumasi, Ghana. This country has a long and rich cultural tradition of creating pottery for cooking and for serving food and water.

◖ **MASTER ARTISANS.** The ancient African kingdom of Benin produced outstanding bronze work. Sculpted by hand and then cast in bronze by the lost-wax method, each piece was created to honor the king.

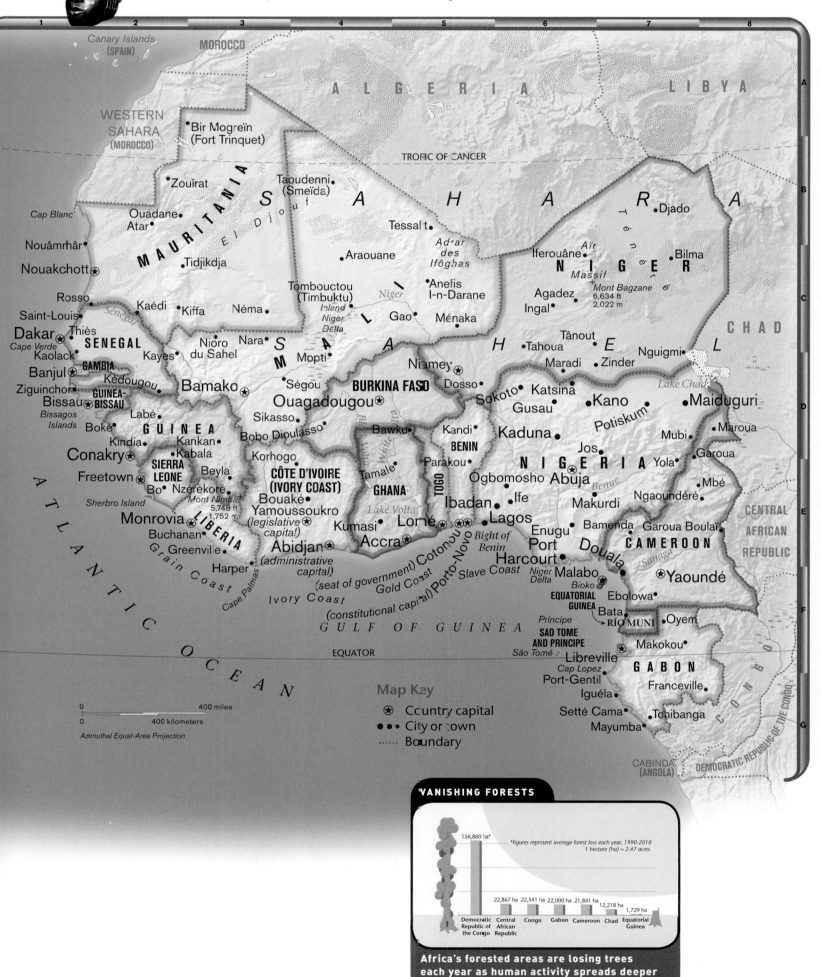

MOROCCO

Canary Islands
(SPAIN)

WESTERN
SAHARA
(MOROCCO)

•Bir Mogreïn
(Fort Trinquet)

A L G E R I A

L I B Y A

TROPIC OF CANCER

•Zouïrat

MAURITANIA

S   A   H   A   R   A

Cap Blanc
Nouâmrhâr•
Nouakchott⊛

Ouadane•
Atar•

El Djouf

•Djado

•Tessalit

Adrar
des
Ifôghas

Ténéré

Iferouâne• Aïr
Massif

•Bilma

•Araouane

N I G E R

Rosso•
Saint-Louis•
Dakar⊛ •Thiès
Cape Verde
Kaolack•
GAMBIA
Banjul⊛
Ziguinchor•
GUINEA-
Bissau⊛ BISSAU
Bissagos
Islands
Boké•

Tidjikdja•

Kaédi•

Kiffa•

Néma•

Tombouctou
(Timbuktu)

Niger

Inland
Niger
Delta

•Anefis
I-n-Darane

•Ménaka

•Gao

Agadez•

Mont Bagzane
6,634 ft
2,022 m

•Tânout

•Ingal

Tahoua•

•Zinder

Nguigmi•

Lake Chad

CHAD

Maradi•

Kayes•

Nioro•
du Sahel

Nara•

Ségou•

Mopti•

Niamey⊛

Dosso•

M   A   L   I

S   A   H   E   L

Katsina•

Kano•

•Maiduguri

Labé•

GUINEA

Kindia•
Conakry⊛
Kabala•
SIERRA
Freetown⊛ LEONE
Bo• •Nzérékoré

Kédougou•

Bamako⊛

Kankan•

Sikasso•

Bobo Dioulasso•

Korhogo•

Mont Nimba
5,748 ft
1,752 m

Ouagadougou⊛

Bawku•

BURKINA FASO

Kandi•

Black Volta

White Volta

BENIN

Sokoto•

Gusau•

Kaduna•

Potiskum•

•Mubi

•Maroua

Jos•

NIGERIA

Beyla•

CÔTE D'IVOIRE
(IVORY COAST)

Tamale•

Parakou•

Yola•

•Garoua

Sherbro Island
Monrovia⊛ LIBERIA
Buchanan•

Bouaké•
Yamoussoukro⊛
(legislative
capital)
Kumasi•

GHANA

TOGO

Lake Volta

Ogbomosho•

Ibadan•

Ife•

Abuja⊛

Benue

•Mbé

Ngaoundéré•

Greenville•

Grain Coast

Abidjan⊛
(administrative
capital)

Loné⊛

Accra⊛

Lagos•

Enugu•

Port
Harcourt

Bamenda•

Douala•

Garoua Boulaï•

CAMEROON

CENTRAL
AFRICAN
REPUBLIC

Harper•

Cape Palmas

Ivory Coast

Gold Coast

Cotonou
Porto-Novo
(seat of government) (constitutional capital)

Bight of
Benin

Slave Coast

Niger
Delta

Malabo⊛

Bioko

EQUATORIAL
GUINEA

Sanaga

⊛Yaoundé

Ebolowa•

Bata•
RÍO MUNI

•Oyem

A   T   L   A   N   T   I   C   O   C   E   A   N

G U L F   O F   G U I N E A

Príncipe

SAO TOME
AND PRINCIPE

São Tomé•

EQUATOR

Makokou•

Libreville⊛

GABON

Cap Lopez
Port-Gentil•

Franceville•

Iguéla•

Setté Cama•

•Tchibanga

Mayumba•

CONGO

DEMOCRATIC REPUBLIC OF THE CONGO

CABINDA
(ANGOLA)

0 ————— 400 miles
0 ————— 400 kilometers
Azimuthal Equal-Area Projection

Map Key
⊛ Country capital
••• City or town
····· Boundary

THE CONTINENT:
AFRICA

THE BASICS

STATS

Largest country
Democratic Republic of the Congo
905,354 sq miles (2,344,858 sq km)

Smallest country
Djibouti 8,957 sq miles (23,200 sq km)

Most populous
Democratic Republic of the Congo
69,117,000

Least populous
Djibouti 923,000

Predominant languages
French, Arabic, English, various
indigenous languages and dialects

Predominant religions
Christianity, Islam, various indigenous
beliefs

Highest GDP per capita
Congo $3,300

Lowest GDP capita
Democratic Republic of the Congo $251

Highest life expectancy
Kenya, Eritrea, Sudan 63 years

Highest literacy rate
Kenya 87%

GEO WHIZ

Lakes Malawi, Tanganyika, and Albert are
part of a chain of lakes that mark where
the Somali Plate (see page 17) is breaking
away from Africa. Millions of years from
now, much of the region from Djibouti to
Mozambique could be one big island.

As part of a coming-of-age ritual, each
Maasai boy must kill a lion. Read the true-
life story of Joseph Lemasolai Lekuton
in *Facing the Lion*, published by National
Geographic Children's Books.

In 2006 the 3.3-million-year-old fossilized
remains of a child were found in the Danakil
area of northern Ethiopia. The find was not
far from where the 2.3-million-year-old
remains of Lucy, an adult female of the
same primitive human species, were found
in 1974.

Only about 700 mountain gorillas remain
on Earth. About half of these magnificent
creatures live in forests on the slopes
of the volcanic Virunga Mountains in
Rwanda, Uganda, and the Democratic
Republic of the Congo. Mountain gorillas
are endangered due to poaching, loss of
habitat, and civil conflict that has disrupted the countries where they are found.

East Africa

The Congo, the region's longest river and chief commercial highway, flows through rain forests that, despite efforts to save them, are being cut for timber and palm oil plantations. In Chad, many people make a living by raising livestock as well as cotton and other crops. Extended drought and diversion of water for agriculture have reduced Lake Chad to one-twentieth of its former size and threatened the animals that live there. Volcanic peaks such as Kilimanjaro—Africa's highest mountain—tower above fertile farmlands in Tanzania and Kenya. Tree-dotted grasslands, called savannas, are home to vast herds of wildlife that attract tourists from around the globe. For more than 50 years, religious and ethnic conflicts fueled warfare in the northeastern part of the region, resulting in political separation—Eritrea from Ethiopia and South Sudan from Sudan.

◒ **EAGER LEARNERS.** Tanzania, a poor country with a literacy rate of only 69 percent, lags in education. Students in this crowded village school compete for the teacher's attention.

◖ **FROM FIELD TO CUP.** A worker on a coffee estate in Kenya holds freshly harvested coffee berries, which will soon be on their way to the world market. Coffee production was introduced to Kenya in 1900. Today, it employs more than six million workers.

◒ **WOMEN'S WORK.** Villagers throughout Africa depend on wood as their main source of fuel to cook and heat their homes. This contributes to widespread deforestation. These women carry wood out of Virunga National Park in the Democratic Republic of the Congo.

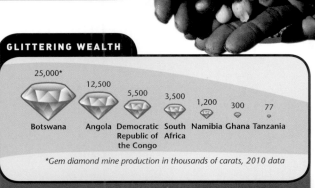

GLITTERING WEALTH

25,000*	12,500	5,500	3,500	1,200	300	77
Botswana	Angola	Democratic Republic of the Congo	South Africa	Namibia	Ghana	Tanzania

Gem diamond mine production in thousands of carats, 2010 data

Diamonds are prized both for jewelry and for industrial uses. More than half of the world's diamond production comes from mines in Africa.

⚫ **CELEBRATING A KING.** The Chokwe people of Central Africa used masks such as this to celebrate the inauguration of a new king. Considered sacred, the mask could only be worn by the current chief of a group.

1 2 3 4 5 6 7 8

TROPIC OF CANCER

LIBYA

EGYPT

SAUDI ARABIA

0   400 miles
0   400 kilometers
Azimuthal Equal-Area Projection

NIGER

SAHARA

Aozou
AOZOU STRIP
Aozi
Tibesti Mts.
Emi Koussi
11,204 ft
3,415 m
Ounianga Kébir
Faya-Largeau
Fada
Ennedi
Koro Toro

Libyan Desert

Lake Nubia
Wadi Halfa
2nd Cataract
Nubian
Desert
3rd Cataract
Dongola
4th Cataract
Merowe
5th Cataract
Atbara

Por. Sudan
Tokar

RED SEA

YEMEN

Mao
Lake Chad
Ati
N'Djamena
Abéché
Biltine

CHAD

SAHEL

Khartoum North
Omdurman
Khartoum

SUDAN

Algena
Agordat
Asmara

ERITREA

Assab
Bab al Mandab

NIGERIA

Am Timan
Chari

Jabal Marra
10,131 ft
3,088 m
El Fasher
DARFUR
Nyala
Gabras

El Obeid
En Nahud
Kadugli

Kosti
Renk
Melut

White Nile
Malakal

Blue Nile

Mek'elē
Gonder
Lake Tana
Bahir Dar

Ras Dejen
14,870 ft
4,533 m
Danakil

Desē
Dirē

-512 ft
-156 m
DJIBOUTI
Djibouti

Cape Gwardafuy

GULF OF ADEN
Bargaal
Berbera
SOMALILAND
Qardho

Moundou
Sarh
Bossangoa
Bouar

Birao
Dar Rounga
Kafia Kingi
Ndélé

Raga

ETHIOPIAN

Addis Ababa
Gorē
Dawa

Arba Minch'
Īmī

HIGHLANDS
Goba

Dirē
Dawa

Eyl
Boundary undemarcated and in dispute

CENTRAL
AFRICAN REPUBLIC

Bambari
Bangassou

Dobane
Obo

S O U T H
S U D A N

Wau
Ler
Rumbek

Mountain Nile
Bor
Bowol

Maji
Nagēlē
Mēga

Gaalkacyo
(Galcaio)

SOMALI PENINSULA

Hilalaye

Berbérati
Nola

Bangui

Berbérati

Gemena
Bumba

Uele

Isiro
(Paulis)

Bondo

Maridi

Juba
Boundary claimed by Kenya

Boundary claimed by South Sudan
Lokichokio
Dolo Bay

Beledweyne

Baydhabo

SOMALIA

Mereeg

Ouesso
Basankusu

Congo

DEMOCRATIC

Kisangani
Boyoma Falls

Albert Nile
Bunia
Lake Albert

Arua
Gulu
Victoria Nile

Lake Turkana
(Lake Rudolf)

Wajir

Dif

Marka

Mogadishu
(historic capital; no central government since 1991)

GABON
Mossaka

Inongo

Mbandaka

REPUBLIC

Lake Edward

UGANDA
Kampala
Jinja

Maralal

Kisumu
Mount Kenya
17,057 ft
5,199 m

KENYA

EQUATOR
Kismaayo
Kaambooni

Pointe-Noire

OF THE CONGO

Bandundu
Kindu

Bukavu
Lake Kivu

RWANDA
Kigali

Leke
Lake Victoria

Nairobi

Bura
Lamu
Malindi

INDIAN

Kananga

Kasai

Kinshasa

Mweka
Kasongo

BURUNDI
Bujumbura

Kilimanjaro
19,341 ft
5,895 m

Arusha
Moshi

Mombasa

OCEAN

Brazzaville
Boma

Mbuji-Mayi
(Bakwanga)

Kalemie
Lake Tanganyika

Tabora
Kigoma

Dodoma
(legislative capital)

Zanzibar
Zanzibar Island

Tanga

Pemba Island

Dar es Salaam
(administrative capital)

ATLANTIC
OCEAN

Kahemba
Sandoa

Kamina

KATANGA
PLATEAU

Pweto

Lake Rukwa

TANZANIA

Iringa

Mbeya
Lake Mweru

Lake Malawi
(Lake Nyasa)

Lindi
Mtwara

Map Key

⚫ Kolwezi
Likasi
Lubumbashi

ZAMBIA

Songea

Kilwa Kivinje

⊛ Country capital
• City or town
⋯ Boundary
⋯ Undefined boundary

ANGOLA

MOZAMBIQUE

COMOROS

MADAGASCAR

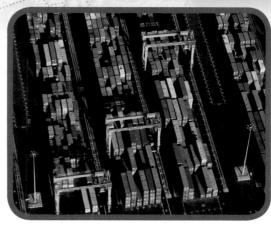

⚫ **INTERNATIONAL PORT.** Shipping containers look like colorful ribbons at a port terminal in Djibouti. The recently modernized and expanded port facility, with its deep natural harbor, is the mainstay of this small East African country's economy.

THE CONTINENT:
AFRICA

THE BASICS

STATS

Largest country
Angola 481,354 sq mi (1,246,700 sq km)

Smallest country
Seychelles 176 sq mi (455 sq km)

Most populous country
South Africa 51,147,000

Least populous country
Seychelles 93,000

Predominant languages
English, French, Portuguese, various indigenous languages and dialects

Predominant religions
Christianity, Islam, various indigenous beliefs

Highest GDP per capita
Seychelles $11,200

Lowest GDP per capita
Malawi $262

Highest life expectancy
Mauritius 75 years

Highest literacy rate
Seychelles
92%

GEO WHIZ

South Africa's Kruger National Park, the largest in Africa, covers more area than the entire country of Israel. Within its boundary are 14 different ecological zones that provide habitat to a great variety of plants, birds, and other animals, including the "big five": lions, elephants, leopards, rhinos, and buffaloes.

Great Zimbabwe National Monument has the largest ancient stone ruins south of the Sahara. This massive fortress city was the center of an empire that flourished from the 11th to the 15th century.

The Makgadikgadi salt pans in the eastern Kalahari of Botswana are what is left of an immense lake. Each spring, rains flood the area and attract herds of migrating zebras and wildebeests.

Namibia is famed for sand dunes that are reportedly the highest in the world. The largest, Big Daddy, towers 1,200 feet (366 m) above the surrounding land. Along Namibia's northwestern coast, treacherous crosscurrents have caused countless shipwrecks, earning it the nickname Skeleton Coast.

Southern Africa

Ringed by uplands, the region's central basin holds the seasonally lush Okavango Delta and scorching Kalahari Desert. The

🛑 **NATURAL WONDER.**
Victoria Falls, third largest waterfall in the world, is 5,500 feet (1,676 m) wide and 355 feet (108 m) high.

mighty Zambezi thunders over Victoria Falls on its way to the Indian Ocean, where Madagascar is home to plants and animals found nowhere else in the world.

Bantu and San are among the indigenous people who saw their hold on the land give way to Portuguese, Dutch, and British traders and colonists. The region offers a range of mineral resources and a variety of climates and soils that in some places yield bumper crops of grains, grapes, and citrus. Rich deposits of coal, gold, and diamonds have helped make South Africa the continent's economic powerhouse.

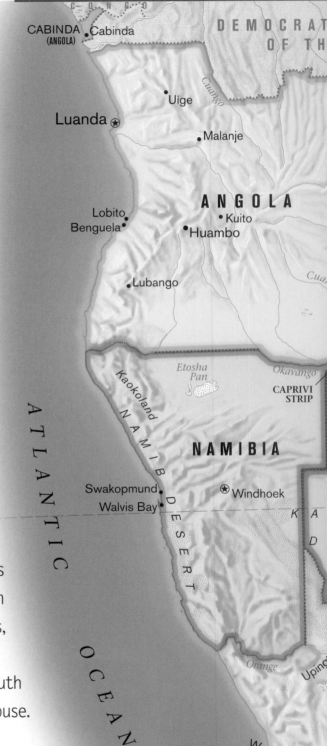

◐ **STARING EYES.**
This ring-tailed lemur sits on a forest tree branch. The ring-tail, found only in Madagascar, spends time both on the ground and in the trees. It eats fruits, leaves, insects, small birds, and even lizards.

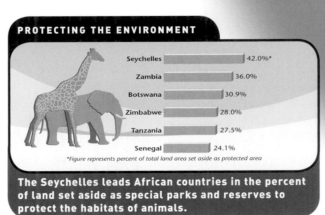

PROTECTING THE ENVIRONMENT

Seychelles	42.0%*
Zambia	36.0%
Botswana	30.9%
Zimbabwe	28.0%
Tanzania	27.5%
Senegal	24.1%

Figure represents percent of total land area set aside as protected area

The Seychelles leads African countries in the percent of land set aside as special parks and reserves to protect the habitats of animals.

EARLY MAN. Dating back perhaps 70,000 years, this skull of "Broken Hill Man," found in Zimbabwe, is thought to represent a transitional type between *Homo erectus* and *Homo sapiens*.

REPUBLIC
CONGO

TANZANIA

Lake Tanganyika

Map Key

★ Country capital
●●● City or town
····· Boundary

0   200 miles
0   300 kilometers
Azimuthal Equidistant Projection

SEYCHELLES

Kasama

Mufulira
Mzuzu
Lake Malawi
Rovuma
Moroni ⊛
COMOROS
Îles Glorieuses (FRANCE)
Cap d'Ambre
Antsiranana

Chingola
Kitwe
Luanshya Ndola
MALAWI
Lugende
Pemba
Île de Mayotte (FRANCE)

Kabwe
Chipata
Lichinga
Nacala
Maromokotro
9,436 ft
2,876 m

ZAMBIA
Lilongwe ⊛
Zomba
Nampula
Moçambique

Mongu
Lusaka ⊛
Blantyre
Tete

Victoria Falls
Livingstone
Lake Kariba
Harare ★
Zambezi
Quelimane
Île Juan De Nova (FRANCE)

Okavango Delta
Chitungwiza
Mutare
MOZAMBIQUE
Mahajanga

Makgadikgadi Pans
ZIMBABWE
Gweru
Chimoio
Mozambique Channel
MADAGASCAR
Antananarivo ★
Antsirabe

Great Zimbabwe
Beira
Toamasina

Francistown
Bulawayo
Bassas da India (FRANCE)
Fianarantsoa

OTSWANA
Serowe
Île Europa (FRANCE)
For Mauritius and Réunion, see maps on pages 126–127.

HARI
Gaborone ⊛
Polokwane (Pietersburg)
TROPIC OF CAPRICORN
Toliara

ERT
Kanye
Pretoria (Tshwane) (administrative capital)
Inhambane
INDIAN OCEAN

Johannesburg
Xai-Xai
Cap Ste. Marie

Soweto
Maputo ★
Klerksdorp
Mbabane (administrative capital)

SOUTH
Welkom
Vereeniging
SWAZILAND
Kroonstad
Lobamba (legislative and royal capital)

Kimberley
Richards Bay
Bloemfontein ★ (judicial capital)
Maseru ★
Pietermaritzburg

AFRICA
LESOTHO
Durban
Orange

Middelburg
Karroo
Queenstown
Oudtshoom
Uitenhage
George
East London
Grahamstown
Port Elizabeth

SOUTHERN METROPOLIS. Third most populous city in South Africa and seat of the national parliament, Cape Town began as a Dutch supply station in 1652. Table Mountain rises in the background.

PHYSICAL

Area and population totals are for the independent countries in the region only.

Land area
3,278,000 sq mi
(8,490,000 sq km)

Highest point
Mount Wilhelm, Papua New Guinea
14,793 ft (4,509 m)

Lowest point
Lake Eyre, Australia
-52 ft (-16 m)

Longest river
Murray-Darling, Australia
2,310 mi (3, 718 km)

Largest lake
Lake Eyre, Australia
3,430 sq mi (8,884 sq km)

POLITICAL

Population
35,759,000

Largest metropolitan area
Sydney, Australia
Pop. 4,429,000

Largest country
Australia
2,969,906 sq mi (7,692,024 sq km)

Most densely populated country
Nauru
1,275 people per sq mi (485 per sq km)

Economy
Farming: livestock, wheat, fruit
Industry: mining, wool, oil
Services

Australia, New Zealand, & Oceania

Australia, New Zealand & Oceania

TROPIC OF CANCER

EQUATOR

TROPIC OF CAPRICORN

Map Key

— Country boundary

SCALE AT THE EQUATOR

1,000 miles

1,000 kilometers

Mercator Projection

Pitcairn Island

TUAMOTU ARCHIPELAGO

Marquesas
Islands

Tahiti

Society Islands

Austral Islands

P O L Y N E S I A

Jarvis Island

Kiritimati

Kingman Reef

Palmyra Atoll

LINE ISLANDS

COOK ISLANDS

Rarotonga

Hawaiian Islands

Hawai'i

Johnston Atoll

Midway Is.

NORTH PACIFIC OCEAN

Wake
Island

Ratak Chain

MARSHALL IS.

Ralik Chain

Bikini Atoll

Gilbert Islands

Howland
Island

Baker I.

Phoenix
Islands

Tokelau

Samoa Is.

Tonga Islands

Tuvalu

Fiji
Islands

Santa Cruz
Islands

Vanuatu

New
Caledonia

Kermadec
Islands

Chatham Islands

North
Island

NEW
ZEALAND

South
Island

Mt. Ruapehu
9,176 ft 2,797 m

Cook Strait

Mt. Cook
12,316 ft
3,754 m

Southern Alps

SOUTH PACIFIC OCEAN

Norfolk Island

Lord Howe Island

Mariana Islands

Yap
Islands

Truk Islands

M I C R O N E S I A

CAROLINE ISLANDS

PHILIPPINE
SEA

PHILIPPINE ISLANDS

A S I A

GREATER
SUNDA
ISLANDS

Lesser Sunda Islands

Timor
Sea

New Guinea

Mount Wilhelm
14,793 ft
4,509 m

Bismarck
Archipelago

Highest Point
in Oceania

Solomon Islands

M E L A N E S I A

CORAL SEA

Arafura Sea

Gulf of
Carpentaria

Kimberley
Plateau

WESTERN
PLATEAU

Great Victoria
Desert

North West
Basin

Darling Range

A U S T R A L I A

Central Lowlands

Uluru
(Ayers Rock)
2,831 ft 863 m

Lake Eyre
Lowest Point
in Oceania
-52 ft -16 m

Eucla Basin

Great
Australian Bight

Spencer Gulf

GREAT DIVIDING RANGE

Darling

Murray

Mt. Kosciuszko
7,310 ft 2,228 m

Bass Strait

Tasmania

TASMAN
SEA

INDIAN
OCEAN

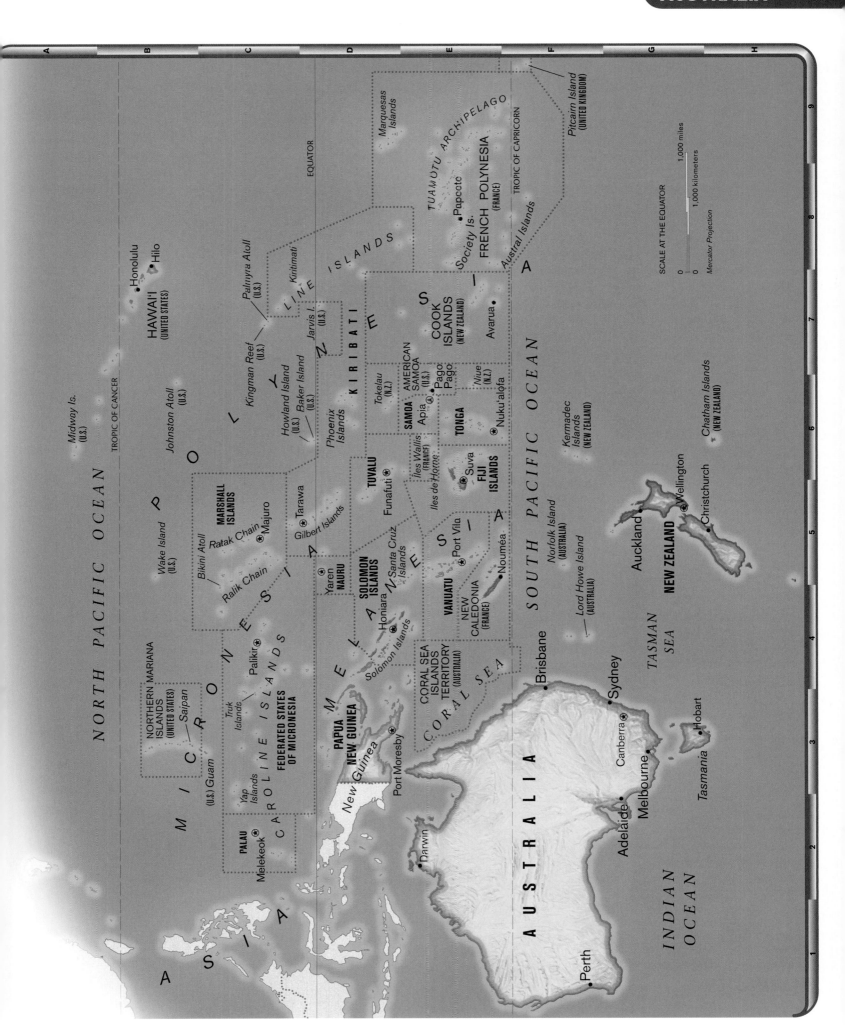

A   B   C   D   E   F   G   H

NORTH PACIFIC OCEAN

Midway Is.
(U.S.)

TROPIC OF CANCER

•Honolulu
•Hilo
HAWAI'I
(UNITED STATES)

Johnston Atoll
(U.S.)

Wake Island
(U.S.)

EQUATOR

Palmyra Atoll
(U.S.)

Kiritimati

Kingman Reef
(U.S.)

Howland Island
(U.S.)

Baker Island
(U.S.)

Jarvis I.
(U.S.)

L I N E

I S L A N D S

Marquesas Islands

TUAMOTU ARCHIPELAGO

TROPIC OF CAPRICORN

Pitcairn Island
(UNITED KINGDOM)

Papeete
Society Is.   **FRENCH POLYNESIA**
(FRANCE)

Austral Islands

SCALE AT THE EQUATOR

1,000 miles
0
1,000 kilometers
0
Mercator Projection

P   O   L   Y   N   E   S   I   A

COOK ISLANDS
(NEW ZEALAND)
•Avarua

Phoenix Islands

KIRIBATI

Tokelau
(N.Z.)

AMERICAN SAMOA
(U.S.)   Pago Pago

Niue
(N.Z.)   Nuku'alofa

SAMOA
Apia

TONGA

Iles Wallis
(FRANCE)

Iles de Horne

Suva
FIJI ISLANDS

TUVALU
Funafuti

M   I   C   R   O   N   E   S   I   A

MARSHALL ISLANDS

Bikini Atoll

Ratak Chain   ⊛Majuro

•Tarawa

Gilbert Islands

Ralik Chain

Yaren⊛
NAURU

M   E   L   A   N   E   S   I   A

SOLOMON ISLANDS
Santa Cruz Islands

Honiara⊛

Solomon Islands

Port Vila⊛
VANUATU

NEW CALEDONIA
(FRANCE)
•Nouméa

SOUTH PACIFIC OCEAN

Kermadec Islands
(NEW ZEALAND)

Wellington
NEW ZEALAND
Auckland•
•Christchurch

Chatham Islands
(NEW ZEALAND)

NORTHERN MARIANA ISLANDS
(UNITED STATES)
—Saipan

(U.S.) Guam

Truk Islands

Yap Islands

Palikir⊛

FEDERATED STATES OF MICRONESIA

C   A   R   O   L   I   N   E   I   S   L   A   N   D   S

PALAU
Melekeok⊛

A   S   I   A

PAPUA NEW GUINEA
Port Moresby•

New Guinea

CORAL SEA ISLANDS TERRITORY
(AUSTRALIA)

C   O   R   A   L   S   E   A

Norfolk Island
(AUSTRALIA)

Lord Howe Island
(AUSTRALIA)

•Brisbane

•Sydney

Canberra⊛
•Melbourne

Adelaide•

TASMAN SEA

•Hobart
Tasmania

A   U   S   T   R   A   L   I   A

•Darwin

•Perth

INDIAN OCEAN

1   2   3   4   5   6   7   8   9

Australia, New Zealand, & Oceania

WORLDS APART

This vast region includes Australia—the world's smallest continent—New Zealand, and a fleet of mostly tiny island worlds scattered across the Pacific Ocean. Apart from Australia, New Zealand, and Papua New Guinea, Oceania's other 11 independent countries cover about 25,000 square miles (65,000 sq km), an area only slightly larger than half of New Zealand's North Island. Twenty-one other island groups are dependencies of the United States, France, Australia, New Zealand, or the United Kingdom. Long isolation has allowed the growth of diverse marine communities, such as Australia's Great Barrier Reef, and the evolution of platypuses, kangaroos, and other land animals that live nowhere else on the planet.

AUSTRALIAN TEDDY BEAR. Koalas, which are not bears at all, are native to the eucalyptus forests of eastern Australia.

ANCIENT VOYAGERS. The Maoris are believed to have sailed to New Zealand from islands far to the northeast. Maori warriors traditionally adorned themselves with elaborate tattoos to frighten enemies.

PLACE OF LEGENDS. Sacred to native Aborigines, Uluru, also known as Ayers Rock, glows a deep red in the rays of the setting sun. Uluru is the tip of a massive sandstone block—part of an ancient seabed exposed by erosion.

TROPICAL HABITAT. Brilliantly colored fish swim among branching corals in the warm waters of the Vatu-i-Ra Channel in the Fiji Islands. The waters around Fiji have some of the richest and most diverse fish populations in the world.

NATIVE COWBOYS. Competition is fierce during a rodeo in Hope Vale, an Aboriginal community on Australia's Cape York Peninsula. Hope Vale is home to several Aboriginal clan groups.

more about
Australia, New Zealand & Oceania

BIG JUMPER. The red kangaroo, the largest living marsupial—an animal that carries its young in a pouch—is at home on the dry inland plains of Australia. It can cover 30 feet (9 m) in a single hop.

WOOLY POPULATION. Sheep outnumber people in Australia and New Zealand. Wool production is an important part of the economy of these two countries.

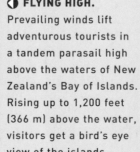

FLYING HIGH. Prevailing winds lift adventurous tourists in a tandem parasail high above the waters of New Zealand's Bay of Islands. Rising up to 1,200 feet (366 m) above the water, visitors get a bird's eye view of the islands.

◐ **A WATER WORLD.** Located just 7 degrees north of the Equator in the western Pacific Ocean, the islands of the Republic of Palau were a United Nations Trust Territory until 1994, when they gained independence.

WHERE THE PICTURES ARE

Tropical islands of Palau pp. 146–147

New Guinea tribesman with painted face p. 151

Aborigine cowboys p. 145

Ambrym volcano p. 150

Catching octopus p. 151

Parasailing p. 146

Lagoon p. 150

Uluru (Ayers Rock) pp. 144–145

Easter Island statue p. 151

Red kangaroo p. 146

Great white shark p. 148

Koala p. 144

Dingo p. 149

Sydney Opera House p. 148

Coral reef with fish pp. 144–145

Auckland skyline pp. 146–147

Maori man p. 144

Sheep in pasture p. 146

Mount Cook p. 147

Jet boat with tourists p. 147

Fiordland National Park p. 149

◐ **A WET RIDE.** Tourists go for a wild ride in a jet boat on the roaring waters of New Zealand's Shotover River.

◐ **SNOWY PEAK.** New Zealand's Mount Cook rises above the clouds. Legend says the peak is a frozen Maori warrior.

◐ **MODERN METROPOLIS.** Modern buildings rise against a twilight sky in Auckland, on New Zealand's North Island. It is home to almost one-third of the country's population.

SHOTOVER JET

THE CONTINENT:
AUSTRALIA

THE BASICS

STATS

Largest country
Australia 2,969,906 sq mi
(7,692,024 sq km)

Smallest country
New Zealand 104,454 sq mi
(270,534 sq km)

Most populous country
Australia 22,035,000

Least populous country
New Zealand 4,437,000

Predominant languages
English, Maori

Predominant religion
Christianity

Highest GDP per capita
Australia $40,800

Lowest GDP per capita
New Zealand $28,000

Highest life expectancy
Australia 82 years

Highest literacy rate
Australia, New Zealand
99%

GEO WHIZ

Australian Aborigines use a small tree
trunk hollowed out by termites to make a
musical instrument called a didgeridoo.

One-fourth of New Zealand's population
lives in Auckland, on North Island,
making it the largest city in Polynesia.

Lake Eyre is Australia's largest lake, but
it is very shallow—not quite 20 feet (6 m)
deep when full. Most of the rivers that
flow into it dry up before reaching it. The
lake has been filled to capacity only three
times over the past 150 years.

Australia's location south of the Equator
earned it the nickname Land Down Under.

The ceilings of grottoes in New Zealand's
Waitomo Caves look like starry night
skies thanks to the light given off by
thousands of glowworms.

The Tasmanian devil is a meat-eating
marsupial that lives only in Tasmania.
Its high-pitched screeches can be
heard at night when the animal is most
active. This protected species is the
symbol of the Tasmanian National
Parks and Wildlife Service.

Australia & New Zealand

Most people in Australia live along the coast, far from the country's dry interior, known as the Outback. The most populous cities and the best croplands are in the southeast. This "Land Down Under" is increasingly linked by trade to Asian countries and to 4.4 million "neighbors" in New Zealand. Twelve hundred miles (1,930 km) across the Tasman Sea, New Zealand is cooler, wetter, and more mountainous than Australia. It is geologically active and has ecosystems ranging from subtropical forests on North Island to snowy peaks on South Island. Both countries enjoy high standards of living and strong agricultural and mining outputs, including wool, wines, gold, coal, and iron ore.

🌐 **KILLER OF THE DEEP.**
Great white sharks inhabit the warm
waters off the coast of southern
Australia. These warm-blooded
marine predators can grow up to
20 feet (6 m) in length.

🌓 **SAILS AT SUNSET.** Reminiscent of
a ship in full sail, the Sydney Opera
House, in Sydney Harbor, has become
a symbol of Australia that is
recognized around the world.

THE CONTINENT:
AUSTRALIA

◑ **DOG OF THE OUTBACK.** The dingo is a wild dog found throughout Australia except for Tasmania. Unlike most domestic dogs, the dingo does not bark, although it howls. Aborigines sometimes use dingos as hunting companions or guard dogs.

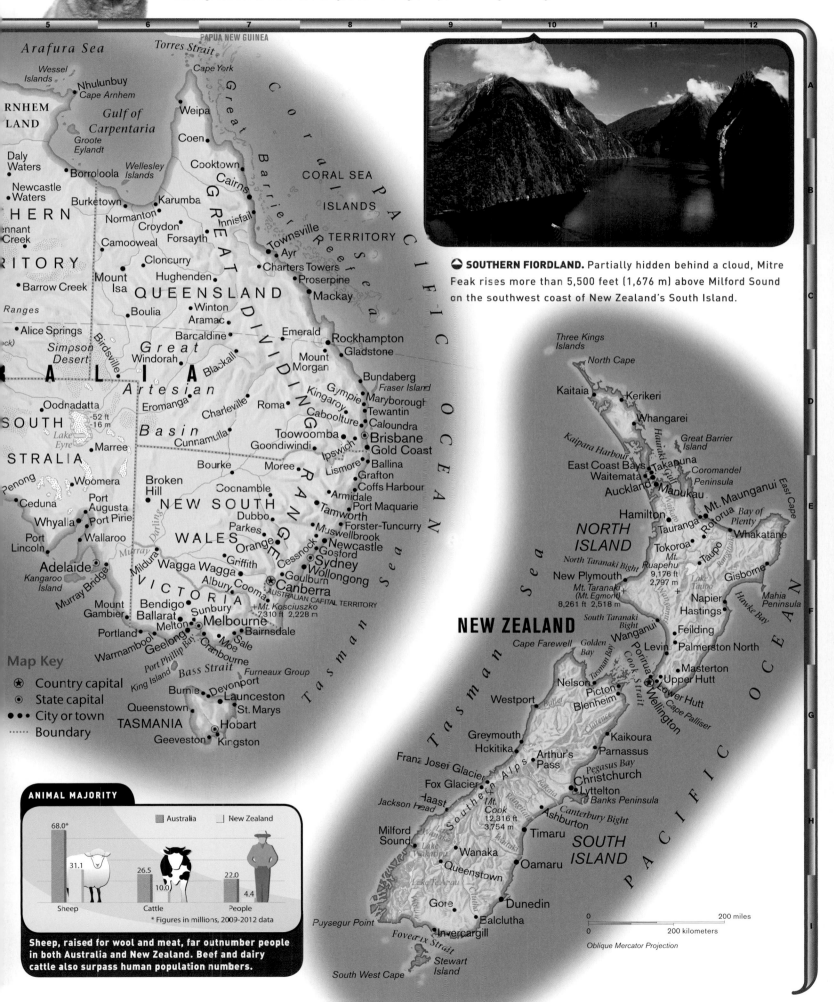

◓ **SOUTHERN FIORDLAND.** Partially hidden behind a cloud, Mitre Peak rises more than 5,500 feet (1,676 m) above Milford Sound on the southwest coast of New Zealand's South Island.

Map Key
- ★ Country capital
- ◉ State capital
- ••• City or town
- ⋯⋯ Boundary

ANIMAL MAJORITY

	Australia	New Zealand
Sheep	68.0*	31.1
Cattle	26.5	10.0
People	22.0	4.4

*Figures in millions, 2009–2012 data

Sheep, raised for wool and meat, far outnumber people in both Australia and New Zealand. Beef and dairy cattle also surpass human population numbers.

200 miles
200 kilometers

Oblique Mercator Projection

THE BASICS

STATS

Largest country
Papua New Guinea
178,703 sq mi (462,840 sq km)

Smallest country
Nauru 8 sq mi (21 sq km)

Most populous country
Papua New Guinea 7,034,000

Least populous country
Nauru 10,200

Predominant languages
English, various indigenous
languages and dialects

Predominant religion
Christianity, various
indigenous beliefs

Highest GDP per capita
Palau $8,100

Lowest GDP per capita
Micronesia $2,200

Highest life expectancy
Tonga 75 years

Highest literacy rate
Samoa
100%

GEO WHIZ

Tuvalu's highest point is roughly 16 feet
(5 m) above sea level. Predictions that
rising sea levels due to global warming
could drown the island within the next
50 years have caused some of its people
to emigrate to New Zealand and other
countries with higher elevations.

For centuries in Fiji, tribal officials would
bring out their best utensils for special
people—not to serve them, but to eat
them. Cannibalism in the islands ended
in the late 1800s, when Christianity was
adopted.

Only 36 of Tonga's 170 islands are inhab-
ited. It was in Tongan waters that the
infamous mutiny aboard the British ship
HMS *Bounty* took place in 1789.

The interior highland region of Papua New
Guinea is so mountainous and forested
that it wasn't explored by outsiders until
the 1930s. Europeans were surprised to
find people living there whose cultures
hadn't changed since the Stone Age.

Kennedy Island, in the Solomon Islands,
is named for U.S. President John F.
Kennedy. During World War II he and
some of his crew swam to this island—
known as Plum Pudding at the time—
after their PT boat was rammed by a
Japanese destroyer.

⬤ **LIVING EARTH.**
Ambrym volcano, in
Vanuatu, is one of the most
active volcanoes in Oceania.
First observed by Captain
Cook in 1774, Ambrym
continues to erupt regularly,
adding to the island's black
sand beaches.

Oceania

Although in its broadest sense Oceania includes
Australia and New Zealand, more commonly it refers
to some 25,000 islands that make up three
large cultural regions in
the Pacific Ocean.
Melanesia, which
extends from
Papua New
Guinea to
Fiji, is closest
to Australia.
Micronesia lies
mostly north of
the Equator and
includes Palau
and the Federated States of Micronesia. New
Zealand, Hawai'i, and Rapa Nui (Easter Island)
mark the western, northern, and eastern limits
of Polynesia, with Tahiti, Samoa, and Tonga near its
heart. Oceania's people often face problems of limited
living space and fresh water. Plantation agriculture,
fishing, tourism, or mining form the economic base
for most of the islands in this region.

⬤ **TROPICAL PARADISE.** A reef
separates an area of sea water
from the ocean, forming a quiet
lagoon around the island of
Bora Bora in the Society Islands
of French Polynesia.

◐ **UNSOLVED MYSTERY.** Carved from volcanic rock, the giant stone heads of Rapa Nui, also known as Easter Island, remain a mystery. Although culturally Polynesian, the island belongs to Chile, 2,400 miles (3,862 km) to the east (see page 32).

◑ **LONG ARMS.** Octopuses live on coral reefs in the warm tropical waters of the South Pacific Ocean. They use the suckers on their tentacles to move around and to catch crustaceans and small fish.

Midway Islands (U.S.)

HAWAI'I (UNITED STATES)

TROPIC OF CANCER

Honolulu O'ahu

Wake Island (U.S.)

Johnston Atoll (U.S.)

Hilo
Hawai'i

P O L Y N E S I A

S O U T H P A C I F I C O C E A N

Bikini Atoll

Ratak Chain

MARSHALL ISLANDS

Ralik Chain

⊛ Majuro

Gilbert Islands

⊛ Tarawa

NAURU
Yaren ⊛

K I R I B A T I

Kingman Reef (U.S.)
Palmyra Atoll (U.S.)

Howland Island (U.S.)
Baker Island (U.S.)

Kiritimati (Christmas I.)

EQUATOR

Jarvis Island (U.S.)

Malden Island
Starbuck Island

L I N E I S L A N D S

TUVALU
⊛ Funafuti

SOLOMON ISLANDS

Santa Cruz Is.

TOKELAU (NEW ZEALAND)

Vostok Island
Caroline Island
Flint Island

MARQUESAS ISLANDS (FRANCE)

Rotuma

Îles Wallis (FRANCE)
Îles de Horne

SAMOA
Apia ⊛

AMERICAN SAMOA (U.S.)
⊙ Pago Pago

Samoa Islands

Cook Islands (NEW ZEALAND)

P O L Y N E S I A

TUAMOTU ARCHIPELAGO

VANUATU
Port Vila ⊛ Éfaté

Vanua Levu

FIJI

Viti Levu ⊛ Suva

ISLANDS

TONGA
⊛ Nuku'alofa

Society Islands
Tahiti ⊙ Papeete

FRENCH POLYNESIA (FRANCE)

Austral Islands

Henderson Island (UNITED KINGDOM)

Mt. Panié + 5,341 ft 1,628 m

⊙ Nouméa

New Caledonia (FRANCE)

TROPIC OF CAPRICORN

S O U T H P A C I F I C O C E A N

Pitcairn Island (U.K.)

Ducie Island (U.K.)

Sala-y-Gómez (CHILE)

Isla de Pascua (Easter Island) (CHILE)

(AUSTRALIA)
Norfolk Island
Phillip Island

Kermadec Islands (NEW ZEALAND)

NEW ZEALAND

Map Key

⊛ Country capital
⊙ State or province capital
••• City or town
...... Boundary

SCALE AT THE EQUATOR

0 ————————— 1,000 miles
0 ————————— 1,000 kilometers

Mercator Projection

◐ **MELANESIAN CUSTOM.** In the Huli culture of Papua New Guinea's Eastern Highlands, men adorn themselves with colorful paints, feathers, and grasses in preparation for festivals.

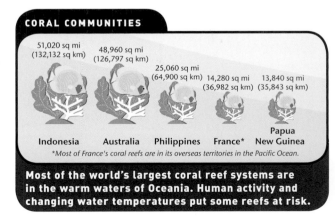

CORAL COMMUNITIES

51,020 sq mi (132,132 sq km)	48,960 sq mi (126,797 sq km)	25,060 sq mi (64,900 sq km)	14,280 sq mi (36,982 sq km)	13,840 sq mi (35,843 sq km)
Indonesia	Australia	Philippines	France*	Papua New Guinea

*Most of France's coral reefs are in its overseas territories in the Pacific Ocean.

Most of the world's largest coral reef systems are in the warm waters of Oceania. Human activity and changing water temperatures put some reefs at risk.

THE CONTINENT:
ANTARCTICA

PHYSICAL

Land area
5,100,000 sq mi (13,209,000 sq km)

Highest point
Vinson Massif
16,067 ft (4,897 m)

Lowest point
Bentley Subglacial Trench
-8,383 ft (-2,555 m)

Coldest place
Plateau Station
Annual average temperature
-70°F (-56.7°C)

**Average precipitation
on the polar plateau**
Less than 2 in
(5 cm) per year

POLITICAL

Population
There are no indigenous inhabitants, but there are both permanent and summer-only staffed research stations.

Number of independent countries
0

Number of countries claiming land
7

Number of countries operating year-round research stations
20

Number of year-round research stations
40

Antarctica

Antarctica

THE BASICS

Antarctica is the only continent that has no sovereign boundaries and no economy or permanent population. Seven countries claim portions of the landmass (see map below), but according to the Antarctic Treaty, which preserves the continent for peaceful use and scientific study, no country rules.

GEO WHIZ

In winter, sea ice averaging 6 feet (2 m) deep more than doubles the size of the continent as it forms a belt ranging from 300 miles (483 km) to more than 1,000 miles (1,620 km) wide.

The Antarctic Convergence, an area where the waters of the Pacific, Atlantic, and Indian Oceans meet the cold Antarctic Circumpolar Current, is one of Earth's richest marine ecosystems.

The largest iceberg ever spotted in Antarctic waters measured 208 miles (335 km) long by 60 miles (97 km) wide, making it slightly larger than Belgium.

Krill, a tiny shrimplike creature that thrives in the waters around the continent of Antarctica, is important in the Antarctic food chain. Whales, seals, and penguins are among the creatures that depend on it for survival.

A small insect known as the wingless midge is Antarctica's largest land animal.

Five species of penguins—considered aquatic animals—live on the continent and on nearby islands. The Emperor penguin is the only one that breeds during the winter.

Fierce, bitter cold winds batter the coast at speeds of as much as 180 miles per hour (300 kph).

Mount Erebus is the world's southernmost volcano. Polar explorer James Clark Ross named it after one of his ships.

The Antarctic Treaty was signed in 1959 by 12 countries. To date, 47 countries have signed the document, agreeing to cooperate in scientific research and forbidding military action, nuclear tests, and the dumping of radioactive waste on the continent and in its waters.

🔵 **SOUTHERN HEIGHTS.**
Standing on the rocky summit of Mount Bearskin, named for a member of the team that established the 1956–57 IGY (International Geophysical Year) South Pole Station, a climber looks out across a vast snowfield.

Antarctica is the coldest, windiest, and even the driest continent. Though its immense ice cap holds 70 percent of the world's fresh water, its interior averages less than 2 inches (5 cm) of precipitation per year. Hidden beneath the ice is a continent of valleys, mountains, and lakes, but less than 2 percent of the land breaks through the ice cover. Reaching toward South America is the Antarctic Peninsula, the most visited of Antarctic regions. Though it is remote and mostly inhospitable, issues of human impact abound: fishing in rich but fragile waters that are sometimes called the Southern Ocean, future mining rights, and concern about the impact of global warming on the ice sheet.

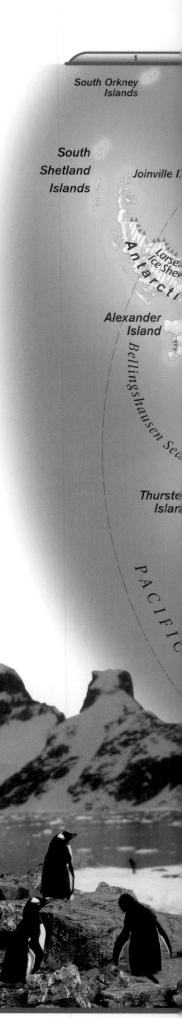

In color are shown 7 nations' territorial claims recognized by the Antarctic Treaty.

0   2,000 mi
0   2,000 km

Azimuthal Equidistant Projection

◐ **STANDING GUARD.** Even while resting, this leopard seal is alert to danger. Although penguins are their main food, leopard seals also eat other species of seals and have even been known to attack humans.

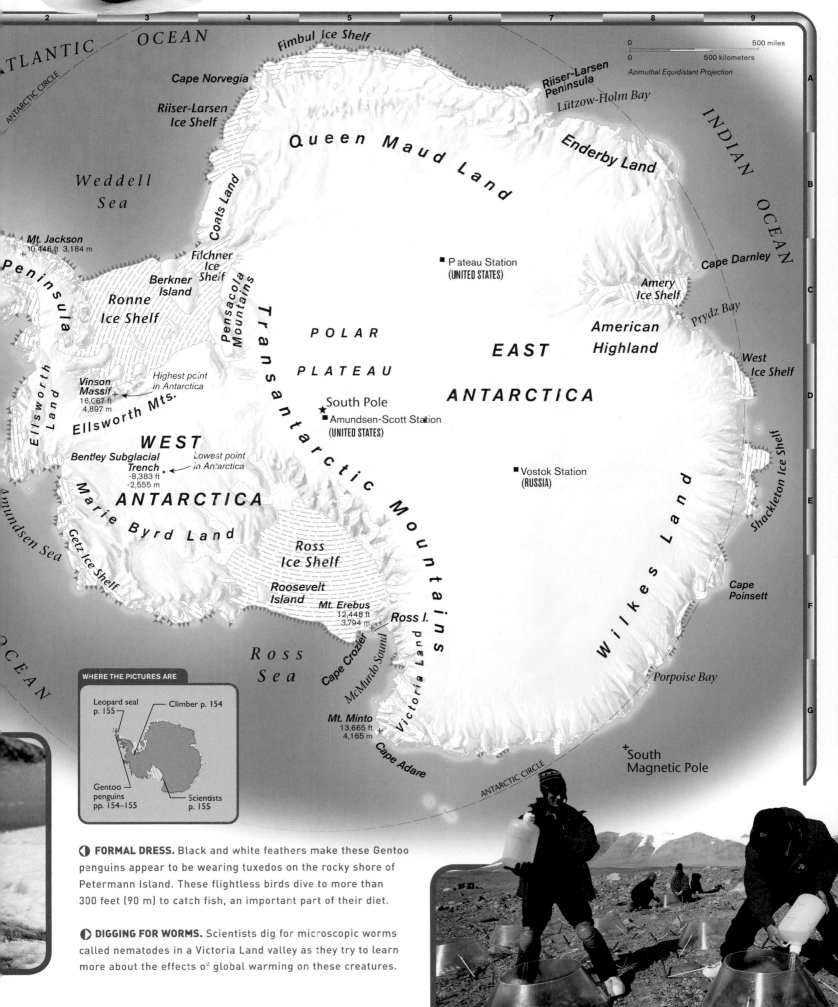

ATLANTIC OCEAN

ANTARCTIC CIRCLE

Fimbul Ice Shelf

Cape Norvegia

Riiser-Larsen
Ice Shelf

Riiser-Larsen
Peninsula

Lützow-Holm Bay

Queen Maud Land

Enderby Land

INDIAN OCEAN

Weddell
Sea

Coats Land

Cape Darnley

Mt. Jackson
10,446 ft 3,184 m

Filchner
Ice
Shelf

Berkner
Island

Ronne
Ice Shelf

Pensacola Mountains

Transantarctic Mountains

Plateau Station
(UNITED STATES)

Amery
Ice Shelf

Prydz Bay

Peninsula

POLAR

PLATEAU

EAST

American
Highland

West
Ice Shelf

Ellsworth Land

Vinson
Massif
16,067 ft
4,897 m

Highest point
in Antarctica

Ellsworth Mts.

South Pole

ANTARCTICA

WEST

Bentley Subglacial
Trench
-8,383 ft
-2,555 m

Lowest point
in Antarctica

Amundsen-Scott Station
(UNITED STATES)

Vostok Station
(RUSSIA)

Shackleton Ice Shelf

ANTARCTICA

Marie Byrd Land

Amundsen Sea

Getz Ice Shelf

Ross
Ice Shelf

Roosevelt
Island

Mt. Erebus
12,448 ft
3,794 m

Ross I.

McMurdo Sound

Cape
Poinsett

Wilkes Land

OCEAN

WHERE THE PICTURES ARE

Leopard seal
p. 155

Climber p. 154

Gentoo
penguins
pp. 154–155

Scientists
p. 155

Ross
Sea

Cape Crozier

Victoria Land

Porpoise Bay

Mt. Minto
13,665 ft
4,165 m

Cape Adare

ANTARCTIC CIRCLE

+South
Magnetic Pole

0   500 miles
0   500 kilometers
Azimuthal Equidistant Projection

◐ **FORMAL DRESS.** Black and white feathers make these Gentoo penguins appear to be wearing tuxedos on the rocky shore of Petermann Island. These flightless birds dive to more than 300 feet (90 m) to catch fish, an important part of their diet.

◐ **DIGGING FOR WORMS.** Scientists dig for microscopic worms called nematodes in a Victoria Land valley as they try to learn more about the effects of global warming on these creatures.

The Oceans

Investigating the Oceans

The map at right shows that more than 70 percent of Earth's surface is underwater, mainly covered by four great oceans. There is growing support for a fifth ocean, called the Southern Ocean, in the area from Antarctica to 60°S latitude. The oceans are really inter-connected bodies of water that together form one global ocean.

The ocean floor is as varied as the surface of the continents, but mapping the oceans is challenging. Past explorers cut their way through jungles of the Amazon and conquered icy heights of the Himalaya, but explorers could not march across the floor of the Pacific Ocean, which in places descends to more than 35,000 feet (10,668 m) below the surface of the water.

0 m	0 ft
-500 m	-1,640 ft
-1,500 m	-4,920 ft
-3,000 m	-9,840 ft
-5,000 m	-16,400 ft
-7,000 m	-22,970 ft
-9,000 m	-29,530 ft
-11,000 m	-36,090 ft

ARCTIC OCEAN

ASIA

NORTH

NORTH PACIFIC OCEAN

AUSTRALIA

INDIAN OCEAN

SOUTH PACIFIC OCEAN

ANTARCTIC

World Bathymetry

🌐 **UNDERWATER LANDSCAPE.** The landscape of the ocean floor is varied and constantly changing. A continental edge that slopes gently beneath the water is called a continental shelf. Mountain ranges, called mid-ocean ridges, rise where ocean plates are spreading and magma flows out to create new land. Other plates plunge into trenches more than six miles (10 km) deep. In addition, magma, rising through vents called hot spots, pushes through ocean plates, creating seamounts and volcanoes.

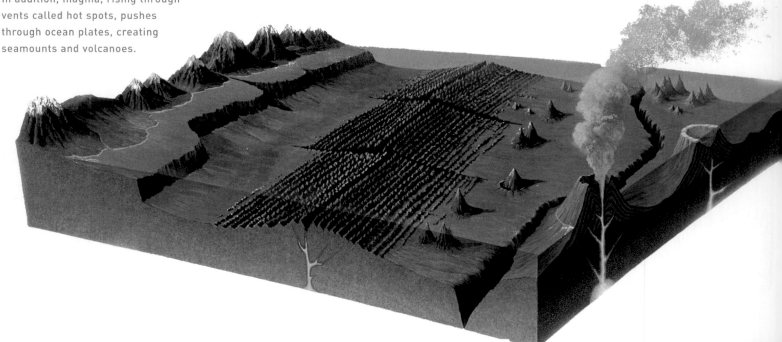

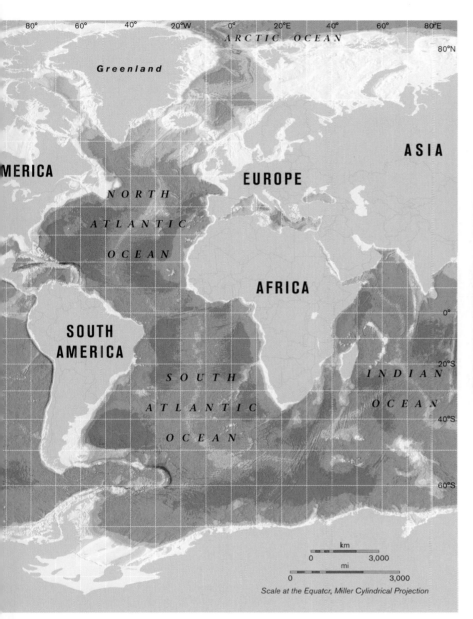

ARCTIC OCEAN

Greenland

ASIA

EUROPE

MERICA

NORTH
ATLANTIC
OCEAN

AFRICA

SOUTH
AMERICA

SOUTH
ATLANTIC
OCEAN

INDIAN
OCEAN

80°N

0°

20°S

40°S

60°S

km
0   3,000
mi
0   3,000
Scale at the Equator, Miller Cylindrical Projection

🌀 **FROM OCEAN TO SATELLITE.** In the 1990s, scientists developed the Argo Float to collect data from below the ocean surface. Argo Floats sink to a preset depth, often thousands of feet, where they gather data, such as temperature and salt content. At regular intervals, the floats rise to the surface (above) and transmit the data collected to a satellite. Then the cycle starts over again.

🌀 **EYE ON THE OCEAN.** The Sea-Viewing Wide Field-of-View Sensor (SeaWiFS) satellite records digital images of ocean colors that are used to identify and follow plant and animal activity in the oceans.

◐ **SEEING WITH YOUR EARS**. Special instruments, such as this acoustic buoy, use sound waves bounced off the ocean floor to record variations in water temperature. This technique, called Acoustic Thermometry of Ocean Climate (ATOC), may someday help monitor long-term climate changes.

THE OCEANS

Pacific Ocean

The Pacific Ocean, largest of Earth's oceans, is about 15 times larger than the United States

⬒ **IN THE MIDST OF DANGER.**
A false-clown anemonefish swims among the tentacles of a sea anemone off the coast of the Philippines, in the western Pacific. This colorful fish is immune to the anemone's paralyzing sting.

and covers more than 30 percent of Earth's surface. The edges of the Pacific are often called the Ring of Fire because many active volcanoes and earthquakes occur where the ocean plate is moving under the edges of continental plates. The southwestern Pacific is dotted with many islands. Also in the western Pacific, the Challenger Deep in the Mariana Trench plunges to 36,070 feet (10,994 m) below sea level. Most of the world's fish catch (see page 48) comes from the Pacific, and its oil and gas reserves are an important energy source.

THE BASICS

STATS

Surface area
65,436,200 sq mi
(169,479,000 sq km)

Percent of Earth's water area
47%

Greatest depth
Challenger Deep
(in the Mariana Trench)
-36,070 ft (-10,994 m)

Surface temperatures
Summer high: 90°F (32°C)
Winter low: 28°F (-2°C)

Tides
Highest: 30 ft (9 m)
near Korean peninsula
Lowest: 1 ft (0.3 m)
near Midway Islands

GEO WHIZ

The Pacific Ocean has more islands—tens of thousands of them—than any other ocean.

The ocean's name comes from the Latin *Mare Pacificum*, meaning "peaceful sea," but earthquake and volcanic activity along the Ring of Fire generate powerful waves called tsunamis, which cause death and destruction when they slam ashore.

With the greatest area of tropical waters, the Pacific is also home to the largest number of coral reefs, including Earth's longest: Australia's 1,429-mile (2,300-km)-long Great Barrier Reef.

The Hawaiian monk seal, the most endangered marine mammal in U.S. waters, lives on only a few islands in the remote northwestern end of the Hawaiian archipelago.

◐ **CIRCLE OF LIFE.**
Atolls, such as this one near Okinawa, Japan, are ocean landforms created by tiny marine animals called corals. These creatures live in warm tropical waters. The circular shape of atolls often marks the coastline of sunken volcanic islands.

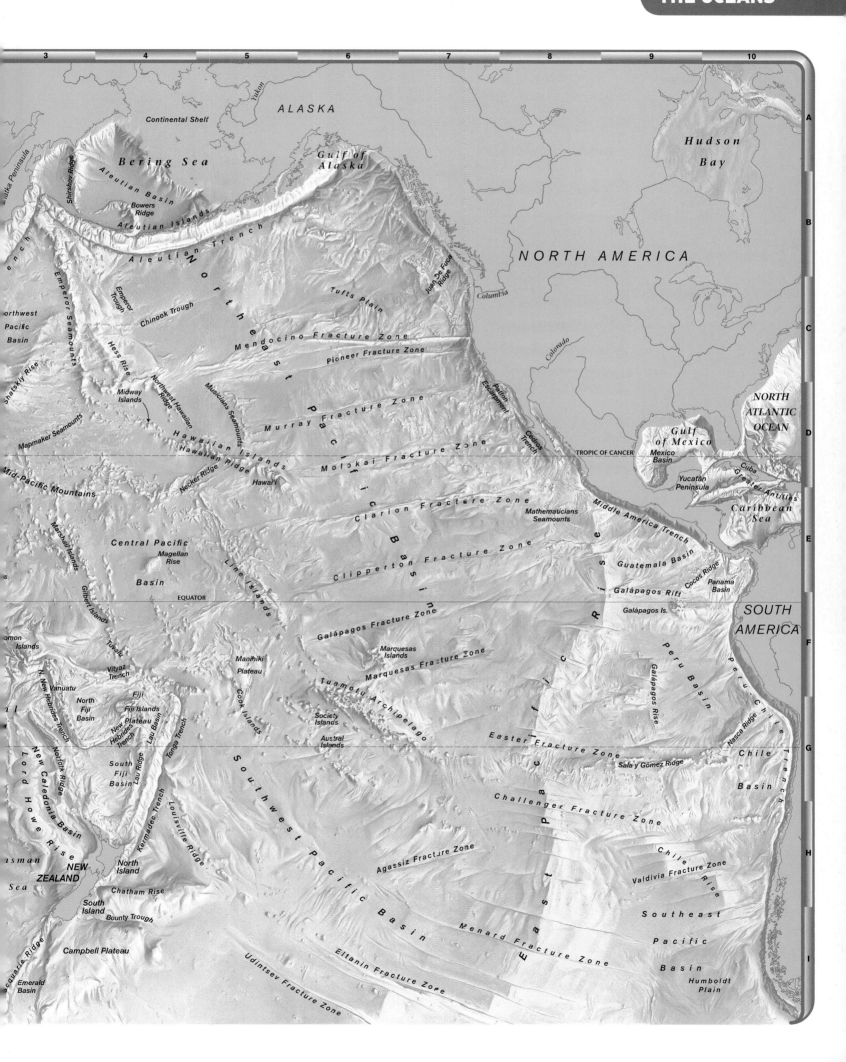

3   4   5   6   7   8   9   10

A

Hudson Bay

B

ALASKA

Bering Sea

Aleutian Basin

Bowers Ridge

Aleutian Islands

NORTH AMERICA

Continental Shelf

Yukon

Gulf of Alaska

Aleutian Trench

Emperor Trough

Shirshov Ridge

Emperor Seamounts

Chinook Trough

Tufts Plain

Juan De Fuca Ridge

Columbia

C

Northwest Pacific Basin

Hess Rise

Mendocino Fracture Zone

Pioneer Fracture Zone

Colorado

Shatskiy Rise

Midway Islands

Northwest Hawaiian Ridge

Musicians Seamounts

Murray Fracture Zone

Encampment

Patton Escarpment

NORTH ATLANTIC OCEAN

D

Mapmaker Seamounts

Hawaiian Islands

Hawaiian Ridge

Necker Ridge

Molokai Fracture Zone

Cedros Trench

TROPIC OF CANCER

Gulf of Mexico

Mexico Basin

Yucatán Peninsula

Cuba

Greater Antilles

Mid-Pacific Mountains

Hawai'i

Clarion Fracture Zone

Mathematicians Seamounts

Middle America Trench

Caribbean Sea

E

Marshall Islands

Central Pacific Basin

Magellan Rise

Line Islands

Clipperton Fracture Zone

Guatemala Basin

Galápagos Rift

Cocos Ridge

Panama Basin

EQUATOR

Galápagos Is.

SOUTH AMERICA

F

Solomon Islands

Gilbert Islands

Tuvalu

Galápagos Fracture Zone

Marquesas Islands

Marquesas Fracture Zone

Peru Basin

Galápagos Rise

N. New Hebrides Trench

Vanuatu

Vityaz Trench

North Fiji Basin

Fiji

Fiji Islands

New Hebrides Trench

Manihiki Plateau

Lau Basin

Cook Islands

Tuamotu Archipelago

Society Islands

Peru-Chile Trench

G

New Plateau

Lau Ridge

Tonga Trench

Austral Islands

Easter Fracture Zone

Sala y Gómez Ridge

Nasca Ridge

Chile Basin

Norfolk Ridge

South Fiji Basin

New Caledonia Basin

Kermadec Trench

Louisville Ridge

Southwest Pacific Basin

Challenger Fracture Zone

Chile Rise

H

Lord Howe Rise

Tasman Sea

NEW ZEALAND

North Island

Chatham Rise

Agassiz Fracture Zone

East Pacific Rise

Valdivia Fracture Zone

South Island

Bounty Trough

Menard Fracture Zone

Southeast Pacific Basin

I

Macquarie Ridge

Campbell Plateau

Emerald Basin

Udintsev Fracture Zone

Eltanin Fracture Zone

Humboldt Plain

THE BASICS

STATS

Surface area
35,338,500 sq mi
(91,526,400 sq km)

Percent of Earth's water area
25%

Greatest depth
Puerto Rico Trench
-28,232 ft (-8,605 m)

Surface temperatures
Summer high: 90°F (32°C)
Winter low: 28°F (-2°C)

Tides
Highest: 52 ft (16 m)
Bay of Fundy, Canada
Lowest: 1.5 ft (0.5 m)
Gulf of Mexico and Mediterranean Sea

GEO WHIZ

In 2005, the Atlantic Ocean produced a record-setting 15 hurricanes. For the first time in a single season, four hurricanes—Emily, Katrina, Rita, and Wilma—reached category 5 level, with sustained winds of at least 155 miles per hour (249 kph).

The Atlantic Ocean is about half the size of the Pacific, but it's growing. Spreading along the Mid-Atlantic Ridge allows molten rock from Earth's interior to escape and form new ocean floor.

Fishermen in the North Atlantic were eyewitnesses to the volcanic eruption that created the island of Surtsey, off the southeastern coast of Iceland, in November 1963.

Each year, the amount of water that flows into the Atlantic Ocean from the Amazon River is equal to 20 percent of Earth's available fresh water.

Atlantic Ocean

Among Earth's great oceans, the Atlantic is second only to the Pacific in size. The floor of the Atlantic is split by the Mid-Atlantic Ridge, which

⊕ **CAMOUFLAGE ON ICE.** A young harp seal, called a pup, rests on the ice in Canada's Gulf of St. Lawrence. Pups are cared for by their mothers for only 12 days. After that, they must survive on their own.

is part of the Mid-Ocean Ridge—the longest mountain chain on Earth. The Atlantic poses many hazards to human activity. Tropical storms called hurricanes form in the warm tropical waters off the west coast of Africa and move across the ocean to bombard the islands of the Caribbean and coastal areas of North America with damaging winds, waves, and rain in the late summer and fall. In the cold waters of the North Atlantic, sea ice and icebergs pose a danger to shipping, especially during winter and spring.

The Atlantic has rich deposits of oil and natural gas, but drilling has resulted in pollution problems. In addition, the Atlantic has important marine fisheries, but overfishing has put some species at risk. Sea lanes between Europe and the Americas are among the most heavily trafficked in the world.

⊕ **HIDDEN DANGER.** Icebergs (above, right) are huge blocks of ice that break away, or calve, from the edges of glaciers. They pose a danger to ships because only about 10 percent of their bulk is visible above the waterline. A tragic disaster associated with an iceberg was the 1912 sinking of the RMS *Titanic*, whose ghostly ruins are shown above, left.

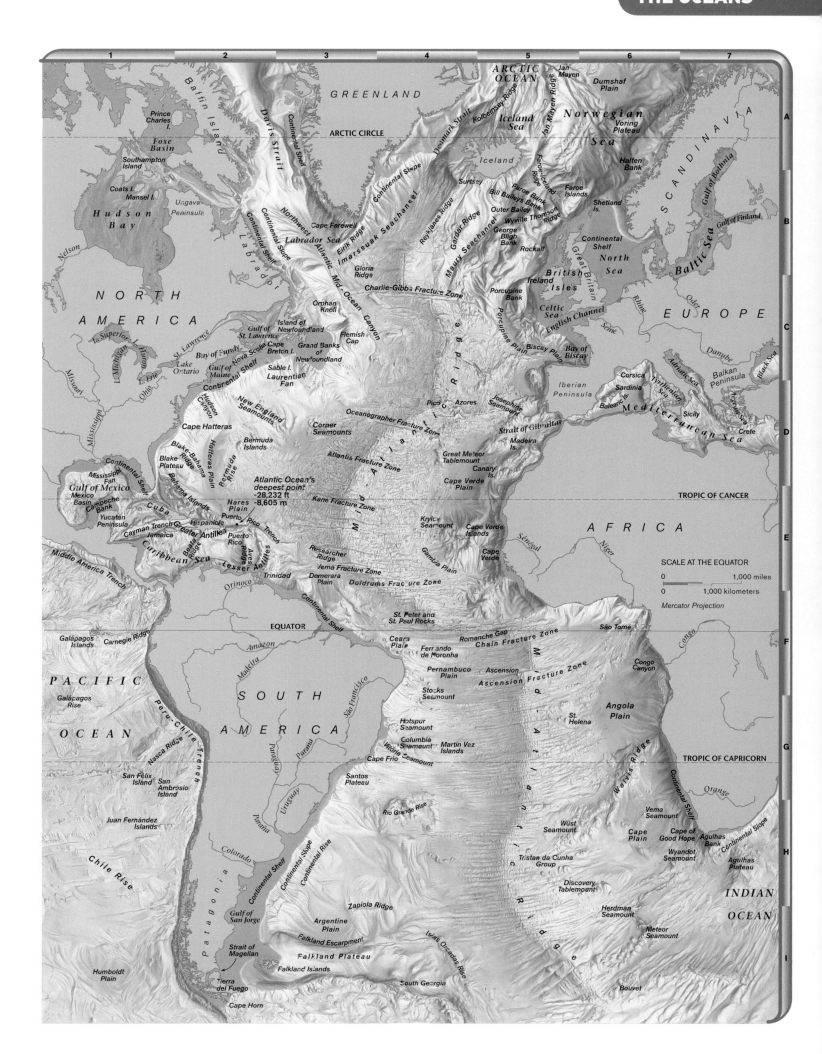

THE BASICS

STATS

Surface area
28,839,800 sq mi
(74,694,800 sq km)

Percent of Earth's water area
21%

Greatest depth
Java Trench
-23,376 ft (-7,125 m)

Surface temperatures
Summer high: 93°F (34°C)
Winter low: 28°F (-2°C)

Tides
Highest: 36 ft (11 m)
Lowest: 2 ft (0.6 m)
Both along Australia's west coast

GEO WHIZ

Each day tankers carrying 17 million barrels of crude oil from the Persian Gulf enter the waters of the Indian Ocean, transporting their cargo for distribution around the world.

Some of the world's largest breeding grounds for humpback whales are in the Indian Ocean, the Arabian Sea, and off the east coast of Africa.

The Bay of Bengal is sometimes called Cyclone Alley because of the large number of tropical storms that occur there each year between May and November.

Sailors from what is now Indonesia used seasonal winds called monsoons to reach Africa's east coast. They arrived on the continent long before Europeans did.

A December 2004 earthquake caused a tsunami that killed more than 225,000 people in countries bordering the Indian Ocean. Waves reached as high as 49 feet (15 m).

The Indian Ocean has several strategic chokepoints—narrow straits through which shipping must pass. They include Bab el Mandeb, between the Gulf of Aden and the Red Sea; the Strait of Hormuz, between the Persian Gulf and the Arabian Sea; the Gulf of Suez, between the Red Sea and the Suez Canal; and the Strait of Malacca, between Sumatra and the Malay Peninsula.

Indian Ocean

The Indian Ocean stretches from Africa's east coast to the southern coast of Asia and the western coast of Australia. It is the third largest of Earth's great oceans. Changing air pressure systems over the warm waters of the Indian Ocean trigger South Asia's famous monsoon climate—a weather pattern in which winds reverse directions seasonally. The Bay of Bengal, an arm of the Indian Ocean, experiences devastating tropical storms, similar to hurricanes, but called cyclones in this region. Islands along the eastern edge of the Indian Ocean plate experience earthquakes that sometimes cause destructive ocean waves, called tsunamis.

The Arabian Sea, Persian Gulf, and Red Sea, also extensions of the Indian Ocean, are important sources of oil and natural gas reserves and account for an estimated 40 percent of the world's offshore oil production. The sea routes of the Indian Ocean connect the Middle East to the rest of world, carrying much needed energy resources on huge tanker ships.

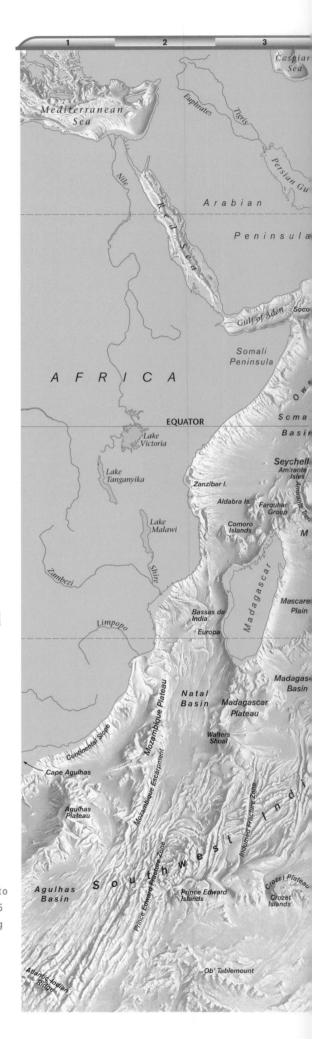

◖ **LIVING FOSSIL.**
A coelacanth swims in the warm waters of the western Indian Ocean off the Comoro Islands. Once thought to have become extinct 65 million years ago along with the dinosaurs, a living coelacanth was discovered in 1938.

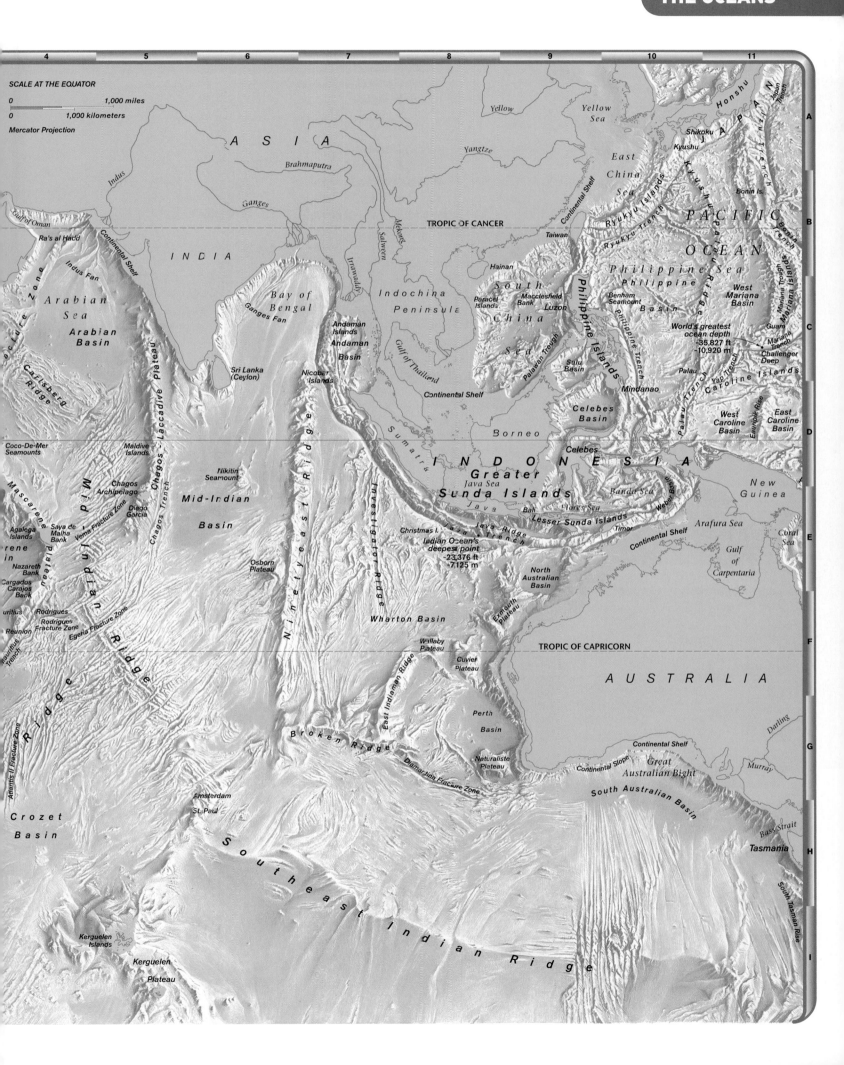

THE OCEANS

THE BASICS

STATS

Surface area
5,390,000 sq mi (13,960,100 sq km)

Percent of Earth's water area
4%

Greatest depth
Molloy Deep: -18,599 ft (-5,669 m)

Surface temperatures
Summer high: 41°F (5°C)
Winter low: 28°F (-2°C)

Tides
Less than a 1-ft (0.3-m) variation throughout the ocean

GEO WHIZ

Satellite monitoring of Arctic sea ice, which began in the late 1970s, shows that the extent of the sea ice is shrinking by approximately 8 percent every 10 years. Scientists think this may be caused by global warming.

The geographic North Pole lies roughly in the middle of the Arctic Ocean under 13,000 feet (3,962 m) of water.

Many of the features on the Arctic Ocean floor are named for early Arctic explorers and for bordering landmasses.

Mapping of the Arctic Ocean floor did not begin until 2001. The initial research was by a joint U.S.-German operation called AMORE (Arctic Mid-Ocean Ridge Expedition). Surprise findings included 12 volcanoes, hydrothermal vents, and a vast continental shelf off Siberia.

ARCTIC OCEAN

The Arctic Ocean lies mostly north of the Arctic Circle, bounded by North America, Europe, and Asia. Unlike the other oceans, the Arctic is subject to persistent cold throughout the year. Also, because of its very high latitude, the Arctic experiences winters of perpetual night and summers of continual daylight. Except for coastal margins, the Arctic Ocean is covered by permanent drifting pack ice that averages almost 10 feet (3 m) in thickness. Some scientists are concerned that the polar ice may be melting due to global warming, putting at risk the habitat of polar bears and other arctic animals.

◗ **ARCTIC RESEARCH.** Scientists wearing cold weather survival suits prepare to measure salt content, nutrients, and plant and animal life in ice and meltwater. They also monitor changes related to global warming, such as the shrinking of the polar ice cap.

◗ **FREE RIDE.** A baby polar bear catches a ride as its mother crosses Canada's Arctic. Polar bear populations are showing signs of stress as sea ice shrinks.

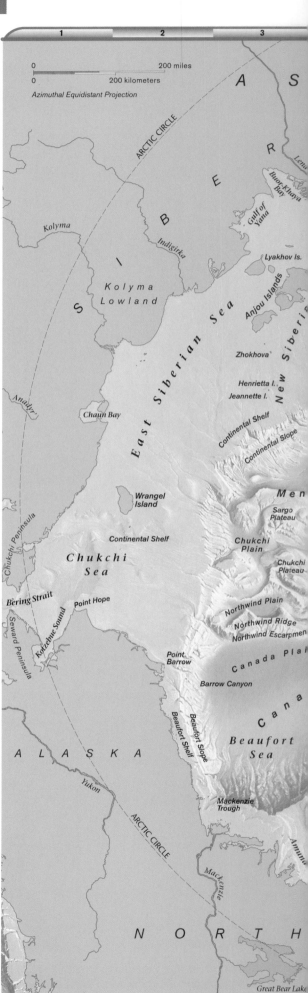

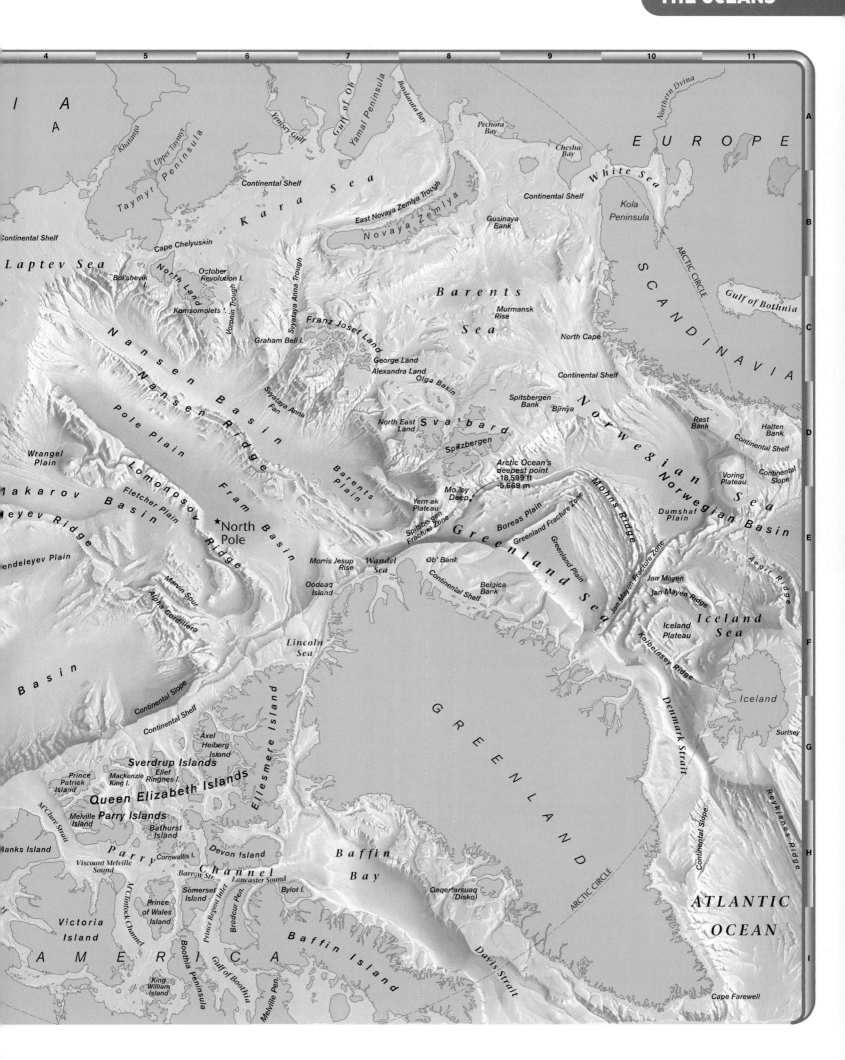

4 5 6 7 8 9 10 11

A

Northern Dvina

Khatanga

Gulf of Ob

Yamal Peninsula

Baydaratia Bay

Pechora Bay

Chesha Bay

E U R O P E

White Sea

A

Upper Taymyr

Yenisey Gulf

K a r a   S e a

Continental Shelf

East Novaya Zemlya Trough

Gusinaya Bank

Continental Shelf

Kola Peninsula

ARCTIC CIRCLE

S C A N D I N A V I A

B

Taymyr Peninsula

Cape Chelyuskin

Novaya Zemlya

Murmansk Rise

Gulf of Bothnia

Continental Shelf

I A

A

Bol'shevik I.

October Revolution I.

B a r e n t s

North Cape

C

L a p t e v   S e a

North Land

Komsomolets I.

Voronin Trough

Syataya Anna Trough

S e a

Continental Shelf

Graham Bell I.

Franz Josef Land

George Land

Alexandra Land

Olga Basin

Continental Shelf

D

Nansen Basin

Syataya Anna Fan

Spitsbergen Bank

Bjørnya

Røst Bank

Halten Bank

Nansen Ridge

North East Land

S v a l b a r d

Continental Shelf

Pole Plain

Barents Plain

Spitzbergen

Arctic Ocean's deepest point -18,599 ft -5,669 m

Voring Plateau

Continental Slope

N o r w e g i a n

E

Wrangel Plain

Lomonosov

Fletcher Plain

Fram

Yermak Plateau

Molloy Deep

Boreas Plain

Mohns Ridge

Dumshaf Plain

M a k a r o v

Ridge

★ *North Pole*

Basin

Spitsbergen Fracture Zone

G r e e n l a n d   S e a

Greenland Fracture Zone

Greenland Plain

Aegic Ridge

Basin

Mendeleyev Plain

B a s i n

Basin

Morris Jesup Rise

Wandel Sea

Ob' Bank

Jan Mayen

N o r w e g i a n   B a s i n

S e a

F

Ridge

Marvin Spur

Oodaaq Island

Continental Shelf

Belgica Bank

Jan Mayen Fracture Zone

Jan Mayen Ridge

Iceland Plateau

I c e l a n d

Alpha Cordillera

Lincoln Sea

Kolbeinsey Ridge

S e a

Iceland

Surtsey

G

Continental Slope

Continental Shelf

Axel Heiberg Island

E l l e s m e r e   I s l a n d

G R E E N L A N D

Denmark Strait

Reykjanes Ridge

Sverdrup Islands

Ellef Ringnes I.

Prince Patrick Island

Mackenzie King I.

H

Queen Elizabeth Islands

M'Clure Strait

Melville Island

Parry Islands

Bathurst Island

Cornwallis I.

P a r r y

Devon Island

B a f f i n

Continental Slope

A T L A N T I C

Banks Island

Viscount Melville Sound

C h a n n e l

Barrow Str.

Lancaster Sound

Bylot I.

B a y

Qeqertarsuaq (Disko)

ARCTIC CIRCLE

O C E A N

I

Victoria Island

M'Clintock Channel

Prince of Wales Island

Somerset Island

Prince Regent Inlet

Brodeur Pen.

B a f f i n   I s l a n d

A M E R I C A

King William Island

Boothia Peninsula

Gulf of Boothia

Melville Peninsula

Davis Strait

Cape Farewell

FLAGS & STATS

These flags and fact boxes represent the world's 195 independent countries—those with national governments that are recognized as having the highest legal authority over the land and people within their boundaries. The flags shown are national flags recognized by the United Nations. Area figures include land, plus surface areas for inland bodies of water. Population figures are for mid-2012, as provided by the Population Reference Bureau. The languages listed are either the ones most commonly spoken within a country or official languages of a country.

NORTH AMERICA

Antigua and Barbuda
Area: 171 sq mi
(442 sq km)
Population: 87,000
Capital: St. John's
Languages: English (official),
local dialects
Currency: East Caribbean
dollar

Bahamas
Area: 5,382 sq mi
(13,939 sq km)
Population: 362,000
Capital: Nassau
Languages: English (official)
Currency: Bahamian dollar

Barbados
Area: 166 sq mi
(430 sq km)
Population: 277,000
Capital: Bridgetown
Language: English
Currency: Barbadian dollar

Belize
Area: 8,867 sq mi
(22,965 sq km)
Population: 326,000
Capital: Belmopan
Languages: Spanish, Creole,
Mayan dialects, English,
Garifuna (Carib), German
Currency: Belize dollar

Canada
Area: 3,855,101 sq mi
(9,984,670 sq km)
Population: 34,860,000
Capital: Ottawa
Languages: English, French
(both official)
Currency: Canadian dollar

Costa Rica
Area: 19,730 sq mi
(51,100 sq km)
Population: 4,481,000
Capital: San José
Languages: Spanish
(official), English
Currency: Costa Rican colón

Cuba
Area: 42,803 sq mi
(110,860 sq km)
Population: 11,219,000
Capital: Havana
Language: Spanish
Currency: Cuban peso

Dominica
Area: 290 sq mi
(751 sq km)
Population: 71,000
Capital: Roseau
Languages: English (official),
French patois
Currency: East Caribbean
dollar

Dominican Republic
Area: 18,704 sq mi
(48,442 sq km)
Population: 10,135,000
Capital: Santo Domingo
Language: Spanish
Currency: Dominican peso

El Salvador
Area: 8,124 sq mi
(21,041 sq km)
Population: 6,264,000
Capital: San Salvador
Languages: Spanish, Nahua
Currency: United States dollar

Grenada
Area: 133 sq mi
(344 sq km)
Population: 115,000
Capital: St. George's
Languages: English (official),
French patois
Currency: East Caribbean
dollar

Guatemala
Area: 42,042 sq mi
(108,889 sq km)
Population: 15,044,000
Capital: Guatemala City
Languages: Spanish,
23 Amerindian languages
Currency: Guatemalan quetzal

Haiti
Area: 10,714 sq mi
(27,750 sq km)
Population: 10,256,000
Capital: Port-au-Prince
Languages: French,
Creole (both official)
Currency: Haitian gourde

Honduras
Area: 43,433 sq mi
(112,492 sq km)
Population: 8,385,000
Capital: Tegucigalpa
Languages: Spanish,
Amerindian dialects
Currency: Honduran lempira

Jamaica
Area: 4,244 sq mi
(10,991 sq km)
Population: 2,716,000
Capital: Kingston
Languages: English,
patois English
Currency: Jamaican dollar

Mexico
Area: 758,449 sq mi
(1,964,375 sq km)
Population: 116,147,000
Capital: Mexico City
Languages: Spanish, Maya,
Nahuatl, other indigenous
languages
Currency: Mexican peso

Nicaragua
Area: 50,193 sq mi
(130,000 sq km)
Population: 5,955,000
Capital: Managua
Languages: Spanish
(official), English,
indigenous languages
Currency: Nicaraguan
córdoba

Panama
Area: 29,157 sq mi
(75,517 sq km)
Population: 3,610,000
Capital: Panama City
Languages: Spanish
(official), English
Currency: Panamanian
balboa/United States dollar

St. Kitts and Nevis
Area: 104 sq mi
(269 sq km)
Population: 54,000
Capital: Basseterre
Language: English
Currency: East Caribbean
dollar

St. Lucia
Area: 238 sq mi
(616 sq km)
Population: 169,000
Capital: Castries
Languages: English (official),
French patois
Currency: East Caribbean
dollar

**St. Vincent and
the Grenadines**
Area: 150 sq mi
(389 sq km)
Population: 108,000
Capital: Kingstown
Languages: English,
French patois
Currency: East Caribbean
dollar

Trinidad and Tobago
Area: 1,980 sq mi
(5,128 sq km)
Population: 1,315,000
Capital: Port of Spain
Languages: English (official),
Caribbean Hindustani,
French, Spanish, Chinese
Currency: Trinidad and
Tobago dollar

United States
Area: 3,794,083 sq mi
(9,826,630 sq km)
Population: 313,858,000
Capital: Washington, D.C.
Languages: English, Spanish
Currency: United States dollar

SOUTH AMERICA

Argentina
Area: 1,073,518 sq mi
(2,780,400 sq km)
Population: 40,829,000
Capital: Buenos Aires
Languages: Spanish (official),
English, Italian, German,
French
Currency: Argentine peso

Bolivia
Area: 424,164 sq mi
(1,098,581 sq km)
Population: 10,836,000
Capitals: La Paz, Sucre
Languages: Spanish,
Quechua, Aymara (all official)
Currency: Bolivian boliviano

Brazil
Area: 3,300,171 sq mi
(8,547,403 sq km)
Population: 194,334,000
Capital: Brasília
Language: Portuguese (official)
Currency: Brazilian real

Chile
Area: 291,930 sq mi
(756,096 sq km)
Population: 17,403,000
Capital: Santiago
Language: Spanish
Currency: Chilean peso

Colombia
Area: 440,831 sq mi
(1,141,748 sq km)
Population: 47,415,000
Capital: Bogotá
Language: Spanish
Currency: Colombian peso

Ecuador
Area: 109,483 sq mi
(283,560 sq km)
Population: 14,865,000
Capital: Quito
Languages: Spanish (official),
Quechua, other Amerindian
languages
Currency: United States dollar

Guyana
Area: 83,000 sq mi
(214,969 sq km)
Population: 796,000
Capital: Georgetown
Languages: English,
Amerindian dialects, Creole,
Hindi, Urdu
Currency: Guyanese dollar

Paraguay
Area: 157,048 sq mi
(406,752 sq km)
Population: 6,683,000
Capital: Asunción
Languages: Spanish, Guaraní
(both official)
Currency: Paraguayan guaraní

Peru
Area: 496,224 sq mi
(1,285,216 sq km)
Population: 30,136,000
Capital: Lima
Languages: Spanish, Quechua
(both official), Aymara, minor
Amazonian languages
Currency: Peruvian nuevo sol

Suriname
Area: 63,037 sq mi
(163,265 sq km)
Population: 542,000
Capital: Paramaribo
Languages: Dutch (official),
English, Sranang Tongo (Taki-
Taki), Hindustani, Javanese
Currency: Surinamese dollar

Uruguay
Area: 68,037 sq mi
(176,215 sq km)
Population: 3,381,000
Capital: Montevideo
Languages: Spanish,
Portunol, Brazilero
Currency: Uruguayan peso

Venezuela
Area: 352,144 sq mi
(912,050 sq km)
Population: 29,715,000
Capital: Caracas
Languages: Spanish (official),
many indigenous languages
Currency: Venezuelan bolívar

EUROPE

Albania
Area: 11,100 sq mi
(28,748 sq km)
Population: 2,833,000
Capital: Tirana
Languages: Albanian
(official), Greek, Vlach,
Romani, Slavic dialects
Currency: Albanian lek

Andorra
Area: 181 sq mi
(468 sq km)
Population: 72,000
Capital: Andorra la Vella
Languages: Catalan (official),
French, Castilian, Portuguese
Currency: Euro

Austria
Area: 32,378 sq mi
(83,858 sq km)
Population: 8,845,000
Capital: Vienna
Languages: German (official),
Slovene, Croatian, Hungarian
Currency: Euro

Belarus
Area: 80,153 sq mi
(207,595 sq km)
Population: 9,457,000
Capital: Minsk
Languages: Belarusian,
Russian
Currency: Belarusian ruble

Belgium
Area: 11,787 sq mi
(30,528 sq km)
Population: 11,121,000
Capital: Brussels
Languages: Flemish (Dutch),
French, German (all official)
Currency: Euro

Bosnia and Herzegovina
Area: 19,741 sq mi
(51,129 sq km)
Population: 3,843,000
Capital: Sarajevo
Languages: Croatian,
Serbian, Bosnian
Currency: Bosnia and
Herzegovina convertible mark

Bulgaria
Area: 42,855 sq mi
(110,994 sq km)
Population: 7,240,000
Capital: Sofia
Languages: Bulgarian,
Turkish, Roma
Currency: Bulgarian lev

Croatia
Area: 21,831 sq mi
(56,542 sq km)
Population: 4,274,000
Capital: Zagreb
Language: Croatian
Currency: Croatian kuna

Cyprus
Area: 3,572 sq mi
(9,251 sq km)
Population: 1,172,000
Capital: Nicosia
Languages: Greek, Turkish,
English
Currency: Euro

Czech Republic
Area: 30,450 sq mi
(78,866 sq km)
Population: 10,490,000
Capital: Prague
Language: Czech
Currency: Czech koruna

Denmark
Area: 16,640 sq mi
(43,098 sq km)
Population: 5,591,000
Capital: Copenhagen
Languages: Danish, Faroese,
Greenlandic, German
Currency: Danish krone

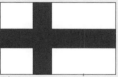

Estonia
Area: 17,462 sq mi
(45,227 sq km)
Population: 1,339,000
Capital: Tallinn
Languages: Estonian
(official), Russian
Currency: Euro

Finland
Area: 130,558 sq mi
(338,145 sq km)
Population: 5,414,000
Capital: Helsinki
Languages: Finnish, Swedish
(both official)
Currency: Euro

FLAGS & STATS

France
Area: 210,026 sq mi
(543,965 sq km)
Population: 63,605,000
Capital: Paris
Language: French
Currency: Euro

Germany
Area: 137,847 sq mi
(357,022 sq km)
Population: 81,825,000
Capital: Berlin
Language: German
Currency: Euro

Greece
Area: 50,949 sq mi
(131,957 sq km)
Population: 10,833,000
Capital: Athens
Languages: Greek, English,
French
Currency: Euro

Hungary
Area: 35,919 sq mi
(93,030 sq km)
Population: 9,947,000
Capital: Budapest
Language: Hungarian
Currency: Hungarian forint

Iceland
Area: 39,769 sq mi
(103,000 sq km)
Population: 320,000
Capital: Reykjavík
Languages: Icelandic,
English, Nordic languages,
German
Currency: Icelandic króna

Ireland
Area: 27,133 sq mi
(70,273 sq km)
Population: 4,683,000
Capital: Dublin
Languages: Irish (Gaelic),
English
Currency: Euro

Italy
Area: 116,345 sq mi
(301,333 sq km)
Population: 60,950,000
Capital: Rome
Languages: Italian (official),
German, French, Slovene
Currency: Euro

Kosovo
Area: 4,203 sq mi
(10,887 sq km)
Population: 2,290,000
Capital: Pristina
Languages: Albanian, Serbian,
Bosnian, Turkish, Roma
Currency: Euro

Latvia
Area: 24,938 sq mi
(64,589 sq km)
Population: 2,049,000
Capital: Riga
Languages: Latvian (official),
Russian, Lithuanian
Currency: Latvian lats

Liechtenstein
Area: 62 sq mi
(160 sq km)
Population: 37,000
Capital: Vaduz
Languages: German (official),
Alemannic dialect
Currency: Swiss franc

Lithuania
Area: 25,212 sq mi
(65,300 sq km)
Population: 3,179,000
Capital: Vilnius
Languages: Lithuanian
(official), Polish, Russian
Currency: Lithuanian litas

Luxembourg
Area: 998 sq mi
(2,586 sq km)
Population: 527,000
Capital: Luxembourg
Languages: Luxembourgish
(official), German, French
Currency: Euro

Macedonia
Area: 9,928 sq mi
(25,713 sq km)
Population: 2,064,000
Capital: Skopje
Languages: Macedonian,
Albanian, Turkish
Currency: Macedonian denar

Malta
Area: 122 sq mi
(316 sq km)
Population: 399,000
Capital: Valletta
Languages: Maltese, English
(both official)
Currency: Euro

Moldova
Area: 13,050 sq mi
(33,800 sq km)
Population: 4,114,000
Capital: Chisinău
Languages: Moldovan
(official), Russian, Gagauz
Currency: Moldovan leu

Monaco
Area: 0.8 sq mi
(2 sq km)
Population: 36,000
Capital: Monaco
Languages: French (official),
English, Italian, Monegasque
Currency: Euro

Montenegro
Area: 5,415 sq mi
(14,026 sq km)
Population: 622,000
Capital: Podgorica
Languages: Serbian (official),
Bosnian, Albanian, Croatian
Currency: Euro

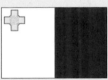

Netherlands
Area: 16,034 sq mi
(41,528 sq km)
Population: 16,749,000
Capital: Amsterdam
Languages: Dutch, Frisian
(both official)
Currency: Euro

Norway
Area: 125,004 sq mi
(323,758 sq km)
Population: 5,019,000
Capital: Oslo
Language: Norwegian (official)
Currency: Norwegian krone

Poland
Area: 120,728 sq mi
(312,685 sq km)
Population: 38,195,000
Capital: Warsaw
Language: Polish
Currency: Euro

Portugal
Area: 35,655 sq mi
(92,345 sq km)
Population: 10,561,000
Capital: Lisbon
Languages: Portuguese,
Mirandese (both official)
Currency: Euro

Romania
Area: 92,043 sq mi
(238,391 sq km)
Population: 21,408,000
Capital: Bucharest
Languages: Romanian
(official), Hungarian, German
Currency: Romanian leu

Russia
Area: 6,592,850 sq mi
(17,075,400 sq km)
Population: 143,165,000
Capital: Moscow
Languages: Russian, many
minority languages
Currency: Russian ruble

San Marino
Area: 24 sq mi
(61 sq km)
Population: 32,000
Capital: San Marino
Language: Italian
Currency: Euro

Serbia
Area: 29,913 sq mi
(77,474 sq km)
Population: 7,102,000
Capital: Belgrade
Languages: Serbian (official),
Romanian, Hungarian, Slovak,
Croatian
Currency: Serbian dinar

Slovakia
Area: 18,932 sq mi
(49,035 km)
Population: 5,394,000
Capital: Bratislava
Languages: Slovak (official),
Hungarian
Currency: Euro

Slovenia
Area: 7,827 sq mi
(20,273 sq km)
Population: 2,058,000
Capital: Ljubljana
Languages: Slovene,
Serbo-Croatian
Currency: Euro

Spain
Area: 195,363 sq mi
(505,988 sq km)
Population: 46,195,000
Capital: Madrid
Languages: Castilian Spanish
(official), Catalan, Galician,
Basque
Currency: Euro

Sweden
Area: 173,732 sq mi
(449,964 sq km)
Population: 9,514,000
Capital: Stockholm
Languages: Swedish, Sami,
Finnish
Currency: Swedish krona

Switzerland
Area: 15,940 sq mi
(41,284 km)
Population: 7,994,000
Capital: Bern
Languages: German, French,
Italian (all official), Romansch
Currency: Swiss franc

Ukraine
Area: 233,090 sq mi
(603,700 sq km)
Population: 45,556,000
Capital: Kiev
Languages: Ukrainian
(official), Russian
Currency: Ukrainian hryvnia

United Kingdom
Area: 93,788 sq mi
(242,910 sq km)
Population: 63,213,000
Capital: London
Languages: English, Welsh,
Scottish form of Gaelic
Currency: British pound

Vatican City
Area: 0.2 sq mi
(0.4 sq km)
Population: 836
Languages: Italian,
Latin, French
Currency: Euro

ASIA

Afghanistan
Area: 251,773 sq mi
(652,090 sq km)
Population: 33,397,000
Capital: Kabul
Languages: Afghan Persian
(Dari), Pashtu (both official),
Turkic languages
Currency: Afghan Afghani

Armenia
Area: 11,484 sq mi
(29,743 sq km)
Population: 3,282,000
Capital: Yerevan
Language: Armenian
Currency: Armenian dram

Azerbaijan
Area: 33,436 sq mi
(86,600 sq km)
Population: 9,284,000
Capital: Baku
Language: Azerbaijani (Azeri)
Currency: Azerbaijan manat

Bahrain
Area: 277 sq mi
(717 sq km)
Population: 1,336,000
Capital: Manama
Languages: Arabic, English,
Farsi, Urdu
Currency: Bahraini dinar

Bangladesh
Area: 56,977 sq mi
(147,570 sq km)
Population: 152,875,000
Capital: Dhaka
Languages: Bangla (Bengali)
(official), English
Currency: Bangladeshi taka

Bhutan
Area: 17,954 sq mi
(46,500 sq km)
Population: 708,000
Capital: Thimphu
Languages: Dzongkha
(official), Tibetan dialects,
Nepali dialects
Currency: Bhutanese
ngultrum/Indian rupee

Brunei
Area: 2,226 sq mi
(5,765 km)
Population: 413,000
Capital: Bandar Seri Begawan
Languages: Malay (official),
English, Chinese
Currency: Brunei dollar

Cambodia
Area: 69,898 sq mi
(181,035 sq km)
Population: 14,953,000
Capital: Phnom Penh
Language: Khmer (official)
Currency: Cambodian riel

China
Area: 3,705,405 sq mi
(9,596,960 sq km)
Population: 1,350,378,000
Capital: Beijing
Languages: Standard Chinese
(Mandarin), Yue, Wu, Minbei,
other dialects and minority
languages
Currency: Chinese yuan

**Timor-Leste
(East Timor)**
Area: 5,640 sq mi
(14,609 sq km)
Population: 1,126,000
Capital: Dili
Languages: Tetum, Portuguese
(official), Indonesian, English
Currency: United States dollar

Georgia
Area: 26,911 sq mi
(69,700 sq km)
Population: 4,519,000
Capital: T'bilisi
Languages: Georgian
(official), Russian, Armenian,
Azeri, Abkhaz
Currency: Georgian lari

India
Area: 1,269,222 sq mi
(3,287,270 sq km)
Population: 1,259,721,000
Capital: New Delhi
Languages: Hindi, English
(both official), 21 other
official languages
Currency: Indian rupee

Indonesia
Area: 742,308 sq mi
(1,922,570 sq km)
Population: 240,990,000
Capital: Jakarta
Languages: Bahasa
Indonesian (official), English,
Dutch, Javanese
Currency: Indonesian rupiah

Iran
Area: 636,296 sq mi
(1,648,000 sq km)
Population: 78,869,000
Capital: Tehran
Languages: Farsi (modern-
day Persian), Turkic, Kurdish
Currency: Iranian rial

Iraq
Area: 168,754 sq mi
(437,072 sq km)
Population: 33,703,000
Capital: Baghdad
Languages: Arabic, Kurdish,
Assyrian, Armenian
Currency: Iraqi dinar

Israel
Area: 8,550 sq mi
(22,145 sq km)
Population: 7,906,000
Capital: Jerusalem
Languages: Hebrew (official),
Arabic, English
Currency: Israeli new shekel

Japan
Area: 145,902 sq mi
(377,887 sq km)
Population: 127,588,000
Capital: Tokyo
Language: Japanese
Currency: Japanese yen

FLAGS & STATS

Jordan
Area: 34,495 sq mi
(89,342 sq km)
Population: 6,318,000
Capital: Amman
Languages: Arabic (official),
English
Currency: Jordanian dinar

Kazakhstan
Area: 1,049,155 sq mi
(2,717,300 sq km)
Population: 16,793,000
Capital: Astana
Languages: Kazakh (Qazaq),
Russian (official)
Currency: Kazakhstani tenge

Korea, North
Area: 46,540 sq mi
(120,538 sq km)
Population: 24,589,000
Capital: Pyongyang
Language: Korean
Currency: North Korean won

Korea, South
Area: 38,321 sq mi
(99,250 sq km)
Population: 48,906,000
Capital: Seoul
Languages: Korean,
English widely taught
Currency: South Korean won

Kuwait
Area: 6,880 sq mi
(17,818 sq km)
Population: 2,892,000
Capital: Kuwait
Languages: Arabic (official),
English
Currency: Kuwaiti dinar

Kyrgyzstan
Area: 77,182 sq mi
(199,900 sq km)
Population: 5,668,000
Capital: Bishkek
Languages: Kyrgyz, Russian
(both official)
Currency: Kyrgyzstani som

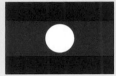

Laos
Area: 91,429 sq mi
(236,800 sq km)
Population: 6,521,000
Capital: Vientiane
Languages: Lao (official),
French, English, other ethnic
Currency: Lao kip

Lebanon
Area: 4,036 sq mi
(10,452 sq km)
Population: 4,304,000
Capital: Beirut
Languages: Arabic (official),
French, English, Armenian
Currency: Lebanese pound

Malaysia
Area: 127,355 sq mi
(329,847 sq km)
Population: 28,975,000
Capital: Kuala Lumpur
Languages: Bahasa Melayu
(official), English, Chinese
dialects, Tamil, Telugu,
indigenous languages
Currency: Malaysian ringgit

Maldives
Area: 115 sq mi
(298 sq km)
Population: 331,000
Capital: Male
Languages: Maldivian
Dhivehi, English
Currency: Maldivian rufiyaa

Mongolia
Area: 603,909 sq mi
(1,564,116 sq km)
Population: 2,873,000
Capital: Ulaanbaatar
Languages: Khalkha Mongol,
Turkic, Russian
Currency: Mongolian tögrög

Myanmar (Burma)
Area: 261,218 sq mi
(676,552 sq km)
Population: 54,585,000
Capitals: Nay Pyi Taw,
Yangon (Rangoon)
Languages: Burmese,
minority ethnic languages
Currency: Burmese kyat

Nepal
Area: 56,827 sq mi
(147,181 sq km)
Population: 30,918,000
Capital: Kathmandu
Languages: Nepali, Maithali,
Bhojpuri, Tharu, Tamang,
English
Currency: Nepalese rupee

Oman
Area: 119,500 sq mi
(309,500 sq km)
Population: 3,090,000
Capital: Muscat
Languages: Arabic (official),
English, Baluchi, Urdu,
Indian dialects
Currency: Omani rial

Pakistan
Area: 307,374 sq mi
(796,095 sq km)
Population: 180,428,000
Capital: Islamabad
Languages: Urdu, English
(both official), Punjabi, Sindhi,
Siraiki, Pashtu
Currency: Pakistani rupee

Philippines
Area: 115,831 sq mi
(300,000 sq km)
Population: 96,218,000
Capital: Manila
Languages: Filipino (based
on Tagalog), English (both
official), 8 major dialects
Currency: Philippine peso

Qatar
Area: 4,448 sq mi
(11,521 sq km)
Population: 1,882,000
Capital: Doha
Languages: Arabic (official),
English
Currency: Qatari riyal

Saudi Arabia
Area: 756,985 sq mi
(1,960,582 sq km)
Population: 28,705,000
Capital: Riyadh
Language: Arabic
Currency: Saudi riyal

Singapore
Area: 255 sq mi
(660 sq km)
Population: 5,294,000
Capital: Singapore
Languages: Mandarin,
English, Malay, Hokkien
Currency: Singapore dollar

Sri Lanka
Area: 25,299 sq mi
(65,525 sq km)
Population: 21,166,000
Capital: Colombo,
Sri Jayewardenepura
Languages: Sinhala
(official), Tamil, English
Currency: Sri Lankan rupee

Syria
Area: 71,498 sq mi
(185,180 sq km)
Population: 22,531,000
Capital: Damascus
Languages: Arabic (official),
Kurdish, Armenian, Aramaic,
Circassian
Currency: Syrian pound

Tajikistan
Area: 55,251 sq mi
(143,100 sq km)
Population: 7,079,000
Capital: Dushanbe
Languages: Tajik (official),
Russian
Currency: Tajikistani somoni

Thailand
Area: 198,115 sq mi
(513,115 sq km)
Population: 69,892,000
Capital: Bangkok (Krung Thep)
Languages: Thai, English,
ethnic and regional dialects
Currency: Thai baht

Turkey
Area: 300,948 sq mi
(779,452 sq km)
Population: 74,885,000
Capital: Ankara
Languages: Turkish (official),
Kurdish, Arabic, Armenian,
Greek
Currency: Turkish lira

Turkmenistan
Area: 188,300 sq mi
(488,100 sq km)
Population: 5,170,000
Capital: Ashgabat
Languages: Turkmen,
Russian, Uzbek
Currency: Turkmenistan manat

United Arab Emirates
Area: 30,000 sq mi
(77,700 sq km)
Population: 8,106,000
Capital: Abu Dhabi
Languages: Arabic (official),
Persian, English, Hindi, Urdu
Currency: United Arab
Emirates dirham

Uzbekistan
Area: 172,742 sq mi
(447,400 sq km)
Population: 29,780,000
Capital: Tashkent
Languages: Uzbek, Russian
Currency: Uzbekistani som

Vietnam
Area: 127,844 sq mi
(331,114 sq km)
Population: 88,984,000
Capital: Hanoi
Languages: Vietnamese
(official), English, French,
Chinese, Khmer
Currency: Vietnamese dong

Yemen
Area: 207,286 sq mi
(536,869 sq km)
Population: 25,569,000
Capital: Sanaa
Language: Arabic
Currency: Yemeni rial

AFRICA

Algeria
Area: 919,595 sq mi
(2,381,741 sq km)
Population: 37,402,000
Capital: Algiers
Languages: Arabic (official),
French, Berber dialects
Currency: Algerian dinar

Angola
Area: 481,354 sq mi
(1,246,700 sq km)
Population: 20,945,000
Capital: Luanda
Languages: Portuguese
(official), Bantu, other African
languages
Currency: Angolan kwanza

Benin
Area: 43,484 sq mi
(112,622 sq km)
Population: 9,374,000
Capitals: Porto-Novo, Cotonou
Languages: French (official),
Fon, Yoruba, tribal languages
Currency: West African
CFA franc

Botswana
Area: 224,607 sq mi
(581,730 sq km)
Population: 1,850,000
Capital: Gaborone
Languages: English (official),
Setswana, Kalanga, Sekgalgadi
Currency: Botswana pula

Burkina Faso
Area: 105,869 sq mi
(274,200 sq km)
Population: 17,482,000
Capital: Ouagadougou
Languages: French (official),
indigenous languages
Currency: West African
CFA franc

Burundi
Area: 10,747 sq mi
(27,834 sq km)
Population: 10,557,000
Capital: Bujumbura
Languages: Kirundi, French
(both official), Swahili
Currency: Burundian franc

Cameroon
Area: 183,569 sq mi
(475,442 sq km)
Population: 20,919,000
Capital: Yaoundé
Languages: French, English
(both official), 24 major
African language groups
Currency: Central African
CFA franc

Cape Verde
Area: 1,558 sq mi
(4,036 sq km)
Population: 510,000
Capital: Praia
Languages: Portuguese,
Crioulo
Currency: Cape Verdean
escudo

**Central African
Republic**
Area: 240,535 sq mi
(622,984 sq km)
Population: 4,575,000
Capital: Bangui
Languages: French (official),
Sangho, tribal languages
Currency: Central African
CFA franc

Chad
Area: 495,755 sq mi
(1,284,000 sq km)
Population: 11,831,000
Capital: N'Djamena
Languages: French, Arabic
(both official), Sara, more
than 120 other languages
and dialects
Currency: Central African
CFA franc

Comoros
Area: 719 sq mi
(1,862 sq km)
Population: 773,000
Capital: Moroni
Languages: Arabic, French
(both official), Shikomoro
Currency: Comorian franc

Congo
Area: 132,047 sq mi
(342,000 sq km)
Population: 4,247,000
Capital: Brazzaville
Languages: French (official),
Lingala, Monokutuba, many
local languages and dialects
Currency: Central African
CFA franc

**Congo, Democratic
Republic of the**
Area: 905,365 sq mi
(2,344,885 sq km)
Population: 69,117,000
Capital: Kinshasa
Languages: French (official),
Lingala, Kingwana, Kikongo,
Tshiluba
Currency: Congolese franc

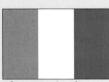

**Côte d'Ivoire (Ivory
Coast)**
Area: 124,503 sq mi
(322,462 sq km)
Population: 20,646,000
Capitals: Abidjan,
Yamoussoukro
Languages: French (official),
Dioula, 60 native dialects
Currency: West African
CFA franc

Djibouti
Area: 8,958 sq mi
(23,200 sq km)
Population: 923,000
Capital: Djibouti
Languages: French, Arabic
(both official), Somali, Afar
Currency: Djiboutian franc

Egypt
Area: 386,874 sq mi
(1,002,000 sq km)
Population: 82,283,000
Capital: Cairo
Languages: Arabic (official),
English, French
Currency: Egyptian pound

Equatorial Guinea
Area: 10,831 sq mi
(28,051 sq km)
Population: 740,000
Capital: Malabo
Languages: Spanish, French
(both official), pidgin English,
Fang, Bubi, Ibo
Currency: Central African
CFA franc

Eritrea
Area: 46,774 sq mi
(121,144 sq km)
Population: 5,581,000
Capital: Asmara
Languages: Afar, Arabic,
Tigre, Kunama, Tigrinya,
other Cushitic languages
Currency: Eritrean nakfa

Ethiopia
Area: 437,600 sq mi
(1,133,380 sq km)
Population: 86,960,000
Capital: Addis Ababa
Languages: Amharic,
Tigrinya, Oromigna,
Guaragigna, Somali
Currency: Ethiopian birr

FLAGS & STATS

Gabon
Area: 103,347 sq mi
(267,667 sq km)
Population: 1,564,000
Capital: Libreville
Languages: French (official),
Fang, Myene, Nzebi,
Bapounou/Eschira
Currency: Central African
CFA franc

Gambia
Area: 4,361 sq mi
(11,295 sq km)
Population: 1,825,000
Capital: Banjul
Languages: English (official),
Mandinka, Wolof, Fula
Currency: Gambian dalasi

Ghana
Area: 92,100 sq mi
(238,537 sq km)
Population: 25,546,000
Capital: Accra
Languages: English (official),
Akan, Moshi-Dagomba, Ewe, Ga
Currency: Ghana cedi

Guinea
Area: 94,926 sq mi
(245,857 sq km)
Population: 11,498,000
Capital: Conakry
Languages: French (official),
indigenous languages
Currency: Guinean franc

Guinea-Bissau
Area: 13,948 sq mi
(36,125 sq km)
Population: 1,637,000
Capital: Bissau
Languages: Portuguese
(official), Crioulo, indigenous
languages
Currency: West African
CFA franc

Kenya
Area: 224,081 sq mi
(580,367 sq km)
Population: 43,013,000
Capital: Nairobi
Languages: English,
Kiswahili (both official),
indigenous languages
Currency: Kenyan shilling

Lesotho
Area: 11,720 sq mi
(30,355 sq km)
Population: 2,217,000
Capital: Maseru
Languages: Sesotho, English
(official), Zulu, Xhosa
Currency: Lesotho loti

Liberia
Area: 43,000 sq mi
(111,370 sq km)
Population: 4,245,000
Capital: Monrovia
Languages: English (official),
20 ethnic group languages
Currency: Liberian dollar

Libya
Area: 679,362 sq mi
(1,759,540 sq km)
Population: 6,469,000
Capital: Tripoli
Languages: Arabic, Italian,
English
Currency: Libyan dinar

Madagascar
Area: 226,658 sq mi
(587,041 sq km)
Population: 21,929,000
Capital: Antananarivo
Languages: French, Malagasy
(both official), English
Currency: Malagasy ariary

Malawi
Area: 45,747 sq mi
(118,484 sq km)
Population: 15,883,000
Capital: Lilongwe
Languages: Chichewa (official),
Chinyanja, Chiyao, Chitumbuka
Currency: Malawian kwacha

Mali
Area: 478,841 sq mi
(1,240,192 sq km)
Population: 16,014,000
Capital: Bamako
Languages: French, Bambara
(both official), numerous
African languages
Currency: West African
CFA franc

Mauritania
Area: 397,955 sq mi
(1,030,700 sq km)
Population: 3,623,000
Capital: Nouakchott
Languages: Arabic (official),
Pulaar, Soninke, French,
Hassaniya, Wolof
Currency: Mauritanian ouguiya

Mauritius
Area: 788 sq mi
(2,040 sq km)
Population: 1,291,000
Capital: Port Louis
Languages: Creole, Bhojpuri,
French (official)
Currency: Mauritian rupee

Morocco
Area: 274,461 sq mi
(710,850 sq km)
Population: 32,597,000
Capital: Rabat
Languages: Arabic (official),
Berber dialects, French
Currency: Moroccan dirham

Mozambique
Area: 308,642 sq mi
(799,380 sq km)
Population: 23,702,000
Capital: Maputo
Languages: Emakhuwa,
Xichangana, Portuguese
(official), Elomwe, Cisena,
Echuwabo
Currency: Mozambican metical

Namibia
Area: 318,261 sq mi
(824,292 sq km)
Population: 2,364,000
Capital: Windhoek
Languages: English
(official), Afrikaans, German,
indigenous languages
Currency: Namibian dollar

Niger
Area: 489,191 sq mi
(1,267,000 sq km)
Population: 16,276,000
Capital: Niamey
Languages: French (official),
Hausa, Djerma
Currency: West African
CFA franc

Nigeria
Area: 356,669 sq mi
(923,768 sq km)
Population: 170,124,000
Capital: Abuja
Languages: English (official),
Hausa, Yoruba, Igbo (Ibo), Fulani
Currency: Nigerian naira

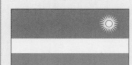

Rwanda
Area: 10,169 sq mi
(26,338 sq km)
Population: 10,815,000
Capital: Kigali
Languages: Kinyarwanda,
French, English (all official),
Kiswahili
Currency: Rwandan franc

São Tomé and Principe
Area: 386 sq mi
(1,001 sq km)
Population: 183,000
Capital: São Tomé
Language: Portuguese (official)
Currency: São Tomé and
Principe dobra

Senegal
Area: 75,955 sq mi
(196,722 sq km)
Population: 13,108,000
Capital: Dakar
Languages: French (official),
Wolof, Pulaar, Jola, Mandinka
Currency: West African
CFA franc

Seychelles
Area: 176 sq mi
(455 sq km)
Population: 93,000
Capital: Victoria
Languages: English (official),
Creole
Currency: Seychellois rupee

Sierra Leone
Area: 27,699 sq mi
(71,740 sq km)
Population: 6,126,000
Capital: Freetown
Languages: English (official),
Mende, Temne, Krio
Currency: Sierra Leone leone

Somalia
Area: 246,201 sq mi
(637,657 sq km)
Population: 10,086,000
Capital: Mogadishu
Languages: Somali (official),
Arabic, Italian, English
Currency: Somali shilling

South Africa
Area: 470,693 sq mi
(1,219,090 sq km)
Population: 51,147,000
Capitals: Pretoria (Tshwane),
Cape Town, Bloemfontein
Languages: IsiZulu, IsiXhosa,
Afrikaans, Sepedi, English,
Setswana
Currency: South African rand

South Sudan
Area: 248,777 sq mi
(644,329 sq km)
Population: 9,385,000
Capital: Juba
Languages: English (official),
Arabic, regional languages
Currency: South Sudanese
pound

Sudan
Area: 967,500 sq mi
(2,505,813 sq km)
Population: 33,494,000
Capital: Khartoum
Languages: Arabic (official),
Nubian, Ta Bedawie, many
local dialects
Currency: Sudanese pound

Swaziland
Area: 6,704 sq mi
(17,363 sq km)
Population: 1,220,000
Capitals: Mbabane, Lobamba
Languages: English, siSwati
(both official)
Currency: Swazi lilangeni

Tanzania
Area: 364,900 sq mi
(945,087 sq km)
Population: 47,656,000
Capitals: Dar es Salaam, Dodoma
Languages: Swahili, English
(both official), Arabic, many
local languages
Currency: Tanzanian shilling

Togo
Area: 21,925 sq mi
(56,785 sq km)
Population: 6,011,000
Capital: Lomé
Languages: French (official),
Ewe, Mina, Kabye, Dagomba
Currency: West African
CFA franc

Tunisia
Area: 63,170 sq mi
(163,610 sq km)
Population: 10,800,000
Capital: Tunis
Languages: Arabic (official),
French
Currency: Tunisian dinar

Uganda
Area: 93,104 sq mi
(241,139 sq km)
Population: 35,621,000
Capital: Kampala
Languages: English (official),
Ganda or Luganda, many
local languages
Currency: Ugandan shilling

Zambia
Area: 290,586 sq mi
(752,614 sq km)
Population: 13,711,000
Capital: Lusaka
Languages: English (official),
75 indigenous languages
Currency: Zambian kwacha

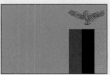

Zimbabwe
Area: 150,872 sq mi
(390,757 sq km)
Population: 12,620,000
Capital: Harare
Languages: English (official),
Shona, Sindebele, tribal dialects
Currency: United States
dollar/South African
rand/Euro/British pound/
Botswana pula

Australia
Area: 2,969,906 sq mi
(7,692,024 sq km)
Population: 22,035,000
Capital: Canberra
Language: English
Currency: Australian dollar

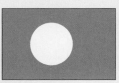

Fiji Islands
Area: 7,095 sq mi
(18,376 sq km)
Population: 844,000
Capital: Suva
Languages: English (official),
Fijian, Hindustani
Currency: Fijian dollar

Kiribati
Area: 313 sq mi
(811 sq km)
Population: 105,000
Capital: Tarawa
Languages: English (official),
I-Kiribati
Currency: Kiribati dollar,
Australian dollar

Marshall Islands
Area: 70 sq mi
(181 sq km)
Population: 55,000
Capital: Majuro
Languages: Marshallese
(official), English
Currency: United States dollar

Micronesia
Area: 271 sq mi
(702 sq km)
Population: 107,000
Capital: Palikir
Languages: English (official),
Trukese, Pohnpeian, Yapese,
Kosrean
Currency: United States dollar

Nauru
Area: 8 sq mi
(21 sq km)
Population: 10,200
Capital: Yaren
Languages: Nauruan
(official), English
Currency: Australian dollar

New Zealand
Area: 104,454 sq mi
(270,534 sq km)
Population: 4,437,000
Capital: Wellington
Languages: English, Maori
(both official)
Currency: New Zealand dollar

Palau
Area: 189 sq mi
(489 sq km)
Population: 20,800
Capital: Melekeok
Languages: Palauan, Filipino,
English, Chinese
Currency: United States dollar

Papua New Guinea
Area: 178,703 sq mi
(462,840 sq km)
Population: 7,034,000
Capital: Port Moresby
Languages: Melanesian pidgin,
715 indigenous languages
Currency: Papua New
Guinea kina

Samoa
Area: 1,093 sq mi
(2,831 sq km)
Population: 187,000
Capital: Apia
Languages: Samoan
(Polynesian), English
Currency: Samoan tala

Solomon Islands
Area: 10,954 sq mi
(28,370 sq km)
Population: 552,000
Capital: Honiara
Languages: Melanesian pidgin,
120 indigenous languages
Currency: Solomon Islands
dollar

Tonga
Area: 289 sq mi
(748 sq km)
Population: 103,000
Capital: Nuku'alofa
Languages: Tongan, English
Currency: Tongan pa'anga

Tuvalu
Area: 10 sq mi
(26 sq km)
Population: 11,300
Capital: Funafuti
Languages: Tuvaluan,
English, Samoan, Kiribati
Currency: Tuvaluan dollar/
Australian dollar

Vanuatu
Area: 4,707 sq mi
(12,190 sq km)
Population: 258,000
Capital: Port Vila
Languages: more than 100
local languages, pidgin
(Bislama or Bichelama)
Currency: Vanuatu vatu

SPOT THE
Difference

Can you spot the ten differences between these two pictures? (Answers on page 184)

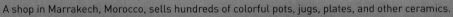

A shop in Marrakech, Morocco, sells hundreds of colorful pots, jugs, plates, and other ceramics.

GIVE IT A Swirl

Use the clues below to figure out which animals appear in these swirled pictures. (Answers on page 184)

1 You don't want to touch the skin of this colorful little creature that lives in the rain forests of central and South America.

2 If you're in the land down under you might see these creatures hopping by with their joeys in tow.

3 These animals live in and around the icy waters of the Antarctic. They may look funny walking on land, but underwater, they are graceful swimmers.

4 Coral reefs are where you'll find these bright and colorful creatures.

5 These funny African animals live in groups called mobs, clans, or gangs.

6 This large North American mammal is great at catching a meal.

7 Cute and cuddly, this furry mammal lives in the land of the Great Wall and is always eating its favorite food.

8 You don't want to get too close to this marine stinger!

9 If you see this insect fluttering around the mountainous meadows of Europe, you might mistake its red spots for eyes.

FIND THE
Hidden Animals

Many animals blend into their environment in order to protect themselves. See if you can identify the camouflaged animals in these pictures. (Answers on page 184)

C Vietnam and China

D Argentina and Chile

A Eastern Atlantic Ocean and Mediterranean Sea

E Gabon

B The Amazon

India **F**

J Nepal

G North America

K Australia

H Costa Rica

L Mexico

I United States

Wild Guess

Compare these pairs, if you dare.
(Answers on page 185)

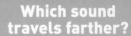

Which sound travels farther?
The howl of a howler monkey or the vocals of a blue whale?

Argentina **India**

Which is bigger?
Countries are not to scale.

Which takes longer?
Travel by car from Rome, Italy, to Istanbul, Turkey, or travel by foot from New York, New York, to Philadelphia, Pennsylvania, U.S.A.?

Which is taller?
Washington Monument in Washington, D.C., U.S.A., or Eiffel Tower in Paris, France?

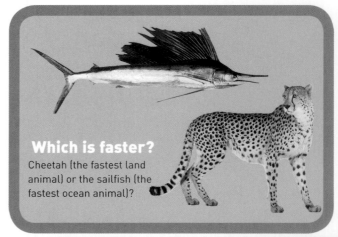

Which is faster?
Cheetah (the fastest land animal) or the sailfish (the fastest ocean animal)?

SPOT THE
Difference

Can you spot the ten differences between these two pictures? (Answers on page 185)

Colorful buoys hang outside a lobster shack in Bar Harbor, Maine, United States.

Name That Place

Name the landmark or feature in these images and the place each is located. (Answers on page 185)

3

5

4

1

6

7

2

8

9

10

11

12

13

14

15

16

Answers

Spot the difference, page 176:

Give it a swirl, page 177:
1. Red poison dart frog in the Amazon rain forest of Peru
2. A mother and baby kangaroo in the Australian wilderness
3. A Gentoo penguin walking on ice in Antarctica
4. Two butterfly fish in the Red Sea off the coast of Egypt
5. Five meerkats looking around outside their burrow in Africa
6. A grizzly bear catching salmon in Alaska, United States
7. A giant panda climbing a tree in China
8. A compass jellyfish swimming in the Cerbère-Banyuls Marine Reserve in France
9. A nomion butterfly sitting on a leaf. This butterfly is found mostly in Europe.

Hidden Animals, page 178-179:
A. A red scorpionfish, found in the Eastern Atlantic Ocean and the Mediterranean Sea
B. A Black caiman in the Amazon
C. A Vietnamese mossy frog, found in northern Vietnam and southern China
D. Sea lions and penguins on the islands of Tierra del Fuego on the southern tip of South America
E. A Gaboon viper snake in the country of Gabon in Africa
F. A tiger in the national park in India
G. A species of green butterfly found in North America
H. A ghost crab on a beach in Costa Rica
I. A snowshoe hare in Maine, United States
J. A crocodile in a national park in Nepal
K. A koala high in a gum tree in Australia
L. A jaguar cub in a jungle in Mexico

Spot the Difference, page 181:

Wild Guess, page 180:

Which sound travels farther?
A blue whale's vocals travel farther than a howler monkey's. A blue whale can be louder than a jet plane and detected from more than 500 miles (805 km) away. On land, the howler monkey's howl can be heard 3 miles (5 km) away.

Which is bigger?
India with a land area of 1,269,219 sq mi (3,287,263 sq km) is larger than Argentina, which has a land area of 1,073,518 sq mi (2,780,400 sq km).

Which is taller?
The Eiffel Tower at 1,063 ft (324 m) is taller than the Washington Monument, which is 555 feet (169 m).

Which takes longer?
It takes longer to travel by foot from New York, New York, to Philadelphia, Pennsylvania (about 29 hours) than to drive from Rome, Italy, to Istanbul, Turkey (about 24 hours).

Which is faster?
The sailfish can travel 68 miles per hour (110 kph), making it faster than the cheetah, which can reach speeds of 60 to 65 mph (96.5 to 104 kph).

Name That Place, pages 182–183:
 1. Taj Mahal in Agra, India
 2. The Incan ruins of Machu Picchu in Peru
 3. Uluru (Ayers Rock) in Australia
 4. Mayan Pyramid Chichen Itza in Mexico
 5. Leaning Tower of Pisa in Italy
 6. The Himalaya in Nepal
 7. Sydney Opera House in Australia
 8. Great Wall of China
 9. Mount Kilimanjaro in Kenya
10. Grand Canyon in Arizona, U.S.A.
11. Colosseum of Rome in Italy
12. The CN Tower in Toronto, Canada
13. Big Ben in London, United Kingdom
14. Christ the Redeemer Monument in Rio de Janeiro, Brazil
15. Golden Gate Bridge in San Francisco, California, U.S.A.
16. The Great Sphinx of Giza guarding a Pyramid in Egypt

GLOSSARY

acid rain precipitation containing acid droplets resulting from the mixture of moisture in the air with carbon dioxide, nitrogen oxide, sulfur dioxide, and hydrocarbons released by factories and motor vehicles

archipelago a group or chain of islands

bathymetry measurement of depth at various places in the ocean or other body of water

bay a body of water, usually smaller than a gulf, that is partially surrounded by land

biomass the total volume of organic material in a certain area or ecosystem that can be used as a renewable energy source

border the area close to a boundary

boundary most commonly, a line that has been established by people to mark the limit of one political unit, such as a country or state, and the beginning of another; geographical features such as mountains sometimes act as boundaries

breakwater a structure, such as a wall, that protects a harbor or beach from pounding waves

caloric supply a measure of the amount of food available to a particular person, household, or community

canal a human-made waterway that is used by ships or to carry water for irrigation

canyon a deep, narrow valley that has steep sides

cape a point of land that extends into an ocean, a lake, or a river

carat a unit of weight for precious stones equal to 200 milligrams

cataract a steplike series of waterfalls or rapids such as occur on the Nile River

cliff a very steep rock face, usually along a coast but also on the side of a mountain

continent one of the seven main landmasses on Earth's surface

country a territory whose government is the highest legal authority over the land and people within its boundaries

delta lowland formed by silt, sand, and gravel deposited by a river at its mouth

desert a hot or cold region that receives 10 inches (25 cm) or less of rain or other kinds of precipitation a year

desertification the spread of desertlike conditions in semiarid regions that is the result of climatic changes and increasing human pressures, such as overgrazing, removal of natural vegetation, and cultivation of land

dialect a regional variation of a language

divide an elevated area drained by different river systems flowing in different directions

elevation distance above sea level, usually measured in feet or meters

escarpment a cliff that separates two nearly flat land areas that lie at different elevations

fault a break in Earth's crust along which movement up, down, or sideways occurs

fork the place in a river where two streams come together

geographic pole 90°N, 90°S latitude; location of the ends of Earth's axis

geomagnetic pole point at which the axis of Earth's magnetic field intersects Earth's surface; compass needles align with Earth's magnetic field so that one end points to the magnetic north pole, the other to the magnetic south pole

glacier a large, slow-moving mass of ice

global warming a theory explaining that the recent increase in Earth's average global temperature is due to a buildup of greenhouse gases, such as carbon dioxide and methane, in excess of natural levels due mainly to human activities

greenhouse gases atmospheric gases, such as carbon dioxide and methane, in excess of natural levels due mainly to human activities

gross domestic product (GDP) the total market value of goods and services produced by a country's economy in a year

gulf a portion of the ocean that cuts into the land; usually larger than a bay

harbor a body of water, sheltered by natural or artificial barriers, that is deep enough for ships

hemisphere literally half a sphere; Earth has four hemispheres: Northern, Southern, Eastern, and Western

highlands an elevated area or the more mountainous region of a country

hybrid car a car that is powered by gasoline and electricity

hydrothermal vent a crack in the ocean floor that releases mineral-rich, superheated water

inlet a narrow opening in the land that is filled with water flowing from an ocean, a lake, or a river

island a landmass, smaller than a continent, that is completely surrounded by water

isthmus a narrow strip of land that connects two larger landmasses and has water on two sides

lagoon a shallow body of water that is open to the sea but also protected from it by a reef or sandbar

lake a body of water that is surrounded by land; large lakes are sometimes called seas

landform a physical feature shaped by tectonic activity, weathering, and erosion; the four major kinds on Earth are plains, mountains, plateaus, and hills

landmass a large area of Earth's crust that lies above sea level, such as a continent

large-scale map a map, such as a street map, that shows a small area in great detail

Latin America cultural region generally considered to include Mexico, Central America, South America, and the West Indies;

Portuguese and Spanish are the prinicipal languages

latitude distance north and south of the Equator, which is 0° latitude

leeward the side away from or sheltered from the wind

lingua franca a language not native to the local population that is used as a common or commercial language

longitude distance east and west of the prime meridian, which is 0° longitude

magma molten rock in Earth's mantle

mesa an eroded plateau, broader than it is high, that is found in arid or semiarid regions

metropolitan area a city and its surrounding suburbs or communities

Middle East term commonly used for the countries of Southwest Asia but which can also include northern Africa from Morocco to Somalia

molten liquefied by heat; melted

mountain a landform, higher than a hill, that rises at least 1,000 feet (300 m) above the surrounding land and is wider at its base than at its top, or peak; a series of mountains is called a range

nation people who share a common culture; often used as another word for "country," although people within a country may be of many cultures

ocean the large body of saltwater that surrounds the continents and covers more than two-thirds of Earth's surface

peninsula a piece of land that is almost completely surrounded by water

permafrost a permanently frozen subsurface soil in frigid regions

plain a large area of relatively flat land that is often covered with grasses

plateau a relatively flat area, larger than a mesa, that rises above the surrounding landscape

poaching the illegal killing or taking of animals from their natural habitats

point a narrow piece of land smaller than a cape that extends into a body of water

population density in a country, the number of people living on each square mile or square kilometer of land (calculated by dividing population by land area)

Prairie Provinces popular name for the Canadian provinces of Manitoba, Saskatchewan, and Alberta

prime meridian an imaginary line that runs through Greenwich, England, and is accepted as the line of 0° longitude

projection the process of representing the round Earth on a flat surface, such as a map

rain shadow the dry region on the leeward side of a mountain range

reef an offshore ridge made of coral, rocks, or sand

renewable resources resources that are replenished naturally, but the supply of which can be endangered by overuse and pollution

Sahel a semiarid grassland in Africa along the Sahara's southern border

savanna a tropical grassland with scattered trees

scale on a map, a means of explaining the relationship between distances on the map and actual distances on Earth's surface

sea the ocean or a partially enclosed body of saltwater that is connected to the ocean; completely enclosed bodies of saltwater, such as the Dead Sea, are really lakes

slot canyon a very narrow, deep canyon formed by water and wind erosion

small-scale map a map, such as a country map, that shows a large area without much detail

sound a long, broad inlet of the ocean that lies parallel to the coast and often separates an island and the mainland

Soviet Union shortened name for the Union of Soviet Socialist Republics (U.S.S.R.), a former Communist republic (1920–1991) in eastern Europe and northern and Central Asia. It was made up of 15 republics, of which Russia was the largest.

spit a long, narrow strip of land, often of sand or silt, that extends into a body of water from the land

staple a chief ingredient of a people's diet

steppe a Slavic word referring to relatively flat, mostly treeless temperate grasslands that stretch across much of central Europe and Central Asia

strait a narrow passage of water that connects two larger bodies of water

territory land that is under the jurisdiction of a country but is not a state or a province

tributary a stream that flows into a larger river

tropics region lying within $23\frac{1}{2}°$ north and south of the Equator that experiences warm temperatures year-round

topography the relief features that are evident on a planet's surface

upwelling process by which nutrient-rich water rises from ocean depths to the surface

valley a long depression, usually created by a river, that is bordered by higher land

virgin forest a forest made up of trees that have never been cut down by humans

volcano an opening in Earth's crust through which molten rock erupts

windward the unsheltered side toward which the wind blows

GEO FACTS & FIGURES

PLANET EARTH

Mass:
6,583,348,000,000,000,000,000 tons
(5,974,000,000,000,000,000,000 metric tons)
Distance around the Equator:
24,901 mi
(40,073 km)
Area: 196,938,000 sq mi
(510,066,000 sq km)
Land area: 57,393,000 sq mi
(148,647,000 sq km)
Water area: 139,545,000 sq mi
(361,419,000 sq km)

The Continents

Asia: 17,208,000 sq mi
(44,570,000 sq km)
Africa: 11,608,000 sq mi
(30,065,000 sq km)
North America: 9,449,000 sq mi
(24,474,000 sq km)
South America: 6,880,000 sq mi
(17,819,000 sq km)
Antarctica: 5,100,000 sq mi
(13,209,000 sq km)
Europe: 3,841,000 sq mi
(9,947,000 sq km)
Australia: 2,968,000 sq mi
(7,687,000 sq km)

Highest Mountain on Each Continent

Everest, Asia: 29,035 ft (8,850 m)
Aconcagua, South America:
22,834 ft (6,960 m)
McKinley (Denali), North
America:
20,320 ft (6,194 m)
Kilimanjaro, Africa: 19,340 ft
(5,895 m)
El'brus, Europe: 18,510 ft
(5,642 m)
Vinson Massif, Antarctica:
16,067 ft (4,897 m)
Kosciuszko, Australia: 7,310 ft
(2,228 m)

Lowest Point on Each Continent

Bentley Subglacial Trench,
Antarctica: –8,383 ft (–2,555 m)
Dead Sea, Asia: –1,385 ft (–422 m)
Lake Assal, Africa: –512 ft
(–156 m)
Death Valley, North America:
–282 ft (–86 m)
Laguna del Carbón, South
America: –344 ft
(–105 m)
Caspian Sea, Europe: –92 ft
(–28 m)
Lake Eyre, Australia: –52 ft
(–16 m)

Longest Rivers

Nile, Africa: 4,241 mi (6,825 km)
Amazon, South America: 4,000 mi
(6,437 km)
Yangtze (Chang), Asia: 3,964 mi
(6,380 km)
Mississippi-Missouri, North
America: 3,710 mi (5,971 km)
Yenisey-Angara, Asia: 3,440 mi
(5,536 km)
Yellow (Huang), Asia: 3,395 mi
(5,464 km)
Ob-Irtysh, Asia: 3,362 mi
(5,410 km)
Congo (Zaire), Africa: 2,715 mi
(4,370 km)
Amur, Asia: 2,744 mi (4,416 km)
Lena, Asia: 2,734 mi (4,400 km)

Largest Islands

Greenland: 836,000 sq mi
(2,166,000 sq km)
New Guinea: 306,000 sq mi
(792,500 sq km)
Borneo: 280,100 sq mi
(725,500 sq km)
Madagascar: 226,600 sq mi
(587,000 sq km)

Baffin: 196,000 sq mi
(507,500 sq km)
Sumatra: 165,000 sq mi
(427,300 sq km)
Honshu: 87,800 sq mi
(227,400 sq km)
Great Britain: 84,200 sq mi
(218,100 sq km)
Victoria: 83,900 sq mi
(217,300 sq km)
Ellesmere: 75,800 sq mi
(196,200 sq km)

Largest Lakes (by area)

Caspian Sea, Europe-Asia:
143,200 sq mi
(371,000 sq km)
Superior, North America: 31,700
sq mi (82,100 sq km)
Victoria, Africa: 26,800 sq mi
(69,500 sq km)
Huron, North America: 23,000 sq
mi (59,600 sq km)
Michigan, North America: 22,300
sq mi (57,800 sq km)
Tanganyika, Africa: 12,600 sq mi
(32,600 sq km)
Baikal, Asia: 12,200 sq mi
(31,500 sq km)
Great Bear, North America:
12,100 sq mi (31,300 sq km)
Malawi, Africa: 11,200 sq mi
(28,900 sq km)
Great Slave Lake, Canada, North
America: 11,000 sq mi
(28,600 sq km)

Oceans

Pacific: 65,436,200 sq mi
(169,479,000 sq km)
Atlantic: 35,338,500 sq mi
(91,526,400 sq km)
Indian: 28,839,800 sq mi
(74,694,800 sq km)
Arctic: 5,390,000 sq mi
(13,960,100 sq km)

BACK OF THE BOOK

Largest Seas (by area)

Coral: 1,615,260 sq mi
  (4,183,510 sq km)
South China: 1,388,570 sq mi
  (3,596,390 sq km)
Caribbean: 1,094,330 sq mi
  (2,834,290 sq km)
Bering: 972,810 sq mi
  (2,519,580 sq km)
Mediterranean: 953,320 sq mi
  (2,469,100 sq km)
Sea of Okhotsk: 627,490 sq mi
  (1,625,190 sq km)
Gulf of Mexico: 591,430 sq mi
  (1,531,810 sq km)
Norwegian: 550,300 sq mi
  (1,425,280 sq km)
Greenland: 447,050 sq mi
  (1,157,850 sq km)
Sea of Japan: 389,290 sq mi
  (1,008,260 sq km)

GEOGRAPHIC EXTREMES

Highest Mountain
Everest, China/Nepal:
29,035 ft (8,850 m)

Deepest Point in the Ocean
Challenger Deep, Mariana
  Trench, Pacific:
-36,070 ft (-10,994 m)

Hottest Place
Dalol, Danakil Depression,
  Ethiopia:
annual average temperature 93°F
  (34°C)

Coldest Place
Plateau Station, Antarctica:
annual average temperature
  -70°F (-56.7°C)

Wettest Place
Mawsynram, Assam, India:
  annual average rainfall 467 in
  (1,187 cm)

Driest Place
Arica, Atacama Desert, Chile:
  barely measurable rainfall

Largest Hot Desert
Sahara, Africa: 3,475,000 sq mi
  (9,000,000 sq km)

Largest Cold Desert
Antarctica: 5,100,000 sq mi
  (13,209,000 sq km)

PEOPLE

Most People by Continent
Asia: 4,191,414,100

Least People by Continent
Antarctica: 4,400 (transient)
Australia: 22,035,000

Most Densely Populated Country
Monaco: 45,000 people per
  sq mi/18,000 per sq km
Least Densely Populated Country
Mongolia: 5 people per sq mi/
  2 per sq km

Most Populated Metropolitan Areas
Tokyo, Japan: 36,669,000
Delhi, India: 22,157,000
São Paulo, Brazil: 20,262,000
Mumbai, India: 20,041,000
Mexico City, Mexico: 19,460,000
New York, United States:
  19,425,000
Shanghai, China: 16,575,000
Kolkata (Calcutta), India:
  15,552,000
Dhaka, Bangladesh: 14,648,000
Karachi, Pakistan: 13,125,000

Countries With the Highest Life Expectancy
Japan: 83 years
San Marino: 83 years
Australia: 82 years
Spain: 82 years
Israel: 82 years
France: 82 years
Switzerland: 82 years
Sweden: 82 years

Countries With the Lowest Life Expectancy
Afghanistan: 44 years
Zimbabwe: 46 years
Guinea-Bissau: 48 years
Swaziland: 49 years
Zambia: 49 years
Dem. Rep. of the Congo: 49 years
Lesotho: 49 years
Central Africa Republic: 50 years

Countries With the Highest Gross Domestic Product per Person
Luxembourg: $104,196
Norway: $102,249
Qatar: $99,839
Switzerland: $76,598
Australia: $69,582

Countries With the Lowest Gross Domestic Product per Person
Dem. Rep. of the Congo: $251
Malawi: $262
Burundi: $317
Niger: $434
Central African Republic: $451

OUTSIDE WEBSITES

The following websites will provide you with additional valuable information about various topics discussed in this atlas.

Antarctic wildlife:
www.antarcticconnection.com/antarctic/wildlife/index.shtml

Biomes:
www.blueplanetbiomes.org

Currency converter:
www.xe.com/ucc

Earth's climates:
www.worldclimate.com

Earth's geologic history:
Earthquakes: earthquake.usgs.gov
Tsunamis: www.tsunami.noaa.gov
Volcanoes: www.geo.mtu.edu/volcanoe/

Extreme facts about the world:
www.extremescience.com

Flags of the world:
www.fotw.us/flags/index.html

Languages of the world:
www.ipl.org/div/hello/

Mapping sites:
earth.google.com
www.skylineglobe.com

National anthems:
www.nationalanthems.info

Political world (lots of statistics):
https://www.cia.gov/library/publications/the-world-factbook/index.html

Religions of the world:
www.adherents.com/Religions_By_Adherents.html

Solar system:
solarsystem.nasa.gov/planets

Time differences between places:
www.worldtimeserver.com

Time zone map:
www.worldtimezone.com

Tracking Quakes (page 33)
www.iris.edu/seismon

Weather around the world right now:
www.weather.com

World heritage sites (important historic places around the world):
whc.unesco.org/en/list

Index

Map references are in boldface (50) type. Letters and numbers following in lightface (D12) locate the place-names using the map grid. (Refer to page 7 for more details.)

Amman — Beni Abbes

Chechnya — Dzhugdzhur Range

Great Artesian Basin — Jambi

Larsen Ice Shelf — Mek'elē

Northern Dvina — Porpoise Bay

Sakarya — Sudan

Sudbury — United Arab Emirates

United Kingdom — Zürich

Aden, Gulf of — Herdman Seamount

Hess Rise — Saya de Malha Bank

Shatskiy Rise — Zhokhova

Illustrations Credits

Abbreviations for terms appearing below: LO = lower; UP = upper; LE = left; RT = right; CTR = center; NGS = National Geographic Society.

All continent opening spreads (52-53, 68-69, 82-83, 100-101, 124-125, 140-141, 152-153, 156-157): ETOPO1/Amante and Eakins, 2009 and GTOPO30 USGS EROS Data Center, 2000.

All graphic illustrations by Stuart Armstrong unless otherwise noted.

All locator globes created by Theophilus Britt Griswold and NGS.

Front Cover

Globe, Anton Balazh/Shutterstock; boy, Roy Toft/National Geographic Stock; city, Richard Nowtiz/National Geographic Stock; tiger, Ron Kimball/ Kimball Stock; Taj Mahal, Shutterstock

Back Cover

Volcano, beboy/Shutterstock; snowboarder, Eric Limon/Shutterstock; monkey, Roy Toft/National Geographic Stock; musician, Arthur Thévenart/Corbis

Front of the Book

1, Premium Stock/Corbis; 2, Premium Stock/Corbis; 2 (Far LE), Roy Toft/NG Image Collection; 2 (LE), Tom Murphy/NG Image Collection; 2 (RT), Cary Wolinsky/NG Image Collection; 2 (Far RT), Richard Nowitz/NG Image Collection; 3 (Far LE), Ron Kimball Stock; 3 (LE), Jose Fuste Raga/Corbis; 3 (RT), scxh; 3 (Far RT), Brand X; 4 (LE), Raymond Gehman/NG Image Collection; 4 (UPRT), Todd Gipstein/NG Image Collection; 4 (LO), Richard Nowitz/NG Image Collection; 5 (LORT), Cary Wolinsky/NG Image Collection; 5 (UP), Frans Lanting/NG Image Collection; 5 (UPRT), Gordon Wiltsie/NG Image Collection; 10 (LO), Mark Theissen/NG Image Collection; 14 (LO), David Aguilar; 20 (Far LE), Maria Stenzel/NG Image Collection; 20 (LE), Bill Hatcher/NG Image Collection; 20 (RT), Carsten Peter/NG Image Collection; 20 (Far RT), Carsten Peter/NG Image Collection; 21 (Far LE), Gordon Wiltsie/NG Image Collection; 21 (LE), James P. Blair/NG Image Collection; 21 (RT), Thomas J. Abercrombie/NG Image Collection; 21 (Far RT), Anne Keiser/NG Image Collection; 24 NG Image Collection; 25 (UP), Kevin Rivoli/Associated Press; 25 (LOLE), Weiss and Overpeck, The University of Arizona; 25 (LORT), Weiss and Overpeck, The University of Arizona; 26 (Far LE), Raymond Gehman/NG Image Collection; 26 (LE), George F. Mobley/NG Image Collection; 26 (RT), Paul Nicklen/NG Image Collection; 26 (Far RT), Raymond Gehman/NG Image Collection; 27 (Far LE), Annie Griffiths Belt/NG Image Collection; 27 (LE), Beverly Joubert/NG Image Collection; 27 (RT), Michael Melford/NG Image Collection; 27 (Far RT), Maria Stenzel/NG Image Collection; 28 (LE), George Grall/NG Image Collection; 28 (LE B), Nicole Duplaix/NG Image Collection; 28 (LE C), Michael Nichols/NG Image Collection; 28 (LE D), William Albert Allard/NG Image Collection; 28 (LE E), Michael Nichols/NG Image Collection; 28 (LE F), Paul Sutherland/NG Image Collection; 28 (RT), James P. Blair/NG Image Collection; 29 (LE), William Thompson/NG Image Collection; 29 (CTR), Steve McCurry/NG Image Collection; 29 (RT), Peter Essick/NG Image Collection; 30 (UP), Ron Gravelle/National Geographic My Shot; 30 (LO), Mehdi Taamallah/AFP/Getty Images; 31 (UP), Pablo Hidalgo/Shutterstock; 31 (LO), Jiji Press/AFP/Getty Images; 35, Justin Guariglia/NG Image Collection; 38, Maria Stenzel/NG Image Collection; 39 (LE), Justin Guariglia/NG Image Collection; 39 (RT), Phillipe Lissac/Godong/Corbis; 40 (LE), Martin Gray/NG Image Collection; 40 (CTR), Randy Olson/NG Image Collection; 40 (RT), Amit Dave/Reuters/Corbis; 41 (LE), Reza/NG Image Collection; 41 (RT), Richard Nowitz/NG Image Collection; 42 (CTR LO), Jon Parker Lee/Alamy; 42 (RT), Justin Guariglia/NG Image Collection; 43 (LE), George F. Mobley/NG Image Collection; 43 (RT), Phil Schermeister/NG Image Collection; 46, Jodi Cobb/NG Image Collection; 49 (LE), James P. Blair/NG Image Collection; 49 (UPRT), Stephen St. John/NG Image Collection; 49 (CTR RT), Joel Sartore/NG Image Collection; 49 (LORT), Michael Nichols/NG Image Collection; 51 (Far Le), Walter Rawlings/Robert Harding World Imagery/Corbis; 51 (LE), Richard Nowitz/NG Image Collection; 51 (RT), Sarah Leen/NG Image Collection; 51 (Far RT), Priit Vesilind/NG Image Collection

North America

56 (UP), Raymond Gehman/NG Image Collection; 56 (LO), Tomasz Tomaszewski/NG Image Collection; 56 (LO), Rex Stucky/NG Image Collection; 57 (UP), Michael Melford/NG Image Collection; 57 (LO), Jeff Vanuga/Corbis; 58 (UPLE), Ira Block/NG Image Collection; 58 (UPRT), NG Image Collection; 58 (LOLE), George F. Mobley/NG Image Collection; 58 (LORT), Martin Gray/NG Image Collection; 58 (UP), Vilainecrevette/iStockphoto; 59 (LORT), Brad Mitchell/Alamy; 59 (LOLE), Photographer/Getty Images; 59 (LORT), Richard Nowitz/NG Image Collection; 60 (UP), Tim Laman/NG Image Collection; 60 (CTR), Alaska Stock/National Geographic Stock; 61 (CTR), William Albert Allard/NG Image Collection; 61 (LO), Michael S. Yamashita/NG Image Collection; 62 (UPLE), Zeljko Radojko/Shutterstock; 62 (LOLE), Todd Gipstein/NG Image Collection; 62 (LORT), Norbert Rosing/NG Image Collection; 62 (UPRT), Brooks Walker/NG Image Collection; 64 (UP), Chris Jenner/Shutterstock; 64 (LO), Kenneth Garrett/NG Image Collection; 65 (UPLE), Macduff Everton/NG Image Collection; 65 (UPRT), Roy Toft/NG Image Collection; 66 (UP), Pablo Corral Vega/Corbis; 66 (LOLE), Steve Raymer/NG Image Collection; 67 (LO), Bill Curtsinger/NG Image Collection; 67 (UP), Michael Melford/NG Image Collection; 67 (LORT), Jose Fuste Raga/Corbis

South America

72 (UP), Tim Laman/NG Image Collection; 72 (LOLE), Pablo Corral Vega/NG Image Collection; 72 (LORT), Anne Keiser/NG Image Collection; 73 (UP), Stephanie Maze/NG Image Collection; 73 (LORT), Todd Gipstein/NG Image Collection; 74 (UPLE), Jimmy Chin/NG Image Collection; 74 (UPRT), Catarina Belova/Shutterstock; 74 (LORT), Pablo Corral Vega/NG Image Collection; 74 (LOLE), Ed George/NG Image Collection; 75 (UP), Richard Nowitz/NG Image Collection; 75 (LOLE), Joel Sartore/NG Image Collection; 75 (LORT), Melissa Farlow/NG Image Collection; 76 (UP), William Albert Allard/NG Image Collection; 76 (LOLE), Pablo Corral Vega/NG Image Collection; 76 (LORT), Meredith Davenport/NG Image Collection; 77 (UP), O. Louis Mazzatenta/NG Image Collection; 78 (UP), Macduff Everton/NG Image Collection; 78 (LO), James L. Amos/NG Image Collection; 79 (LO), Priit Vesilind/NG Image Collection; 79 (UP), Joel Sartore/NG Image Collection; 80 (UP), O. Louis Mazzatenta/NG Image Collection; 80 (LO), Dmitry Saparov/Shutterstock; 81 (UP), Maria Stenzel/NG Image Collection; 81 (CTR), Joel Sartore/NG Image Collection

Europe

86 (UP), Richard Nowitz/NG Image Collection; 86 (LOLE), Priit Vesilind/NG Image Collection; 86 (UP), Melissa Farlow/NG Image Collection; 86-87, Pavel Svoboda/Shutterstock; 87 (UPRT), Richard Nowitz/NG Image Collection; 88 (UPLE), Taylor S. Kennedy/NG Image Collection; 88 (LOLE), Steve

Published by the National Geographic Society
John M. Fahey, *Chairman of the Board and Chief Executive Officer*
Declan Moore, *Executive Vice President;*
President, Publishing and Travel
Melina Gerosa Bellows, *Executive Vice President;*
Chief Creative Officer, Books, Kids, and Family

Prepared by the Book Division
Hector Sierra, *Senior Vice President and General Manager*
Nancy Laties Feresten, *Senior Vice President,*
Kids Publishing and Media
Jay Sumner, *Director of Photography, Children's Publishing*
Jennifer Emmett, *Vice President, Editorial Director, Children's Books*
Eva Absher-Schantz, *Design Director, Kids Publishing and Media*
R. Gary Colbert, *Production Director*
Jennifer A. Thornton, *Director of Managing Editorial*

Staff for This Book
Priyanka Lamichhane, *Project Editor*
David M. Seager, *Art Director*
Lori Epstein, *Senior Illustrations Editor*
Ariane Szu-Tu, *Editorial Assistant*
Callie Broaddus, *Design Production Assistant*
Hillary Moloney, *Illustrations Assistant*
Carl Mehler, *Director of Maps*
Matthew W. Chwastyk, *Map Project and Production Manager*
Sven M. Dolling, Steven D. Gardner, Thomas L. Gray, Michael
McNey, Nicholas P. Rosenbach, Tibor G. Tóth, Gregory
Ugiansky, Mapping Specialists, and XNR Productions, *Map
Research and Production*
Martha Sharma, *Contributing Writer*
Grace Hill, *Associate Managing Editor*
Joan Gossett, *Production Editor*
Lewis R. Bassford, *Production Manager*
Susan Borke, *Legal and Business Affairs*

Manufacturing and Quality Management
Phillip L. Schlosser, *Senior Vice President*
Chris Brown, *Vice President, NG Book Manufacturing*
George Bounelis, *Vice President, Production Services*
Nicole Elliott, *Manager*
Rachel Faulise, *Manager*
Robert L. Barr, *Manager*

The National Geographic Society is one of the world's largest
nonprofit scientific and educational organizations. Founded in 1888
to "increase and diffuse geographic knowledge," the Society's
mission is to inspire people to care about the planet. It reaches
more than 400 million people worldwide each month through its
official journal, *National Geographic,* and other magazines; National
Geographic Channel; television documentaries; music; radio; films;
books; DVDs; maps; exhibitions; live events; school publishing
programs; interactive media; and merchandise. National
Geographic has funded more than 10,000 scientific research,
conservation and exploration projects and supports an education
program promoting geographic literacy.

For more information, please visit www.nationalgeographic.com,
call 1-800-NGS LINE (647-5463), or write to the following address:
National Geographic Society
1145 17th Street N.W.
Washington, D.C. 20036-4688 U.S.A.

Visit us online at www.nationalgeographic.com/books

For librarians and teachers: www.ngchildrensbooks.org

More for kids from National Geographic: kids.nationalgeographic.com

For information about special discounts for bulk purchases, please
contact National Geographic Books Special Sales: ngspecsales
@ngs.org

For rights or permissions inquiries, please contact National
Geographic Books Subsidiary Rights: ngbookrights@ngs.org

Paperback ISBN: 978-1-4263-1403-2
Hardcover ISBN: 978-1-4263-1405-6
Reinforced Library Binding ISBN: 978-1-4263-1404-9

Printed in U.S.A.
13/RRDW-CML/1

McCurry/NG Image Collection; 88 (LORT), Sisse Brimberg/NG Image Collection; 88-89 (UP),
Richard Nowitz/NG Image Collection; 89 (LOLE), Richard Nowitz/NG Image Collection; 89 (CTR),
Nicole Duplaix/NG Image Collection; 89 (LORT), James P. Blair/NG Image Collection; 90 (UP),
Karen Kasmauski/NG Image Collection; 90 (LOLE), Priit Vesilind/NG Image Collection; 90 (LORT),
Gregory Davies/Alamy; 91 (UP), The Art Archive/Corbis; 92 (CTR), Skip Brown/NG Image Collection;
92 (LORT), Jim Richardson/NG Image Collection; 92 (UP), Richard Nowitz/NG Image Collection;
93 (UP), Richard Nowitz/NG Image Collection; 94 (UP), Catherine Karnow/NG Image Collection; 94
(LO), Catherine Karnow/NG Image Collection; 95 (UPLE), Sisse Brimberg/NG Image Collection; 95
(RT), Sissie Brimberg/NG Image Collection; 96 (RT), James P. Blair/NG Image Collection; 96 (LORT),
Richard I'anson/Lonely Planet Images/Getty Images; 96 (LOLE), Todd Gipstein/NG Image Collection;
97 (UP), James L. Stanfield/NG Image Collection; 98 (UP), Steve Raymer/NG Image Collection; 98
(LO), Steve Raymer/NG Image Collection; 99, Richard Nowitz/NG Image Collection

Asia
104 (UP), Taylor S. Kennedy/NG Image Collection; 104 (LOLE), Steve McCurry/NG Image Collection;
105 (UP), Steve Raymer/NG Image Collection; 105 (LOLE), Justin Guariglia/NG Image Collection;
105 (LORT), David Edwards/NG Image Collection; 106 (UPLE), Fred de Noyelle/Godong/Corbis; 106
(LOLE), Jodi Cobb/NG Image Collection; 106 (LORT), Justin Guariglia/NG Image Collection; 106-
107 (UP), Todd Gipstein/NG Image Collection; 107 (LOLE), Michael Nichols/NG Image Collection;
107 (LORT), Justin Guariglia/NG Image Collection; 108 (UP), Maria Stenzel/NG Image Collection;
108 (LO), Steve Winter/NG Image Collection; 109 (UP), Steve Raymer/NG Image Collection; 109
(LO), Cary Wolinsky/NG Image Collection; 110 (UP), Medford Taylor/NG Image Collection; 110 (LO),
Gordon Wiltsie/NG Image Collection; 111 (UP), David Edwards/NG Image Collection; 111 (LO), Dean
Conger/NG Image Collection; 112 (UP), H. Kim/NG Image Collection; 112 (LO), Justin Guariglia/
NG Image Collection; 113 (UP), O. LOuis Mazzatenta/NG Image Collection; 113 (LO), Roy Toft/NG
Image Collection; 114 (UP), James L. Stanfield/NG Image Collection; 114 (LO), Alex Webb/NG Image
Collection; 115 (UP), Martin Gray/NG Image Collection; 115 (LO), Priit Vesilind/NG Image Collection;
116 (UPLE), Morteza Nikoubazl/Reuters/Corbis; 116 (UPRT), Arthur Thèvenart/Corbis; 116 (LO),
Robb Kendrick/NG Image Collection; 117 (UP), Bill Lyons/NG Image Collection; 118 (UP), Ed George/
NG Image Collection; 118 (LO), Bobby Model/NG Image Collection; 119 (UP), iStockphoto.Com; 119
(LO), James P. Blair/NG Image Collection; 120 (UPLE), Paul Chesley/NG Image Collection; 120
(UPRT), Macduff Everton/NG Image Collection; 120 (LO), Deepblue-Photographer/Shutterstock; 121
(UP), Jack Fields/Corbis; 121 (LO), Steve Raymer/NG Image Collection; 122 (UP), Reuters/Corbis;
122 (LO), Richard Nowitz/NG Image Collection; 123 (UPLE), Paul Chesley/NG Image Collection; 123
(UPRT), Tim Laman/NG Image Collection; 123 (LO), Tim Laman/NG Image Collection

Africa
128 (UP), George F. Mobley/NG Image Collection; 128 (LOLE), Michael Nichols/NG Image Collection;
128 (LORT), Instinia/Shutterstock; 129 (UP), Skip Brown/NG Image Collection; 129 (LOLE), Bill
Curtsinger/NG Image Collection; 129 (LORT), Cary Wolinsky/NG Image Collection; 130 (UP), Georg
Gerster/NG Image Collection; 130 (LOLE), Digital Vision/Getty Images; 130 (LORT), Kenneth Garrett/
NG Image Collection; 131 (UP), Cary Wolinsky NG Image Collection; 131 (LOLE), Bill Curtsinger/NG
Image Collection; 131 (LORT), Michael Nichols/NG Image Collection; 132, Thomas J. Abercrombie/
National Geographic Stock; 132, Jose Fuste Raga/Corbis; 133 (LORT), Richard Nowitz/NG Image
Collection; 133 (UPLE), Kenneth Garrett/NG Image Collection; 133, Teb Nad/iStockphoto; 134 (UP),
W. Robert Moore/NG Image Collection; 134 (LOLE), Adisa/Shutterstock; 134 (LORT), NG Image
Collection; 135 (UP), James L. Stanfield/NG Image Collection; 136 (UP), Randy Olson/NG Image
Collection; 136 (LOLE), Michael Lewis/NG Image Collection; 136 (LO), Michael Nichols/NG Image
Collection; 137 (UPRT), Bobby Haas/NG Image Collection; 137 (UPLE), Werner Forman/Corbis; 138
(UP), George F. Mobley/NG Image Collection; 138 (LO), Tim Laman/NG Image Collection; 139 (UP),
Kenneth Garrett/NG Image Collection; 139 (LO), Bob Krist/Corbis

Australia New Zealand and Oceania
144 (UP), Nicole Duplaix/NG Image Collection; 144 (LOLE), Frans Lanting/NG Image Collection;
145 (UP), Art Wolfe/NG Image Collection; 145 (LOLE), Tim Laman/NG Image Collection; 145
(LORT), Nicole Duplaix/NG Image Collection; 146 (UPLE), Medford Taylor/NG Image Collection;
146 (LOLE), Danita Delimont Creative/Alamy; 146 (CTR), N.Minton/Shutterstock; 146-149 (UP), Tim
Laman/NG Image Collection; 146-149 (LO), Travellight/Shutterstock; 147 (CTR), Paul Chesley/NG
Image Collection; 147 (LORT), Mark Cosslett/NG Image Collection; 148 (LOLE), Bill Curtsinger/
NG Image Collection; 148 (LORT), Sam Abell/NG Image Collection; 149 (UPLE), Jason Edwards/
NG Image Collection; 149 (UPRT), Paul Chesley/NG Image Collection; 150 (UP), Randy Olson/NG
Image Collection; 150 (LO), Carsten Peter/NG Image Collection; 151 (UPLE), Martin Gray/NG Image
Collection; 151 (UPRT), Randy Olson/NG Image Collection; 151 (LO), Jodi Cobb/NG Image Collection

Antarctica
154 (UP), Gordon Wiltsie/NG Image Collection; 154 (LO), Gordon Wiltsie/NG Image Collection; 155
(UP), Paul Nicklen/NG Image Collection; 155 (LO), Maria Stenzel/NG Image Collection

The Oceans
159 (LOLE), Scripps Institute of Oceanography; 159 (UPRT), NOAA; 159 (LORT), NASA; 160 (UP),
Wolcott Henry/NG Image Collection; 160 (LO), Karen Kasmauski/NG Image Collection; 162 (UP), Tom
Murphy/NG Image Collection; 162 (LOLE), Emory Kristof/NG Image Collection; 162 (LORT), John
Eastcott and Yva Momatiuk/NG Image Collection; 164, Hans Fricke/NG Image Collection; 166 (LO),
Norbert Rosing/NG Image Collection; 166 (UP), Paul Nicklen/NG Image Collection

Back of the Book
176, Philip Lange/Shutterstock; 177 (1), Dirk Ercken/Shutterstock; 177 (2), Melissa Woods/iStock-
photo; 177 (3), Greg Smith/National Geographic My Shot; 177 (4), Natursports/Shutterstock; 177 (5),
tratong/Shutterstock; 177 (6), Manamana/Shutterstock; 177 (7), Hung Chung Chih/Shutterstock; 177
(8), Vilainecrevette/Shutterstock; 177 (9), psamtik/Shutterstock; 178 (A), scubaluna/Shutterstock;
178 (B), Mariusz S. Jurgielewicz/Shutterstock; 178 (E), Michael Nichols/National Geographic Stock;
178 (D), Anton Ivanov/Shutterstock; 178 (C), alslutsky/Shutterstock; 179 (F), Michael Nichols/
National Geographic Stock; 179 (J), Galyna Andrushko/Shutterstock; 179 (G), Viktor Kitaykin/iStock-
photo; 179 (K), Pleio/iStockphoto; 179 (H), Nancy Nehring//Shutterstock; 179 (I), Bruce Dale/National
Geographic Stock; 179 (L), Adalberto Rios Szalay/Sexto Sol/Photodisc/Getty Images; 180 (1), Flip
Nicklin/Minden Pictures/National Geographic Stock; 180 (2), Anton Ivanov/Shutterstock; 180 (3),
Atlaspix/Shutterstock; 180 (4), Atlaspix/Shutterstock; 180 (5), ollyy/Shutterstock; 180 (6), Dudarev
Mikhail/Shutterstock; 180 (7), Lissandra Melo/Shutterstock; 180 (8), WDG Photo/Shutterstock; 180
(9), holbox/Shutterstock; 180 (10), Eric Isselee/Shutterstock; 181, Alicia Dauksis/Shutterstock; 182
(3), Maggie Lin/National Geographic My Shot; 182 (5), Steven Bostock/Shutterstock; 182 (4), holbox/
Shutterstock; 182 (1), Mazzzur/Shutterstock; 182 (6), Craig Cassover/National Geographic My Shot;
182 (7), Susan Harris/Shutterstock; 182 (2), Dan Breckwoldt/Shutterstock; 182 (8), feiyuezhangjie/
Shutterstock; 182 (9), iStockphoto; 183 (10), Keneva Photography/Shutterstock; 183 (11), JeniFoto/
Shutterstock; 183 (12), Suranga Weeratunga/Shutterstock; 183 (13), S. Borisov/Shutterstock;
183 (14), Mark Schwettmann/Shutterstock; 183 (15), Radoslaw Lecyk/Shutterstock; 183 (16), Ian
Stewart/Shutterstock

Metric Conversion Tables

CONVERSION TO METRIC MEASURES

SYMBOL	WHEN YOU KNOW	MULTIPLY BY	TO FIND	SYMBOL
		LENGTH		
in	inches	2.54	centimeters	cm
ft	feet	0.30	meters	m
yd	yards	0.91	meters	m
mi	miles	1.61	kilometers	km
		AREA		
in^2	square inches	6.45	square centimeters	cm^2
ft^2	square feet	0.09	square meters	m^2
yd^2	square yards	0.84	square meters	m^2
mi^2	square miles	2.59	square kilometers	km^2
—	acres	0.40	hectares	ha
		MASS		
oz	ounces	28.35	grams	g
lb	pounds	0.45	kilograms	kg
—	short tons	0.91	metric tons	t
		VOLUME		
in^3	cubic inches	16.39	milliliters	mL
liq oz	liquid ounces	29.57	milliliters	mL
pt	pints	0.47	liters	L
qt	quarts	0.95	liters	L
gal	gallons	3.79	liters	L
ft^3	cubic feet	0.03	cubic meters	m^3
yd^3	cubic yards	0.76	cubic meters	m^3
		TEMPERATURE		
°F	degrees Fahrenheit	5/9 after subtracting 32	degrees Celsius (centigrade)	°C

CONVERSION FROM METRIC MEASURES

SYMBOL	WHEN YOU KNOW	MULTIPLY BY	TO FIND	SYMBOL
		LENGTH		
cm	centimeters	0.39	inches	in
m	meters	3.28	feet	ft
m	meters	1.09	yards	yd
km	kilometers	0.62	miles	mi
		AREA		
cm^2	square centimeters	0.16	square inches	in^2
m^2	square meters	10.76	square feet	ft^2
m^2	square meters	1.20	square yards	yd^2
km^2	square kilometers	0.39	square miles	mi^2
ha	hectares	2.47	acres	—
		MASS		
g	grams	0.04	ounces	oz
kg	kilograms	2.20	pounds	lb
t	metric tons	1.10	short tons	—
		VOLUME		
mL	milliliters	0.06	cubic inches	in^3
mL	milliliters	0.03	liquid ounces	liq oz
L	liters	2.11	pints	pt
L	liters	1.06	quarts	qt
L	liters	0.26	gallons	gal
m^3	cubic meters	35.31	cubic feet	ft^3
m^3	cubic meters	1.31	cubic yards	yd^3
		TEMPERATURE		
°C	degrees Celsius (centigrade)	9/5 then add 32	degrees Fahrenheit	°F